Physical The

A Critical Reader

Physical Theatres: A Critical Reader is an invaluable resource for students of physically orientated theatre and performance, drawing on a wide range of sources from all aspects of a hitherto underserved area of study. This book aims to trace the roots and development of physicality in theatre by combining practical experience of the field with a strong historical and theoretical underpinning.

In exploring the histories, cross-overs and intersections of physical theatres, this critical reader provides:

- six new, specially written essays, covering each of the book's main themes, from technical traditions to contemporary practices
- discussion of issues such as the foregrounding of the body, training and performance processes, and the origins of theatre in both play and human cognition
- a focus on the relationship and tensions between the verbal and the physical in theatre
- contributions from Augusto Boal, Stephen Berkoff, Étienne Decroux, Bertolt Brecht and Aristotle.

This book can be used as a stand-alone text, or together with its companion volume *Physical Theatres: A Critical Introduction*, to provide a comprehensive illustration of the physical in theatre and performance.

John Keefe is a senior lecturer at London Metropolitan University Undergraduate Centre, and a lecturer and Visiting Fellow at Queen's University (Canada) ISC specialising in performance-theatre-film studies. He is also a freelance director and performance dramaturg.

Simon Murray is a performer, director and academic. He is currently Director of Theatre at Dartington College of Arts, and author of *Jacques Lecoq* (2003).

Physical Theatres

A Critical Reader

Edited by John Keefe
and Simon Murray

Routledge
Taylor & Francis Group

LONDON AND NEW YORK

First published 2007
by Routledge
2 Park Square, Milton Park, Abingdon, Oxon OX14 4RN

Simultaneously published in the USA and Canada
by Routledge
270 Madison Ave, New York, NY 10016

Routledge is an imprint of the Taylor & Francis Group, an informa business

Selection and editorial matter © 2007 John Keefe and Simon Murray

Individual chapters © the contributors

Typeset in Perpetua and Helvetica by
Florence Production Ltd, Stoodleigh, Devon
Printed and bound in Great Britain by
Antony Rowe Ltd, Chippenham, Wiltshire

British Library Cataloguing in Publication Data
A catalogue record for this book is available from the British Library

Library of Congress Cataloging in Publication Data
Physical theatres : a critical reader/edited by John Keefe and Simon Murray
    p. cm.
  Includes bibliographical references and index.
  1. Movement (Acting) 2. Mime. 3. Dance.   I. Keefe, John, 1950–
II. Murray, Simon David, 1948–
PN2071.M6P46   2007
792.02′8–dc22   2007016777

ISBN10: 0–415–36251–2 (hbk)
ISBN10: 0–415–36252–0 (pbk)

ISBN13: 978–0–415–36251–1 (hbk)
ISBN13: 978–0–415–36252–8 (pbk)

For Ivy, David (Manjusvara) and Will
In memory of Bill

For Wendy and Isla

Contents

List of figures   xiii
Notes on contributors   xv
Thanks, acknowledgements and permissions   xxiii

John Keefe and Simon Murray
INTRODUCTION   1

SECTION 1
Genesis, Contexts, Namings   7

ESSAY 1   CLAIRE HEGGEN GOES FISHING   9
Dick McCaw

  1   **Étienne Decroux**
    MY DEFINITION OF THEATRE   17

  2   **Ana Sánchez-Colberg**
    ALTERED STATES AND SUBLIMINAL SPACES: CHARTING THE
    ROAD TOWARDS A PHYSICAL THEATRE   21

  3   **David E.R. George**
    PERFORMANCE EPISTEMOLOGY   26

4   **J.-J. Rousseau, Citizen of Geneva**
LETTER TO M. D'ALEMBERT ON THE THEATRE   31

5   **Augusto Boal**
THEATRE, HUMAN BEINGS   32

6   **Marcel Mauss**
BODY TECHNIQUES   38

7   **Terry Eagleton**
MORALITY   42

SECTION 2
Roots:Routes   45

ESSAY 2   ROOTS OR ROUTES; THE TECHNICAL TRADITIONS OF
CONTEMPORARY PHYSICAL THEATRE   47
Jonathan Pitches

A   DEEP TRADITIONS: CLASSICAL AND POPULAR   55

8   **Aristotle**
THE ART OF POETRY   57

9   **David Wiles**
THE PERFORMER   60

10   **Alan S. Downer**
IRVING   63

11   **Jeff Pressing**
IMPROVISATION: METHODS AND MODELS   66

12   **Mel Gordon**
LAZZI: THE COMIC ROUTINES OF THE COMMEDIA DELL'ARTE   79

13   **Jeff Nuttall**
A JEWEL ON THE NATION'S ARSE   88

14   **Peter J. Arnold**
SPORT, THE AESTHETIC AND ART: FURTHER THOUGHTS   92

15 **Joan Littlewood**
GOODBYE NOTE FROM JOAN   95

B HYBRID PATHWAYS   97

16 **Mel Gordon**
GERMAN EXPRESSIONIST ACTING   99

17 **Anaïs Nin**
THE THEATRE AND THE PLAGUE   103

18 **Allan Kaprow**
A STATEMENT (REWRITTEN FROM A RECORDED INTERVIEW)   106

19 **Patrick Campbell and Helen Spackman**
SURVIVING THE PERFORMANCE: AN INTERVIEW WITH
FRANKO B.   109

20 **Enrique Pardo**
THE ANGEL'S HIDEOUT: BETWEEN DANCE AND THEATRE   112

SECTION 3
Contemporary Practices   115

ESSAY 3   GESTURING TOWARDS POST-PHYSICAL PERFORMANCE   117
Franc Chamberlain

21 **Steven Berkoff**
INTRODUCTION AND *EAST*, SCENE 4   123

22 **Samuel Beckett to music by John Beckett**
ACT WITHOUT WORDS: A MIME FOR ONE PLAYER   127

23 **Emilyn Claid**
RE-DRESSING THE GIRLS   131

24 **Norbert Servos**
BLUEBEARD   134

25 **Forced Entertainment; Text by Tim Etchells**
CLUB OF NO REGRETS   136

26   **Mike Pearson and Cliff McLucas, John Keefe, Simon Murray**
      'ON BRITH GOF', A MONTAGE OF MATERIAL ABOUT AND
      CONCERNING THE WORK OF BRITH GOF, A WELSH THEATRE
      COMPANY   142

27   **Franc Chamberlain**
      MAG – THE NEXT FIVE YEARS 1997–2002   151

SECTION 4
Preparation and Training   157

ESSAY 4   REFRAMING THE JOURNEY   159
Lorna Marshall

28   **Étienne Decroux; Photographs by Étienne Bertrand Weill**
      PHOTO ESSAY: *SPORTS*   165

29   **Michael Chekhov**
      TO THE ACTOR; APPENDIX: A PRACTICAL GUIDE TO THE APPLICATION OF
      THE MICHAEL CHEKHOV PSYCHOLOGICAL GESTURE (PG) TECHNIQUE.
      TRANSLATION AND COMMENTARY BY ANDREI MALAEV-BABEL   169

30   **Anne Dennis**
      THE ARTICULATE BODY: THE PHYSICAL TRAINING OF THE ACTOR   184

31   **Jacques Lecoq**
      MOVEMENT TECHNIQUE   187

32   **Myra Felner**
      CIRCUS AND THE ACTOR: AN INTERVIEW WITH HOVEY BURGESS   193

33   **Yoshi Oida and Lorna Marshall**
      MOVING   196

SECTION 5
Physicality and the Word   199

ESSAY 5   PHYSICAL THEATRE AND TEXT   201
Phelim McDermott

34   **Bertolt Brecht**
      ON EVERYDAY THEATRE (POEMS OF THE CRISIS YEARS
      1929–1933)   209

35   **Jonathan Kalb**
     ROCKABY AND THE ART OF INADVERTENT INTERPRETATION, and
     CONSIDERATIONS OF ACTING IN THE EARLY PLAYS   213

36   **Mike Alfreds**
     A SHARED EXPERIENCE: THE ACTOR AS STORY-TELLER   217

37   **Albert Hunt and Michael Kustow**
     US 'NARRATIVE ONE' AND 'NARRATIVE TWO'   221

38   **Trevor Griffiths**
     COMEDIANS   229

39   **Robert Kimball and Stephen Sondheim**
     'INTRODUCTORY ESSAY', 'BEAUTIFUL', 'SUNDAY' (*SUNDAY
     IN THE PARK WITH GEORGE*)   233

SECTION 6
Bodies and Cultures

                                                                            237

ESSAY 6   ASSEMBLING OUR DIFFERENCES: BRIDGING
IDENTITIES-IN-MOTION IN INTERCULTURAL PERFORMANCE   239
David Williams

40   **Patrice Pavis**
     INTRODUCTION: TOWARDS A THEORY OF INTERCULTURALISM
     IN THEATRE   249

41   **Eugenio Barba and Nicola Savarese**
     PRE-EXPRESSIVITY   255

42   **Peter Brook**
     THE WORLD AS A CAN OPENER   259

43   **C.L.R. James**
     WHAT IS ART?   262

44   **Edward W. Said**
     ORIENTALISM NOW   265

Afterwords   273
Index   275

List of figures

5.1	*What is theatre?*	35
9.1	The chorus	61
12.1	VII. *Lazzo of the zig-zag* (E08) from *The Go-Between* in the *Grevenbroch Album*, Civic Museum, Venice, circa 1700	82
12.2	IX. *Lazzo of the enema* (F01) from *A Third of the Time* in the Corsini MSS., Rome, circa 1610	84
28.1	*Sports*	166
28.2	*Sports*	166
28.3	*Sports*	167
28.4	*Sports*	167
28.5	*Sports*	168
28.6	*Sports*	168
29.1	Drawing 1	170
29.2	Drawing 2	171
29.3	Drawing 3	172
29.4	Drawing 4	173
29.5	Drawing 5	174
29.6	Drawing 6	175
29.7	Drawing 7	176
29.8	Drawing 8	176
29.9	Drawing 9	177
29.10	Drawing 10	178
29.11	Drawing 11	179
29.12	Drawing 12	180

29.13 Drawing 13   181
29.14 Drawing 14   182
29.15 Drawing 15   183
31.1   Lecoq diagram of 'undulatory movement', 'undulation', 'eclosion'   190

Notes on contributors

Mike Alfreds is the founder of Shared Experience Theatre (1975–1986) and Method and Madness (1991–1999). Developing a 'story-teller narrative' style, productions include *Arabian Nights* (1975), *Bleak House* (1977), and *Pamela* (1985). His forthcoming book on his work and rehearsal processes, *Different Every Night*, will be published in autumn 2007.

Aristotle (384–322 BCE) is regarded as one of the founders, with Socrates and Plato, of modern Western philosophy. He established his own school, the Lyceum, in 335 BCE in Athens. His work on metaphysics, ethics, biology and psychology is unified by the concepts of natural kinds and teleology, or pertaining to optimal states and goals. Writings include *Physics, Nicomachean Ethics, On Plants, and Politics*.

Peter J. Arnold was Head of Education Department, Moray House Institute (now Edinburgh University). His works include *Education, Movement and the Curriculum* (1988) and *Sports, Ethics and Education* (1997).

Eugenio Barba is a theatre director, writer and theorist. After working with Jerzy Grotowski, he founded the Odin Teatret in 1964, based in Halstebro, Denmark. In 1979 he founded the International School of Theatre Anthropology (ISTA). His books include *The Paper Canoe* (1995) and *Land of Ashes and Diamonds* (1999), and he has written many essays and articles for various leading theatre journals.

Samuel Beckett (1906–1989) was an Irish-French dramatist. Often labelled 'absurdist', he is more a profound humanist using extreme situations to reflect on the human condition, writing drama for theatre, radio, film and television and novels. His plays include *Waiting for Godot* (1953/1955), *Endgame* (1957), *Krapp's Last Tape* (1958), *Eh Joe* (1965), *Footfalls* (1975), *Rockaby* (1981), *What Where* (1983).

Steven Berkoff is a writer, actor and director. After training in London and Paris (with Jacques Lecoq) he formed the London Theatre Group (LTG) in 1968. His plays-productions include *Metamorphosis* (1969), *Greek* (1980), *Decadence* (1981), and *West* (1983). The LTG style may be described as a 'heightened physical theatre'.

Augusto Boal is a theatre director, writer and politician. He is best known for his founding of the political theatre forum 'Theatre of the Oppressed' (see also Paulo Freire's 'Pedagogy of the Oppressed') which seeks to rework Aristotle's and Brecht's ideas on theatre as social instrument. His books include *Theatre of the Oppressed* (1979) and *Games for Actors and Non-Actors* (1992/2002).

Bertolt Brecht (1898–1956) was a dramatist, director and dramaturg, developing a style of performance he called 'epic theatre' based on distancing and estranging devices of staging. His plays include *The Threepenny Opera* (1928), *Mother Courage and Her Children* (1941), *The Good Person of Setzuan* (1943), and *The Caucasian Chalk Circle* (1948), in collaboration with Kurt Weill, Hans Eisler, Elisabeth Hauptmann, Helene Weigel, Casper Neher and others. His major theoretical writings are published in English as *Brecht on Theatre* (1964).

Peter Brook is a theatre director. Coming to prominence with the Royal Shakespeare Company, his productions included *King Lear* (1962), *The Marat-Sade* (1964), *A Midsummer Night's Dream* (1971) and the 'Theatre of Cruelty' season (1964). In 1970 he founded the International Centre for Theatre Research in Paris; productions include *The Ik* (1975) and *The Mahabharata* (1985). Among his theatre writings are *The Empty Space* (1969) and *There Are No Secrets* (1993).

Hovey Burgess is a practitioner and teacher of circus arts including juggling, balancing and clowning, working with many of the world's leading circuses. Since 1966 he has taught circus techniques at the Tisch School, New York University. His writing work includes *Circus Techniques* (1976).

Patrick Campbell was Principal Lecturer in English and Leader in MA, Performing Arts at Middlesex University. His works include *Analysing Performance* (ed. 1996).

Franc Chamberlain teaches Drama and Theatre Studies at University College Cork, Ireland, and is Visiting Professor in Performance Studies and Creative Practice at the University of Northampton, UK. He is editing the *Decroux Companion* with Thomas Leabhart and working on a new edition of Craig's *On the Art of the Theatre*.

Michael Chekhov (1891–1955) was a Russian actor, director, and theorist of acting techniques. A protégé of Stanislavski, he both rejected and developed the latter's ideas especially in the area of the actor's body as a story-telling device and tool, using archetypes.

Emilyn Claid is Professor of Choreography at Dartington College of Arts, Devon. Previously Artistic Director of Extemporary Dance Company, she is also co-director of the 'Music & Dance Exchange Project'. From 2001 to 2004 she was co-director, with Valerie Briginshaw, of the 'Embodying Ambiguities' research and writing project.

Étienne Decroux (1898–1991) was a student of Jacques Copeau and Charles Dullin, going on to develop his own influential form of 'corporeal mime' as an art of dramatic movement. He appeared in many films including *Les Enfants du Paradis* (1945). He opened his own school in 1962, where he taught many of the leading mimes of the twentieth century, a number of whom have themselves become teachers.

Anne Dennis trained as a dancer, actor and mime before continuing her studies with Étienne Decroux. Formerly Head of Movement at Rose Bruford College of Speech and Drama, London, she is now based in Barcelona and London working as both teacher and director.

Alan S. Downer (no information available)

Terry Eagleton is John Edward Taylor Professor of English Literature at the University of Manchester. Best known for his Marxist approach to literary and cultural theory, his books include *Criticism and Ideology* (1976), *Literary Theory* (1983/1996), and *The Idea of Culture* (2000).

Tim Etchells (artistic director) and **Forced Entertainment** have been working as an 'ensemble of six artists who make performance' since 1984, based in Sheffield. Their productions include *Jessica in the Room of Lights* (1984), *Marina and Lee* (1991), *Emanuelle Enchanted* (1992), *Speak Bitterness* (1994), *Who Can Sing a Song to Unfrighten Me?* (1999), *Bloody Mess* (2004), and *Exquisite Pain* (2005/7).

Myra Felner is a teacher and writer, focusing on mime and physical theatre. Her other writings include *Apostles of Silence: The Modern French Mimes* (1985).

David E. R. George is a theatre director and writer based in Australia. He is a specialist in Asian theatre, carrying out extensive fieldwork in India, Bali, and Sri Lanka. His books include *Indian Ritual Drama* (1986), *Balinese Ritual Drama* (1990/91), and *Buddhism As/In Performance* (1999), and he has also written a number of journal articles.

Mel Gordon is Professor in Theatre, Dance and Performance Studies at the University of California, Berkeley. He has also taught at the Lee Strasberg Institute and the Michael Chekhov Studio. His books include *Expressionist Texts* (1986) and *Dada Performance* (1987).

Trevor Griffiths is a dramatist writing for both theatre and television. He was a member of Portable Theatre (1968–73) and may be characterised as a writer of 'critical realism', the tension between the materialism of detail and of power forces. His plays include *The Party* (1974), *Occupations* (1980), *Fatherland* (1987), and *Thatcher's Children* (1994).

Albert Hunt is best known for his innovatory theatre and performance practices developed at the Bradford Regional College of Arts. He describes this work and its implications in *Hopes for Great Happenings* (1976) as explorations in situations, street performance and happenings. He also wrote extensively for *Encore* magazine, as well as becoming a collaborator with Peter Brook.

C. L. R. James (1901–89) was a writer on sport and colonialism, a novelist and a dramatist. For many years a journalist on the *Manchester Guardian*, his historical writing includes *World Revolution 1919–1936* (1937), *The Black Jacobins* (1938), and *Cricket* (1986). His writing on cricket places it in a historical, social and cultural context within the politics of colonialism and post-colonialism.

Jonathan Kalb is Professor of Theatre at Hunter College, City University of New York, and a theatre critic. Areas of research interest include theatre history and theory, and dramaturgy. His books include *The Theatre of Heiner Muller* (1998/2003).

Allan Kaprow (1927–2006) was a painter, assemblagist and pioneer of the practice and theory of the 'Environment' and the 'Happening', creating some 200 of the latter. He has written extensively on these forms and concepts, seeing the lines between life and art, artist and audience as necessarily blurred.

Robert Kimball is a music critic for the *New York Post* and co-author or editor of a number of books on musical theatre. These include the *Complete Lyrics* series, and *Reading Lyrics* with Robert Gottlieb.

Michael Kustow is a writer, producer and broadcaster, including work with the RSC, as Director of the Institute of Contemporary Arts, at the National Theatre, London, and as first Arts Commissioning Editor at Channel 4. He is currently working on various independent projects.

Jacques Lecoq (1921–99) was a mime, actor and teacher of theatre. His early training in physical education and work with Commedia dell'Arte led to an interest in the use of mask and mime in both training and performance. In 1957 he opened his l'École Internationale de Théâtre Jacques Lecoq in Paris. He is regarded, along with Decroux, as one of the key figures in the use and place of the corporeal body on stage.

Joan Littlewood (1914–2002) was a theatre director and pioneer of a physical style of staging. She was co-founder with Jimmie Miller of Theatre of Action/ Theatre Union (*Waiting for Lefty, Good Soldier Schweyk*), and with Gerry Raffles of Theatre Workshop in 1945. Littlewood was instrumental in introducing the work of Brecht and Laban to the UK; productions include *Mother Courage and Her Children* (1955), *The Quare Fellow* (1956), *A Taste of Honey* (1958) and *Oh What a Lovely War* (1963).

Dick McCaw co-founded the Actors Touring Company in 1979 and the Medieval Players in 1981. In 1993 he was appointed Artistic Director of the International Workshop Festival, which he left in 2001 to go freelance. With Peter Hulton he has edited eight DVD-ROM documentations of leading practitioners in the performing arts. He has published a book on Warren Lamb, a pupil of Rudolf Laban, and has been commissioned to edit and introduce the *Routledge Companion to Laban*. In 2007 he qualified as a Feldenkrais practitioner.

Phelim McDermott is a theatre director and workshop leader, founder of 'dereck dereck Productions' and Improbable Theatre. Theatre work includes *Improbable Tales*, *Shockheaded Peter* (with The Tiger Lillies), *70 Hill Lane*, *Lifegame*, and *Theatre of Blood*

(National Theatre collaboration). His most recent work includes *Satyagraha* by Philip Glass (English National Opera collaboration, 2007). He is also a regular improvising guest with the Comedy Store Players.

Clifford McLucas (1945–2002) was a designer and artist focusing on the use of location and space; the architectonics of scenography. His work with Brith Gof includes *Gododdin, Tri Bywyd, and Draw Draw Yn . . ..* The *Three Landscapes Project* (2001) was undertaken when he was Senior Fellow, Stanford University Humanities Centre. His last project was for the National Eisteddford (St. Davids) in 2002. His writings include *Ten feet and three quarters of an inch of theatre* (2000).

Lorna Marshall is Honorary Research Fellow (RADA), and Advisor on Training (New National Theatre Studio, Tokyo). She also runs workshops for actors, singers, and directors around the world. She has a long-standing collaboration with Yoshi Oida (from Peter Brook's company), working with him on three books (*An Actor Adrift, The Invisible Actor,* and *An Actor's Tricks*) and various productions.

Marcel Mauss (1872–1950) was a sociologist who developed the work and theories of Émile Durkheim into the areas of reciprocity and gift economies within ethnography and anthropology. His best known work is *The Gift* (1990) and a number of collaborations with members of Annèe Sociologique.

Anaïs Nin (1903–1977) was a writer and diarist – seven volumes spanning over sixty years, 1931–1974 (published between 1966–1981) – based in Paris. She appeared in films by Kenneth Anger and Maya Deren; her other books include *Delta of Venus* (1977).

Jeff Nuttall (1933–2004) was a performer, director and political campaigner, co-founding The People Show in 1967, pioneering live-performance art in the UK. His writings include *Bomb Culture* (1968) and *Performance Art: 1 Memoirs, 2 Scripts* (1979).

Yoshi Oida trained in Noh theatre and Kabuki dance before joining Peter Brook's theatre company in Paris and appearing in many of its key productions. He is an acclaimed acting teacher, and his books include *An Actor Adrift* (1992).

Enrique Pardo trained and worked with the Roy Hart Theatre, developing ideas and techniques for the use of voice and movement in theatre. He formed Pantheatre (with Linda Wise) in 1981, mixing myth-archetype-voice-gesture to create 'choreographic theatre'. He is also a teacher and theorist.

Patrice Pavis is Professor of Theatre at the University of Paris VIII-Saint-Denis. A leading scholar of Marivaux, he is a key figure in the study of theatre semiotics and theatre interculturalism. His books include the *Dictionary of Theatre* (1980/98) and *Analysing Performance* (2003).

Mike Pearson is Professor of Performance Studies at Aberystwyth, University of Wales. Between 1972 and 1997 he co-founded and worked with the innovatory performance companies RAT Theatre, Cardiff Laboratory Theatre and Brith Gof. His other writing includes *Theatre/Archeology* (2001), with Michael Shanks, and 'Horses' in *Patterned Ground* (2003), plus a number of journal articles.

Jonathan Pitches is Professor and Chair in Theatre and Performance in the School of Performance and Cultural Industries at Leeds University. His books include *Vsevolod Meyerhold* (2003) and *The Stanislavsky Tradition of Acting* (2005). His most recent article was published in *Contemporary Theatre Review* in February 2007 – an examination of Michael Chekhov, Anatoly Vasiliev and Platonic acting.

Jeff Pressing (1946–2002) was a musician, theorist and writer in the field of motor behaviour, physicality and corporeality of music improvisation, and cognitive science at the University of Melbourne. His writings include *Synthesizer Performance and Real-Time Techniques* (1992) and many articles in collections on art and music.

Jean-Jacques Rousseau (1712–1778) was a political and social philosopher, influential in both the Enlightenment and Romanticism and later periods, propounding ideas on nature, society, education and political freedoms. He was also an autobiographer and novelist. His works include *Discourse on the Origin and Basis of Inequality* (1754), *Émile* (1762), *The Social Contract* (1762), and *The Confessions* (1782).

Edward W. Said (1935–2003) was a writer, literary theorist and Palestinian political activist, and a key writer in post-colonial theory. His publications include *The World, The Text and the Critic* (1983), *Culture and Imperialism* (1993), *The Politics of Dispossession* (1994) and *The Edward Said Reader* (2000). In 1999 he co-founded the West-East Divan Orchestra with Daniel Barenboim.

Ana Sánchez-Colberg is Senior Lecturer in Performance at the Central School of Speech and Drama, London. A specialist in Tanztheater, she also leads master classes and seminars. Her writings include *Dance and the Performative* (2002, co-edited with Valerie Preston-Dunlop) and many journal articles.

Nicola Savarese is Professor of Disciplines of the Performing Arts at the University of Rome, and a founding member of ISTA with Eugenio Barba. His research interests include the origins of performance techniques and body techniques in the cultures of East and West. His most recent book is *Te@tri in the Net* (2004).

Norbert Servos is a critic, choreographer and director, and has written extensively on Tanztheater. His other works include *The Routledge Dance Studies Reader* (ed. 1998) and an edited volume on Susanne Link (2005).

Stephen Sondheim is a composer and lyricist, widely regarded as the leading writer of music theatre of the last 50 years. Since writing the lyrics for *West Side Story* (1957), he has produced a number of key theatre works using a complex approach to music, lyrics and staging, including *A Little Night Music* (1973), *Pacific Overtures* (1976), *Sweeny Todd* (1979), *Merrily We Roll Along* (1981), and *Into the Woods* (1987).

Helen Spackman is Senior Lecturer in Performing Arts and Theatre Studies at London Metropolitan University. She is also a performance artist, frequently in collaboration with Ernst Fischer, focusing on work that is politically engaged, interdisciplinary and site-specific. She has recently formed the artists' collective Leibniz with Fischer.

David Wiles is Professor of Theatre at Royal Holloway, University of London, with specialist research interests in Greek theatre. His books include *The Masks of Menander* (1991), *Tragedy in Athens* (1997) and *Mask and Performance in Greek Tragedy* (2007).

David Williams is currently Professor of Theatre at Dartington College of Arts, Devon. As well as contributing to many books and performance journals internationally, over the past ten years he has been a contributing editor on the journal *Performance Research*. Recent collaborations include projects with British performance duo Lone Twin, and the choreographers Emilyn Claid and Jane Mason.

Every effort has been made to ensure the accuracy of these notes. Any queries or corrections should be sent to the publishers in the first instance.

Thanks, acknowledgements and permissions

Our thanks go to Talia Rodgers and Minh Ha Duong for commissioning this project and for their generous support, advice and encouragement as the volumes have progressed.

Our thanks must also go to our 'essayists' – Dick McCaw, Jonathan Pitches, Franc Chamberlain, Lorna Marshall, Phelim McDermott and David Williams – for accepting our invitation to contribute original material to this Reader and for providing such a stimulating range of responses to our choices and ideas, and for their engagement in the project and productive conversations around their particular contributions and more generally the subject matters of the books.

Particular thanks go to Madame Jacqueline Weill in Jerusalem for all her help in securing the six Decroux 'Sports' images taken by her late husband Étienne Bertrand Weill. We are most grateful to Jacqueline for enabling and granting permission for these rare images to be reprinted here.

We both owe an acknowledgement to all those friends, students, practitioners and colleagues who have been part of our learning journeys over many years and which continue to delve into the 'messy' nature of theatres.

John Keefe
My thanks go to all my colleagues at London Metropolitan University, Sir John Cass Department of Art, Music and Design, and Queen's University (Canada) International Study Centre for their understanding and stimulation as this project has wended its way forward.

David Bevan, at the International Study Centre, and Brian Falconbridge and Lewis Jones at London Metropolitan University gave their support, advice and encouragement in matters of research and writing which have been greatly appreciated.

Without Eugene Svoboda, the marvellous librarian at the International Study Centre, the research for these volumes would not have been possible; I am indebted to him for his help with obtaining the books and journals needed. I must also thank Julia Ferguson, Robin McLean and Brian Jones, also of the ISC, for their patience and assistance with scanning and technical advice. My thanks go to Peter Carrier and Bettina Nethercott for help with translations, to Eric Litwack for help with Wittgenstein, and to Steffi Sachsenmaier for many lively discussions. My thanks to Karen Aram for her patience. Thanks go to my son Will for his bemused tolerance of my preoccupations whilst nevertheless having his own sense of play.

Finally, thanks to Simon Murray for being a fellow traveller over many years in physical and total theatres, which has led to these books.

Simon Murray

Dartington College of Arts provided me with four months' research leave at a very busy time in 2006 to start preparing for these books and therefore thanks here to Antonia Payne in particular for helping to make this happen.

My special thanks to David Williams, Joe Richards, Catriona Scott, Misha Myers, Misri Dey, Paul Clarke, Simon Persighetti and Sue Palmer from the Theatre team at Dartington for supporting my various absences to write and construct these books. These Dartington colleagues are amongst the most generous people I have ever worked with, and have consistently generated a culture of thoughtful questioning and stimulating dialogue around contemporary theatre practices that in turn has sharpened my own thinking about the perplexing nature of physical theatres. In this and many other respects, thanks, also, to Alan Fairbairn for numerous conversations around contemporary mime and physical theatres. And thanks to my co-writer and editor, John Keefe, for embarking on this journey with me, for challenging my received wisdoms and for sharing a perspective which has led to these publications.

Finally, unquantifiable thanks to Wendy Kirkup for her unflagging support in helping to make these projects happen, and to my daughter Isla for reminding me that there is much more to life than writing books about physical theatres.

Augusto Boal, 'Theatre, the first human invention' from *The Rainbow of Desire*, pp. 13–20. Original text © 1995 Augusto Boal. Introduction and translation © 1995 Adrian Jackson. Reprinted by permission of Routledge; Taylor & Francis Books UK. http://www.tandf.co.uk

Marcel Mauss, 'Body techniques' from *Sociology and Psychology* pp. 97–123. Translated by Ben Brewster. © Presses Universitaires de France 1950. English translation © Routledge & Kegan Paul Ltd 1979. Reprinted by permission of Routledge; Taylor & Francis Books UK. http://www.tandf.co.uk

Terry Eagleton from 'Morality', in *After Theory*, pp. 164–7. First published 2003, Penguin Books. Copyright © Terry Eagleton 2003. Reprinted by permission of the Penguin Group.

Aristotle, *The Art of Poetry*, trans. Ingram Bywater, pp. 28–39. © 1920, 1967 Oxford University Press. Reprinted by permission of Oxford University Press.

David Wiles, from 'The performer', *Greek Theatre Performance*, pp. 131–5. Published by Cambridge University Press, 2000. © David Wiles 2000. Reprinted by permission of Cambridge University Press.

Alan S. Downer, from 'Players and painted stage: nineteenth century acting', pp. 522–76. *PMLA*, Vol. 61, No. 2 (June, 1946). © 1946 PMLA; Modern Language Association. Every effort has been made to trace and contact the known copyright holder for this publication but without success. With respect to further information or queries please contact the publishers in the first instance.

Jeff Pressing from 'Improvisation: methods and models' in *Generative Processes in Music: The Psychology of Performance, Improvisation, and Composition*. Edited by John A. Sloboda, pp. 129–78. Oxford University Press, 1988. © John A. Sloboda and the contributors listed on pp. xvii, 1988.

Mel Gordon from *Lazzi: The Comic Routines of the Commedia dell'Arte* © 1983 Copyright by Performing Arts Journal Publications. © 1983 Copyright by Mel Gordon. Reprinted by permission of Performing Arts Journal Publications.

Jeff Nuttall, from 'A jewel on the nation's arse' in *King Twist – A Portrait of Frank Randle*, pp. 17–24. © Jeff Nuttall 1978. First published in 1978 by Routledge & Kegan Paul Ltd. Reprinted by permission of Routledge; Taylor & Francis Books UK. http://www.tandf.co.uk

Peter J. Arnold, from 'Sport, the aesthetic and art: further thoughts' in *British Journal of Educational Studies* 38:2 (May 1990), pp. 160–79. © The author and BJES 1990. Reprinted by permission of Blackwell Publishing.

Joan Littlewood, 'Goodbye note from Joan' in *New Theatre Voices of the Fifties and Sixties: Selections from* Encore *Magazine 1956–1963*, pp. 132–4. Edited by Charles Marowitz, Tom Milne, Owen Hale. © 1965 Encore Publishing Company. Published in Great Britain 1965, 1981 Eyre Methuen Ltd. Reprinted by permission of Methuen Publishing Ltd.

Mel Gordon, from 'German expressionist acting', *TDR/The Drama Review*, 19.3 (T67, Fall 1975), pp. 34–42. © The Drama Review. Reprinted by permission of *The Drama Review*.

Anaïs Nin, Gunther Stuhlmann, 'The theatre and the plague; its first performance by Antonin Artaud, April 1933, at the Schoolroom of the Sorbonne. As told by Anaïs

Nin', *The Diary of Anaïs Nin 1931–1934, Volume 1*, pp. 191–3. © 1966 by Anaïs Nin and renewed 1994 by Rupert Pole and Gunther Stuhlmann. Reprinted by permission of Harcourt, Inc.

Allan Kaprow, from 'A statement' in *Happenings, An Illustrated Anthology,* written and edited by Michael Kirby, pp. 44–52. E. P. Dutton & Co., Inc. 1965. Copyright © 1965 by Michael Kirby and 'Statement' copyright © 1965 by Allan Kaprow. Reprinted by permission of the estate of Allan Kaprow.

Patrick Campbell and Helen Spackman, from 'Surviving the performance: an interview with Franko B.', *TDR/The Drama Review* 42:4 (T160, Winter 1998), pp. 67–74. © 1998 by New York University and the Massachusetts Institute of Technology. Reprinted by permission of MIT Press.

Enrique Pardo, from 'The angel's hideout: between dance and theatre', *Performance Research* 3:2 (1998), pp. 19–26. © Routledge 1998. Reproduced by permission of Taylor & Francis Books UK. http://www.tandf.co.uk

Steven Berkoff, from 'Introduction' and 'East' in *Playscript 78*, pp. 11, 20–3. © Steven Berkoff 1977, 1978. First published in Great Britain 1977 by John Calder (Publishers) Ltd. New and revised edition printed 1978. Reissued as *Plays 1* by Faber and Faber 1996, and 2000.

Extract from 'East' reprinted by permission of Faber and Faber.

Every effort has been made to trace and contact the permissions holder for the 'Introduction (Producer's Note)' but without success. With respect to further information or queries please contact the publishers in the first instance.

Samuel Beckett, 'Act without words: a mime for one player' (1956), in *Collected Shorter Plays*, pp. 41–6. Translated from the original French by the author. © 1959 Samuel Beckett; 1984 Faber and Faber Limited. Reprinted by permission of Faber & Faber.

Emilyn Claid, from 'Re-dressing the girls' in *Yes? No! Maybe . . . Seductive Ambiguity in Dance*, pp. 189–92. © 2006 Emilyn Claid. First published 2006 by Routledge. Reproduced by permission of Taylor & Francis Books UK. http://www.tandf.co.uk

Norbert Servos, from 'Bluebeard' in *Pina Bausch – Wuppertal Dance Theatre or The Art of Training a Goldfish*, pp. 53–5. Published by Ballet-Bühnen-Verlag Köln, 1978/1984. Translated by Patricia Stadié. © Norbert Servos. Reprinted by permission of the author.

Tim Etchells, from 'Club of No Regrets' in *Certain Fragments, Contemporary Performance and Forced Entertainment*, pp. 162–76. © 1999 Tim Etchells. Reprinted by permission of Routledge; Taylor & Francis Books UK. http://www.tandf.co.uk

'On Brith Gof', a montage of material about and concerning the work of Brith Gof, a Welsh Theatre Company.

Mike Pearson, from 'My Balls/Your Chin' in *Performance Research* 3:2, Summer 1998. © Routledge 1998. Reprinted by permission of Taylor & Francis Books UK. http://www.tandf.co.uk

Mike Pearson and Cliff McLucas, from *Y Llyfyr Glas 1988–1995*, 1995. © Mike Pearson and Cliff McLucas 1995. Reprinted by permission of Mike Pearson.

Simon Murray and John Keefe, from 'Chasing Shadows' in *Total Theatre* 6:4, Winter 1994. © Simon Murray & John Keefe & Mime Action Group 1994. Reprinted by permission of the authors.

John Keefe, 'Brith Gof: "Arturius Rex"', *Total Theatre* 7:1, Spring 1995 © John Keefe & Mime Action Group 1995. Reprinted by permission of the author.

John Keefe, 'Brith Gof: "Tri Bywyd"', *Total Theatre* 7:4, Winter 1995 © John Keefe & Mime Action Group 1995. Reprinted by permission of the author.

Franc Chamberlain, *MAG – The Next Five Years 1997–2002*. Previously unpublished report. © Franc Chamberlain 1996. Reprinted by permission of the author.

Mme Jacqueline Weill, *Sports*. © Mme Jacqueline Weill. Reprinted by permission of the copyright holder.

Michael Chekhov, Nicolai Remisoff, from 'Appendix' in *To the Actor*, pp. 183–215. ©1953 Michael Chekhov. Michael Chekhov Biography and Appendix © 2002 Book Publishers Enterprises, Inc. and Mala Powers. First published in America 1953 by Harper & Row, New York. This edition first published 2002 by Routledge. Reprinted by permission of Taylor & Francis Books UK. http://www.tandf.co.uk
Every effort has been made to trace and contact the known copyright holder for the drawings by Nicolai Remisoff but without success. With respect to further information or queries please contact the publishers in the first instance.

Anne Dennis, from *The Articulate Body: The Physical Training of the Actor*, pp. 52–9. © 1995 by Anne Dennis. Excerpt from *The Articulate Body: The Physical Training of the Actor* by Anne Dennis reprinted by permission of – in the USA – Drama Book Publishers, a division of Quite Specific Media, www.quitespecificmedia.com and – in the UK – Nick Hern Books, www.nickhernbooks.co.uk

Jacques Lecoq, from 'Movement technique' in *The Moving Body: Teaching Creative Theatre*, pp. 66–74, 164–9. Translated from *Le corps poétique* by David Bradby. First published in French by Actes Sud-Papiers. © 1997 the Estate of Jacques Lecoq, Jean-Gabriel Carasso, Jean-Claude Lallias 1997. Translation copyright © David Bradby 2000. Reprinted by permission of Methuen Publishing Ltd and A&C Black.

Myra Felner, from 'Circus and the actor: an interview with Hovey Burgess', *TDR/The Drama Review*, 16.1 (T53, Winter 1972), pp. 39–46. © The Drama Review. Reprinted by permission of *The Drama Review*.

Yoshi Oida and Lorna Marshall, from 'Moving' in *The Invisible Actor*, pp. 19–22. © 1997, Yoshi Oida and Lorna Marshall. First published by Methuen. Reprinted by permission of A&C Black.

Bertolt Brecht, 'On everyday theatre' from *Poems*, pp. 176–9, 549, edited by John Willett and Ralph Manheim with the co-operation of Erich Fried. © 1976, 1979, 1981 by Eyre Methuen Ltd. First published in Great Britain in 1976 by Eyre Methuen Ltd, by arrangement with Suhrkamp Verlag, Frankfurt am Main. Reprinted by permission of Methuen Publishing Ltd.

Jonathan Kalb, from '*Rockaby* and the art of inadvertent interpretation', and 'Considerations of acting in the early plays', *Beckett in Performance*, pp. 9–11, 17, 21; 33–7. First published 1989 Cambridge University Press. First paperback edition 1991. © Jonathan Kalb 1989. Reprinted by permission of Cambridge University Press.

Mike Alfreds, from 'A shared experience: the actor as storyteller', *Dartington Theatre Papers* 3:6, pp. 3–20. © 1979 Theatre Papers. Reprinted by permission of Peter Hulton/Theatre Papers and the author.

Albert Hunt, Michael Kustow, Peter Brook, Denis Cannan, Adrian Mitchell, Geoffrey Reeves, from 'Narrative 1' and 'Narrative 2', *US*, pp. 12–30; 132–41. First published in 1968 by Calder and Boyars Limited. © The authors 1968. Reprinted by permission of Calder Publications.

Trevor Griffiths, *Comedians*, pp. 49–53. © Trevor Griffiths 1976. First published in 1976 by Faber & Faber Limited. Reprinted by permission of Faber & Faber.

Robert Kimball from 'Introductory essay', Stephen Sondheim, 'Beautiful' and 'Sunday', *Sunday in the Park with George* by Stephen Sondheim and James Lapine. (RCA HBC1–5042) © 1984 Revelation Music Publishing Corp. and Rilting Music Inc., and James Lapine, and Robert Kimball. Reprinted by permission of Alfred Publishing Co. Inc.

Patrice Pavis, from 'Introduction: towards a theory of interculturalism in theatre' in *The Intercultural Performance Reader*, pp. 2–5, 8–10. © 1996 Patrice Pavis. First published 1996 by Routledge. Reprinted by permission of Taylor & Francis Books UK. http://www.tandf.co.uk

Eugenio Barba and Nicola Savarese, from 'Pre-expressivity' in *The Secret Art of the Performer*, pp. 186–90. First published in 1991 by Routledge. The English-language edition of 'The secret art of the performer' has been edited and compiled by Richard Gough, translated by Richard Fowler. © 1991 Eugenio Barba and Nicola Savarese. Reprinted by permission of Routledge; Taylor & Francis Books UK. http://www.tandf.co.uk

Peter Brook, from 'The world as a can opener' in *The Shifting Point: Forty Years of Theatrical Exploration 1946–1987*, pp. 129–33. First published in paperback in 1989 by Methuen Drama. © 1987 by Peter Brook. Reprinted by permission of Methuen Publishing Ltd and A&C Black.

C. L. R. James, from 'What is art?' in *Beyond a Boundary*, pp. 257–79, © 1963 and 2005 executor to the estate of C. L. R. James and Yellow Jersey Press. Reprinted by permission of Curtis Brown Group Ltd. The publishers make grateful acknowledgement for permission to reproduce previously published material: *Don Bradman* by Philip Lindsay (Phoenix House); *Maurice Tate* by John Arlott (Phoenix House) and *The Island Cricketers* by Clyde Walcott (Hodder and Stoughton Ltd).

Edward W. Said, from 'Orientalism now' in *Orientalism*, pp. 199–208. Copyright © Edward W. Said 1978, 1995, 2003. First published by Routledge & Kegan Paul Ltd 1978. Published in Peregrine Books 1985. Reprinted with a new afterword 1995. Reprinted with a new preface 2003. Published by arrangement with Pantheon Books, a Division of Random House Inc. Reprinted by permission of Pantheon Books, a division of Random House Inc.

Every effort has been made to trace and contact known copyright holders before publication. Please communicate any queries or clarifications concerning copyright and permissions to the publishers in the first instance.

Editors' Note

The notes given in each article are retained from the original publication, as applicable to the reprinted text, for ease of reference to the original.
Similarly, bibliographical details are given as found in the original publication.
Sub-headings, italics, capitals, and names are retained as these appear in the original publication or essay.

Introduction

■ John Keefe and Simon Murray

Zizou: thanks for the memories

The game, the event, is not necessarily experienced or remembered in real time. My memories are fragmented – whenever something amazing happened I would remember playing in another place, at another time. Someone passed the ball to me and, before even touching it, I knew exactly what was going to happen. I knew I was going to score

Zinedine Zidane, 9 July 2006, Observer newspaper

Calcio (Football) Three qualities required for success:
Fantasia – surprise, unpredictability, imagination, flair
Furbizio – cunning, slyness, bending the rules, trickery, gamesmanship
Tecnica – technique, highly developed core skills

(Translation: David Williams)

THIS BOOK (as with its companion volume *Physical Theatres: A Critical Introduction* – hereafter *PT:I*) is about intersections, cross-overs and spillages. They are books which are trying to understand some key features of contemporary Western theatre practice, at the same time striving to unearth and (re)articulate modes of theatre history which often seem to have been hidden from view or subject to a strange amnesia.

The impulse for the project – two connected volumes on physical theatres – may be identified partly through the personal (theatre) biographies of the two editors, but also in a wish to unravel and map out that complex network of propositions, actions, events and dispositions which arguably constitute – and have constituted – the landscape of *physical theatres/the physical in theatres.*

There are an increasing number of books of all shapes and sizes that explore, set out, methodologise; give history and shape to our understanding of theatre. What is worth noting is the increasing prevalence of the plural in such articulation of theory(ies), history(ies), practice(s). The impulse to acknowledge, and indeed celebrate, complexity is not a perverse desire to complicate for the sake of complication, far rather a recognition that histories, influences and theatre makings are rarely ever simple and linear. To pretend that they are is alluring, but does little to take us towards an understanding of how theatre works in all its creative and often frustrating 'messiness'.

But when we first began forming the ideas and perspectives which lie behind these two volumes, we had been following such pluralities for some years in our own teaching, practice and understanding of what theatre was and is. Our individual and collaborative contributions towards the shaping and execution of the international 'Moving into Performance' workshop-symposium in 1994 in Manchester speak of and reinforce the productiveness of such a perspective. Perhaps these ideas and approaches to theatres derive much from our particular political and social backgrounds; perhaps from our own particular education and professional paths; perhaps thus from ways of looking at and being in the postwar world, a world in flux from the second half of the twentieth century. And, as such, this is reflected in the choice of material in this volume of extracts, and the original essays commissioned for this project.

We both began our theatre careers at a point when the languages of physical theatre were being enthusiastically articulated, promulgated and – from some quarters – denigrated within the landscape of non-literary and experimental theatre. Twenty-six years on, the locus of innovation, risk and challenge has – arguably – moved elsewhere in the cosmology of theatre and performance making. Perhaps, the moment of physical theatre has passed and consequently some of the selections below may have an elegiac quality, wistfully remembering a period and a particular cultural context, highly significant in its time, but no longer possessing the same charge for contemporary makers and thinkers of theatre.

Paradoxically, however, physical theatre has become embedded in the language of educationalists, actor trainers and their students. Within the landscape of professional theatre, too, the vocabulary, aspiration and rhetoric of physicality, and of an actor's movement qualities, have become widely articulated and claimed.

So, regardless of whether the cultural moment of physical theatre has passed, it remains present and – at times – clamorous both in the language of performance and in a variety of diverse contemporary theatre practices. What that 'it' is, and whether the 'it' has substance beyond shadow and phantom, is opened up through a 'dialogue' between the extracts and essays that follow.

So why pluralities?

There may be a dominant set of theatre conventions in any one era, perhaps of style or language. But such 'establishment' work will also draw on the ideas or energies of the unofficial, the submerged, the subversive, and the 'popular', all of which exist underneath or alongside the *official*.

Thus there have always been 'many theatres', but only 'one theatre' that has dominated by virtue of its culturally and politically awarded-ascribed status, its presence in published or preserved manuscripts and other texts, taking on a powerful presence and influence. It is in this spirit that we ground our insistence on talking about 'physical theatres/the physical in theatres' rather than a single form or practice. This has led to arguments with fellow practitioners and academics over many years about whether the plays of Beckett or Chekhov are 'physical theatre', the work of Littlewood or Brecht is 'physical theatre', the stage practices of Shakespeare or Aeschylus are 'physical theatre'.

In a word, yes – they are, it is.

Our aim is to reflect this plurality of theatre practice-theory-history as the through-lines of principles of theatre itself represented in the selections here. Principles and practices that are in a dialectical or interactive relationship to each other. But physicality is too often relegated to a mere supporting role to the word, reduced to the routine gestures and mannerisms sufficient to convey the stock character inhabiting and making familiar the world of the play.

It is such practices that give rise to the truism that all theatre is physical.

The case for there being 'simply theatre' has all the attraction that a comfortable and safe position provides (the arguments for this are restated in *PT:I*). Here, this may be summarised as the 'physical' in physical theatre is redundant excess since all theatrical performance is an embodied activity.

Likewise the perspective that makes ambitious claims for innovative – physical – theatre is a seductive one. Again this is set out in *PT:I*, but here summarised: that in its enthusiasm for proclaiming newness and innovation it fails to acknowledge theatre histories, and in so doing becomes fixated upon the contemporary.

Our books are predicated upon the basis that both these propositions possess their own truths. Consequently, we believe that it is a potentially productive quest to open up the contours and possibilities of the physical *in* theatres, whilst illuminating the claims that seem implicit in assertions made for new and discrete theatre genres which are indeed peculiarly physical and gestural. From the outset of this project we felt that if we were to risk constructing two books which signalled a conditional acceptance of the validity of the physical theatre label – both through their titles and in their structure – then we would employ only the plural usage. Hence, we have been ruthlessly insistent on *physical theatres* with all their consequent implications for suggesting a diversity of forms built from both common and different roots and technical traditions.

To this end *Physical Theatres: A Critical Reader* (hereafter *PT:R*) and *PT:I* are being published as companion volumes, allowing a movement across and between the (paradoxical) network of issues and ideas embraced by the term 'physical theatres'.

We intend these books to be 'portals', pointing readers to many other sources of information which arise from these critical introductions. Whilst it suits us that these will be two books among many that address similar issues, they do form a particular set of engagements with a field that is characterised by a diversity of approaches and differences in emphasis. In this spirit we also hope the books demonstrate a principle of openness that is a reflection of the always messy, hybrid nature of theatres, an approach which always resists attempts to clean these up, to 'purify'.

Thus there is a necessary minimum of division and categorisation needed for reasons of coherence in structuring these books. But it must be emphasised that our organising coda is one that allows the principles of theatre to flow to and from one practitioner or style to another, thus encouraging the virtues of a clash of contrapuntal voices as these appear and reappear in different places and guises.

If we are considering physical theatres/the physical in theatres then, as with all theatres, our response as spectator and audience will be physical, visceral, psychological and emotional. We feel ideas, we think about feelings. We understand, sometimes, on a level of grasping meaning almost without being able to articulate it to ourselves but simply *knowing* through our senses as we see and hear the physical in theatre.

In this sense theatre is practical – of practice – and it is experienced and experiential. Whatever (re)framing, (re)conceptualising or (re)fashioning of ideas and practices occurs, theatre remains an empirical, utterly human phenomenon which we come to from the equally sentient experience of play. In this way the act of theatre also embraces the experience itself of presenting and receiving that act.

Like all such constructions, 'physical theatre' is value-laden, and our selections must in themselves reflect our own values; thus the perspectives and prejudices we own up to. Such alternative modes of enquiry may be seen as of value in themselves, discussed by Richard Rorty as issues not to be settled but differences to be lived with and used, by Thomas Kuhns as the impossibility of there being value-free ways of looking at and advancing understanding (see *PT:I* for more on this matter).

Thus the terms 'physical theatres/physical in theatres' may be regarded as 'lenses' or 'frames' by which to approach the following selections that reflect the mise-en-scène of theatre. It is in this spirit that both volumes are intentionally heterogeneous with paradoxes, seeming contradictions and oppositions left in place. Hence the range of viewpoints that reflects the messy reality of what theatre is: an unavoidable hybrid of inherited, borrowed, stolen and invented practices and ideas.

This book

As an innovatory response to this multi-perspectival approach we have commissioned six original essays, placed at the front of each section. Each essay reflects on the theme of that section as a personal response – neither as simple comment on nor as a banal overview, but a meditation on the issues represented. The essays are very much a personal statement from each writer, discussed with the editors but not complying with any 'party' line.

Likewise following the innovatory practice in *PT:I*, we have included a 'choric quote' placed in a box at the head of each section. The intention is to help readers through the flow of principles and materials within each section and across the sections. Both the essays and the boxed quotes thus act as signposts, as provocations and commentaries on the ideas being presented.

They both also serve as introductions and hence little will be said about each section here. But the broad agenda outlined in our opening statements above will be realised through the selected material, organised into six sections.

Genesis, Contexts, Namings establishes a landscape for the whole project predicated on the genesis of the human as somatic, playful and cognitive, and mapping the range of concerns and issues around physical theatres that follow:

- the fluidity and mutability of language and terminology;
- contemporary practices and historical contexts;
- the acting-performing-theatre-play continuum;
- the body in its philosophical and cultural contexts;
- celebrating the hybridity and multiplicity of theatre.

Roots:Routes is discussed as a coinage by Jonathan Pitches, and seeks to indicate the pluralities of the roots and routes of theatres. This section sets out our overall engagement with physical theatres as both contemporary practices and in their historical and physiological-neurological contexts. Schematically, we articulate two routes of practices which feed contemporary physical theatres, and the *deeper* roots that these rest on: multiple and hybrid *routes* from multiple *roots.*

Deep traditions: classical and popular – a recognition of the importance of the physical in theatres traced through 'classical' drama, medieval drama, the street, circus, music hall/vaudeville, clown and agitprop, sport, etc. But here we also illustrate the deeper cognitive and neurological foundations of mimesis and play (cf. Section 1) which we believe underlie the physicality of all theatres. Here we can point to the routes that theatres may take as the description of Frank Randle becomes an eerie ghost of Gethin Price in *Comedians* (Section 5).

Hybrid pathways – a recognition of nineteenth- and twentieth-century intertwinings of dance-mime-perfomance-theatrical avant garde practices and ideas which prefigure or illustrate the range of physical theatres. Again, these trace the connotations of issues such as gazing-looking and perspectives on the body; of challenges to the theatrical body (cf. *PT:I*).

Contemporary Practices looks at ideas and work which exemplify some of the key concerns of Western physical theatres. Material that explicitly and unapologetically foregrounds the visual and physical dimensions of theatre making and performing, embracing a multiplicity of aesthetics and compositional forms – the spoken word, objects and props, scenography, technology. Here we aim to allow a reiteration of earlier ideas as well as prefiguring some of the concerns found in 'Physicality and the word' (Section 5). We also see how stage directions become the basis for improvisation, in Berkoff's 'restaging' of the battle of Cable Street. (See *PT:I* for a wider discussion of this issue.)

Preparation and Training attempts to trace a late twentieth-century Western theatre training which embraces the mind–body symbiosis, and therefore the impossibility of that mind–body/voice–movement dualism we disavow. We show the assumptions and conceptual paradigms which lie behind selected training strategies; how these deal with the body and physical expression in the creation and representation of character; which reflect on nuances and tensions between notions of 'preparation' and 'technical training'. The unique 'photo-essay' aims to let the body-in-action speak for itself.

Physicality and the Word considers how, when the word is dominant, other theatrical languages – corporeality, movement and scenographies, for example – must work with the word. Where such dramaturgical relationships between words and bodies are necessary to both staging and acting across a range of theatre-drama styles. Beckett's work, for example, operates with the same precision that a choreographer might use for making dance. But this same precision is just as necessary in the storytelling represented by Alfreds, the making of a picture onstage in Sondheim, or the grotesque clown of Gethin Price.

Bodies and Cultures is an acknowledgement – previously implicit – that this selection is inevitably a partial one in that its centre of attention is on Western practices and histories. We felt it better to be explicit and – in a sense – unapologetic about this centricity rather than risk tokenising the rich complexities of Asian, African or South American theatre forms which might otherwise fit into our frame of reference.

However, what this section does offer is an overview of certain performance perspectives which have fed and influenced many debates – sometimes passionate and angry – about cultures and their relationships and engagements. We consider the tension between a cultural exchange that is generous and mutual, and one that has often been accused of exoticism and cultural colonialism, is inevitably framed by the politics of contemporary global culture.

Ownership and omissions

In the creating and production of both books we have divided up the tasks of writing and selection, but they are finally our joint and shared responsibility as a collaboration of dialogue and constructive argument – an 'agon'.

What follows from this is a sharp realisation of the many omissions that any volume such as this has to come to terms with. We are all too aware we have both given attention to specific physical elements within theatre practice and not examined physical theatres through specific theatrical genres as such, although these resonate across our choices.

Rather we have tried to find a mix of material which does justice to the field through which we are charting a path. Pieces which may seem over-familiar will, we trust, take on a freshness when seen alongside the unfamiliar, with both designed to open up some new ('strange') perspectives on our themes of 'the physical' and 'theatres'. For example, how the popular body in sport, seen from the very different perspectives of Peter Arnold and C. L. R. James, can be regarded as sharing overlapping dynamics with the body in theatre. Hence the deliberately eclectic nature of this collection, forcing juxtapositions to make the familiar strange and the strange familiar.

Coda: in three senses

In this sense the meaning of the performance or production text is to be found in the inter-textual manifestation on stage of the constituent parts of theatre (see Kowzan in *PT:I*).

It is in this sense that we would wish to play with the notion of 'blurred genres' or categories. By its very nature, theatres are blurred: at the centre, at the edges and in their processes (see Geertz in *PT:I*).

It is in this sense that we would consider theatre to have always been 'total' as well as 'blurred' as well as 'physical'.

SECTION 1

Genesis, Contexts, Namings

Letter to a young practitioner
Value the work of your hands and body

This physical body is the meeting place of worlds.
Spiritual, social, political, emotional, intellectual worlds are all interpreted through this physical body. When we work with our hands and body to create art, or simply to project an idea from within, we imprint the product with a sweat signature, the glisten and odour which only the physical body can produce. These are the by-products of the meeting of worlds through the physical body. It is visible evidence of work to move from conception to production. Our bodies are both art elements and tools that communicate intuitively.

Goat Island: C.J. Mitchell, Bryan Saner, Karen Christopher,
Mark Jeffery, Matthew Goulish and Lin Hixson
Theatre in Crisis? eds Maria Delgado and Caridad Svich,
Manchester University Press, 2002: 241.

Essay 1

Claire Heggen goes fishing

■ Dick McCaw

IN THE BEGINNING WAS THE WORD? For many people involved in theatre, the process begins with being given a script, the playwright's words, which serve as the basis of the production. But what about a theatre which doesn't rely on words? This used to be called mime, but the term started to lose its currency – in Britain, at any rate – in the early 1990s. Now if you leaf through the programme of the London International Mime Festival you will find many different theatres – physical theatre, theatre of objects, visual theatre – and maybe the one thing they all have in common is that they don't begin with or rely upon the word.

In this essay I shall examine the work of Claire Heggen, co-founder of Paris-based Théâtre du Mouvement and an ex-pupil of the legendary French mime Étienne Decroux. I shall show how her creative process (i.e. the means by which she and her company create performances) starts not with words but movement. If she uses words it is to elicit movement from her fellow artists. For this reason her use of words, her terminology, is very precise – the wrong formula of words might not elicit the quality or type of movement that she is after. The words that I shall be quoting[1] come from a CD-ROM that Peter Hulton[2] and I made of a workshop given by Claire Heggen at the International Workshop Festival[3] (IWF) in 2000.

I use a conversation with Clive Barker to explain how we used the CD/DVD-ROM format to document the work of (mostly movement-oriented) teachers invited to IWF. When Clive Barker (a great friend and mentor) and I were once looking at footage that Peter had taken of a workshop on his theatre games, he muttered that, 'It is all very well seeing *what* I did, but you had no idea of what was in my mind as to *why* I did it.' This is exactly what the DVD-ROM format allows for. The process begins by Peter editing an hour or so from footage of a workshop he has filmed. That hour will be of exercises or moments that Peter considers central to their teaching. I then take the edited footage to the workshop leader and we watch it together. When they want to comment on a particular moment, I record their comments and then we continue viewing. At no point during the first viewings do I ask any questions. I then transcribe the comments and at that point we discuss what we gathered. Very often the teacher will start to recognise certain recurrent preoccupations, or I will ask for an explanation of certain terms, and in this way we build up a very detailed commentary on the exercise. So, we do get a fairly close approximation of what that teacher was thinking when they chose to lead that particular exercise in that particular way. In these documentations the movement or actions come first, and the verbal commentary second. Only by examining a process in detail can one understand exactly how the genesis, terminology and realisation of a piece of physical theatre is different from that of text-based theatre. For this reason I propose to study passages from Heggen's commentary on her workshop.

Claire Heggen goes fishing

Towards the end of a week-long workshop Heggen proposes a 30-minute exercise, or, as she prefers to call it, a protocol. It begins with a very simple movement *constraint* (trying to explore all the movement possible whilst keeping one hand on the floor) and develops into an exercise of theatrical creativity and composition. Her protocol has no cognitive content as such – it is simply a very carefully constructed series of rules for movement. Terminology is important: she resists using the word 'exercises' because they 'are treated as recipes. [. . .] One heaps up exercises one after the other but they lose their ultimate objective which is to make theatre.' She goes on to explain that each moment of an exercise 'can be a moment of drama. There is no such thing as an exercise – it is already theatre.' Heggen echoes Grotowski in her rejection of training as an accumulation of skills (the actor's performing capital), and in her insistence that the moment you start to work is already potentially a moment of theatre. Far from being a means of postponing the moment of theatre-making her training is journey towards it:

> The aim is to experience a very simple journey, which will become progressively more complex and which will reach points of synthesis along the way. Beginning from simply touching the ground with one's hand and from that contact, to move the arm around the shoulder blade, to find out that sense of pushing oneself back [*se repousser*] (according to Gerda Alexander's method); then, through the repetition of this simple movement (using only one side of the body, one can discover the effect that it has on you as in the Feldenkrais method), to become aware of the body from this point. You can't make a movement unless there is a point of support [*point d'appui*], a fixed point [*point fixe*]: for example, when you're walking, you move from one point of support to another. All movements require a fixed point in order that they can be developed. The only rule in this particular protocol is to keep the hand on the floor, not to move it or to let it slide.

The nature and purpose of this exercise are implied in her calling this a *journey* which she is inviting participants to 'experience'. The first level of experience is the physiological – exploring the sensation of rotating your shoulder blade through a movement of the arm; becoming aware of how you push yourself back from the floor.

She mentions the terms *points d'appui* and *points fixes*, but I don't know that it is useful to think of these as *terms* that can be understood discursively. The only way to understand either the *point d'appui* or the *point fixe* is through the action of your weight in relation to the floor and your surrounding space – in other words these terms can even be fully understood in terms of Newtonian mechanics. The exploration in this early part of the protocol is precisely to grasp what they mean in terms of movement. Could one call them kinaesthetic concepts? Their value as terms is that they identify a particular form of relation between the actor and space.

So, the participant begins by re-confirming or rediscovering their sense of internal contact (sensing the connection of the hand with the shoulder) and contact with the floor, and experiencing the contradiction (an important word for Heggen) between being asked to discover a range of movement within the given limitation (one hand on the floor). The next stage of the protocol is to find a fixed point somewhere in the studio – another kind of contact and another level of difficulty: how to find the possibilities for movement whilst trying to keep your eye on one point *and* still keep your hand on the floor? It is a movement conundrum – an adventure you are invited to join in. The protocol has value because it enables – or rather obliges – participants to make discoveries about their physiology, about the nature of theatrical space, and, finally, to happen upon material that might be useful in a performance. She explains that this 'is a process that I am increasingly developing in my teaching: I start with a little form or exercise, and shift gradually from the level of sensation to the level of metaphor'. In other words, you don't tell someone what they might find out, but let them make their own discoveries: her whole approach is *heuristic.*

Heggen doesn't give instructions for movement, she sets out parameters to be explored through movement, and then feeds in suggestions – in the nature of Viola Spolin's side-coaching – that might help stimulate the participant to develop and define their discoveries as they journey along their path, helping them to take creative responsibility for what they are doing. They are being encouraged to be internally responsive to the feedback they are getting from the movement.[4] The words aren't instructions about how to do a movement, but relays by means of which you develop movements within the given constraints. In an article called *The Rhetoric of the Image*,[5] Roland Barthes distinguished between photo captions that serve as a *relay*, and those that serve as an *anchorage*: the first develops upon the meaning of the image while the second merely enforces it by saying it again. Heggen, following her master Decroux, was emphatically opposed to tautology.

Heggen encourages the actor to start looking beyond and through the bodily sensation of movement: 'Be aware of different states within the body: postures, different states of breathing, different states of muscular tonicity.' She asks them to 'Taste the movement', to 'Take the time to experiment', 'Be satisfied with what the body gives you, let it make its own actions, let it happen to you.' The actor has a double engagement: first finding out what movements are possible within the given limitations – a problem-solving and active role; second, listening out for what happens *as a result* of making or finding out these movements – feedback which she invites participants to savour.

It is a body that thinks, it is as though movement develops exploration. It's not just that I am moving to make movements, I move with a savour for the movement, savour in the sense of savoir.

(In *Leçon*[6] Roland Barthes notes how he prefers to engage in the bodily intellection of *saveur* (which translates as 'savour') rather than the purely cognitive knowledge of *savoir* (which translates as 'cognitive knowledge').) You are asked to use your senses to find out what is happening, rather than trying to make sense of what is happening: 'Feed yourself from the situation itself and don't add things: the situation is already there: that is enough, you don't need any supplementary comments.' Her commentary contains useful warnings: 'You mustn't have a preconceived idea of what your body will give you when moving within this constraint. You must allow yourself to be astonished by what happens to you as you follow the path set out by the exercise.' (The late Barney Simon of the Market Theatre Johannesburg called one of his workshops 'The Astonished Eye'.)

I've noted that Heggen delights in contradiction, and this peculiar mixture of activity and passivity might seem to an English reader just another example of the perversity of French thinking. However, it is neither perverse nor alien to English practitioners. Think of Clive Barker, who talks about 'body think' in *Theatre Games*,[7] and is always watching out when an actor's or student's centre rises to their head – when they self-consciously think about an exercise rather than engage in and take information from the exercise itself. In the two workshops I've attended by Phelim McDermott he has asked participants to look after and to listen out for 'what the exercise needs'. In 2001 he began a workshop with an exercise by Viola Spolin:

> Turn your palms towards each other and have an idea that there's some space in between your hands and you don't know what this is yet, but you're going to play with this stuff in between you. Remember that it's a game. Find out. Start feeling what it feels like. What is its texture, its temperature? Is it thick or thin? [. . .] For the moment, concentrate on what is between your hands. Has it got colour? Is it soft or hard? If it changes, let it change. Notice when you go into your head and say to yourself, 'Oh, it's . . .' Then come back to what's out there.[8]

Once again we are dealing with invitations to discover through your senses what is actually happening. McDermott is sensitive to the problem of 'going into your head' and makes no big deal of it – simply take note of where you've gone and come back out again 'to what's out there'.

Later in the workshop he notes 'that this process involves waiting and giving over to something. We can't make a good scene happen. I'm talking about tricking your brain into doing something really good.' Elsewhere his advice is even simpler: 'Don't get in your own way.' The problem is that our impatient, analytic brain wants to get on with the process, and this stops us listening. Heggen notes that, 'Normally, we are sensorially handicapped but if you open the door to this kind of information, the universe which is thereby discovered can be a very rich source of nourishment for the actor.'

It must be clear by now that Heggen's protocol operates entirely via bodily movement. As McDermott observed above, the conscious mind actually takes our attention away from where the action is happening. Heggen points out that in terms of creative movement the body can 'outplay' the mind:

You must explore every possibility – in fact there is no such thing as the impossible: this only exists in our minds – it does not exist in the movement. The body always has ways of escaping the nets of our mind.

I have already noted that during the course of the protocol the student's attention shifts 'gradually from the level of sensation to the level of metaphor'. While the two levels are functionally related, it is the second which leads to theatrical material. She points out that 'images, emotions, potential significations for the actor' are all 'produced by the contradiction between what the body wants to do and what it cannot because part of it is fixed to the ground'. When I have said that the protocol is devoid of content I mean that it is completely open to interpretation. She has set the actor a challenge, and the 'images, emotions and potential significations' are what result from the actor's negotiation with this challenge. The protocol is what we go fishing with:

> The object is for the actor to discover a new body, what I call the fictitious body, a habitual body which enters an unfamiliar dimension, unfamiliar in terms of its distance from the everyday. The protocol can be used as a hook with which to fish. The difference between the real and the fictitious body lies in this question of the habitual and the non-habitual. It is also because we are not in a realist form of theatre, but in a theatre of forms: we are not asking the body to create a mimesis of the real, thus the body is fictional, it is imaginary.

If there are echoes of Eugenio Barba's distinction between the daily and the extra-daily body and Heggen's habitual and fictitious body, it may well be because both have been inspired by Decroux's aphorism that 'The mime is only comfortable when uncomfortable' ('C'est dans la malaise que le mime est à l'aise'). Heggen is describing a complex and functional interrelation of the physical, mental and emotional. Torn between keeping an eye fixed on the point in space and one hand fixed on the floor, and then exploring all the movement possibilities within these rigorous constraints, the actor is led to discover and to create some really unhabitual shapes – this is the imaginary, non-everyday body. Heggen's argument is that this process of exertion and discovery is not simply physical – it sets up emotional resonances, provokes internal images. She suggests that there may be a correlation with degrees of physical unease and creativity, but that it is an unpredictable process:

> It isn't a case of us doing what we want to do because we don't know what will appear, but we know that it might be an important image. Sometimes when you have an image you aren't sure what it means, you don't know quite what to do with it. You think sometimes that you are dealing with one thing and it turns out to be something else – and it is this something else, this unintended intention, which turns out to be more important.

What distinguishes Heggen's type of theatre is the fact that it is not mimetic – the artistry lies in the suggestibility rather than the verisimilitude of the form (both for the actor-creator and the spectator).

So the process is neither linear nor predictable. You simply have to be open and alert to what may happen if you put yourself through a difficult physical process. It is not a cognitive but a physical process, thus you 'know' that you have something because it feels right, rather than because it looks like the something you are trying to represent. (In this sense Decroux's mime differs profoundly from that of Marceau.) Heggen tells the story of a woman who was hugely moved by the 'child-birth' scene in one of their shows. There wasn't such a 'scene' in the show – it is what the spectator interpreted from the movements and body-shapes – but Heggen recognised what she was talking about and found it difficult to escape the association thereafter.

Even though meaning may be open, there is a definite structure, a specific morphology to the form. In this sense, 'The form is a support. It is a place to which you can come back when you are lost, so you know what to do. This way you know that you are not ridiculous.' It also means that when working as a director she can give directions to the actor 'which are uniquely to do with space, dynamics or parts of the body without having resort to psychology'. When she describes this as fixing 'problems within the gestural score', she comes close to Grotowski, who compared the actor's score of physical actions to river banks[9] which channel the flow of emotional or imagistic associations, or to a glass cowl which protects the naked candle flame. The dynamic of Heggen's protocol derives from the productive but unpredictable interplay between interior and exterior, the physical and the emotional/imaginal – the whole thing driven by the contradiction between restriction and movement:

> This, in turn, produces *forms* which then *inform* the body and which induce trans*form*ations in the body and which in turn induce per*form*ance – identifying the exterior and interior forms that it produces.

Behind this seeming paradox is another Decroux aphorism: 'The actor is at the same time the subject and the object of art' ('L'Acteur est sujet et objet d'art à la fois'). The actor, far from being an interpreter of an already-written text, is the author of the performance text – that 'gestural score' mentioned above. This might recall Meyerhold's description of the biomechanical actor as a *conscious* operator of his acting machinery. His 'formula for acting' was $N = A1 + A2$ 'where N = the actor; A1 = the artist who conceives the idea and issues the instructions necessary for its execution; A2 = the executant who executes the conception of A1' (*Meyerhold, A Revolution in Theatre*, Edward Braun (Methuen, 1995), p. 173). But there is a huge difference here. Meyerhold is taking a behaviourist approach (he corresponded with Ivan Pavlov), whereby certain movements are deemed to elicit given – i.e. predictable – effects upon a spectator. Although Heggen makes no reference to contemporary neuro-physiology, her model allows for far greater nuance and complexity in the feedback loops between external movement and internal forms of experience (images, memories, emotions). I think this difference between the mechanical model of the behaviourists and the neuro-physiological approach of Heggen is crucially important.

Finally I think we are ready to offer some answers to the questions I posed at the beginning of this essay. Where does Heggen begin to work when starting a new production? The answer is with play rather than a play:

Another aphorism that is important for us is 'Theatre must be played before it is written'. This means that you don't start with a story and then look for forms with which to express it. Instead you begin by working on forms, and little by little things appear and you can compose your story from the things that result from this exploration. That is how we always work.

She doesn't create from nothing. She invents in the etymological sense of the word – she finds things out (Latin *invenire* – 'to come upon, to discover') through listening to her body's actions and reactions; a body which is constantly informed and transformed through this process of discovering. Training or education in this context is not some accumulation of ever greater quantities of knowledge (the *gourmand* or guzzler), but the development of a palate capable of making ever finer distinctions of taste, and which learns through successive tastings (the *gourmet*). One of Heggen's favourite expressions is borrowed from Antonio Machado – *Voyageur, il n'y a pas de chemin, le chemin se fait en marchant* ('Traveller, there is no path; the path is made by walking it').*

So, in the beginning was the movement. Or rather a protocol which obliges the practitioner to exercise their movement imagination and sensibility. She makes use of a few terms as she guides the practitioner through the exploration of this protocol, but their validity can only be understood when tested out through movement. The whole process is heuristic, and depends on the creative activity of the practitioner: nothing here is given; it has to be created by the mover-researcher. And it is not simply an exercise – a trial run for the 'real' thing to come – it is 'already theatre'. Heggen has gone into the emotional – imaginary – physiological realm of movement with a precision similar to that of Grotowski. But it is a process that starts with, and when lost can go back to the physiological, to the bodily sensation, provoked by making a particular movement.

Despite our long conversations together I don't know how familiar Heggen is with recent research into the complex and global nature of neural connectivity within the brain and throughout the body. Most certainly, the sophistication and open-endedness of her method reflects such an understanding. Heggen demonstrates a physical process whereby ideas or images come through acts of movement. First the actor works at the level of physical sensation, then, hopefully, come the images and ideas by association. The physical body is transformed through this psycho-physical connection into the fictional body (the one that suggests images in the mind of the audience). Both genesis and process are physical. The training she proposes is a 'tuning' by means of which the actor can listen to the emotional and imaginal 'resonances' created by movements. The means of communication with the audience is physical rather than discursive – the audience is physically moved by the actor's movement.

Notes

1   There will be no page references, since the text in the CD-ROM is unpaginated.
2   Peter Hulton is director of the Arts Documentation Unit.
3   I was Artistic Director of IWF from 1993 to 2001.

4   In this sense her instructions are very much like Moshe Feldenkrais' very carefully worded lessons in *Awareness through Movement*. They are 'open' (i.e. give no fixed content) precisely to allow the student to discover the movements that they imply.

5   'Rhétorique de l'image', in *Oeuvres completes, Tome 1* (Éditions du Seuil, Paris, 1993), p. 1422.

6   In *Oeuvres completes, Tome 3* (Éditions du Seuil, Paris, 1995), p. 814. *Sapientia: nul pouvoir, un peu de savoir, un peu de sagesse, et le plus de saveur possible* (Sapientia: no power, a little knowledge, a little wisdom, and the greatest possible amount of savour).

7   In *Theatre Games* (Methuen, London, 1977), pp. 29–31.

8   In *Space, Improvisation, Creativity* (Arts Archives, Exeter, 2005).

9   In his essay 'Exercises' (in *Il Teatro Laboratorium di Jerzy Grotowski*, Fondazione Pontedera Teatro, 2001) and in *At Work with Grotowski on the Physical Actions* (Routledge, London and New York, 1995), p. 21.

Editors' Note

*   From Spanish original 'Caminante no hay camino/se hace el camino al andar'.

CHAPTER 1

Étienne Decroux

My definition of theatre

to Georges Pomies

Partial incarnation of the future actor

I

T**HE LARGE NUMBER OF ELEMENTS** that generally go into the composition of the theatre must contain material for a definition. So what do we find? Worthy arts, each gifted with the power to capture the Universe in its studio, and which should not wish for either expansion or branches. Yet in a place called theatre we find painter, sculptor, architect, musician, singer, dancer and actor united together in an effort to produce something grand. The 'closed to the public' sign which adorns the entrance door to the stage was therefore not put up for them. But let there be no mistake: every art that has access to the stage also has a rigid code allowing it to express in its particular way everything that exists . . . let us boldly underline the rule: every art enjoys the privilege of expressing the world in its own way, without calling on any other art . . .

Where does one see the art of the actor as one sees painting: in its pure state? . . .

Meanwhile, we are approaching the port of the definition, so let us try to land: since the actor is the only artist without a home of his own, the theatre must become his property.

2

Of all the people with claims to the stage, only one has never been absent from it: the actor . . .

Even in productions with words there are silences during which the actor meditates and develops; long moments during which the text is of no value and in which the actor creates emotion through the way he acts. Does the converse exist?

Have we ever, for even a second, heard a text without the speaker? Never, of course.

The only art unceasingly present on the stage is therefore the art of the actor.

3

The arts united in the theatre obey only the actor's orders; that is obvious. They all help him to create the illusion of reality and also to sweeten the unsavouriness of his work . . .

But whatever happens, the actor will remain the harmonic centre of the other arts, the orchestral conductor with perhaps rather faulty aim, but the tuning-fork of the theatre and, even if he is replaced by delightful silk puppets, it will still be philosophical and correct to remark: 'He is respected, therefore he was.'

4

What will our definition be? We have seen that the actor is the only artist without a home of his own.

This encourages us to put him up in the theatre. We have seen that every art occupying the stage is still governed by the action, which is nothing more than the actor in motion: this makes us inclined to see him as 'the rightful inhabitant of the venerable tower'. We have seen above all – and this is decisive – that the actor is the only artist eternally present in the theatre. Such a statement eliminates all the other arts . . . none other is the essential of theatre.

Put another way: none can be included in its definition.

That leaves us to find the logical form of this definition, which we shall express in substance as follows:

Theatre is the actor art. (Trans. note: Decroux's original *l'art d'acteur* is as awkward in French as 'the actor art' is in English.)

4a

So those who define theatre as a 'synthesis of all the arts' have their answer . . . If scenery, along with other accidents, is no more essential to theatre than a jacket is to man, this does not prevent the actor from appearing inside a set any more than it does a man from appearing in a detachable collar. The converse does not exist: if theatre were defined as a synthesis of all the arts or even two of them, any dramatic effort to suggest scenery, words, music, etc., would be driven from the stage.

Theatre is the actor art.

5

What does all this prove? . . . That if the actor art on its own produces pure theatre, then our theatre is suffocating under a heap of rubble. In theatre companies one expects success from a good writer, and disaster from a bad one. The evil is so deeply rooted that it is revealed in the vocabulary: what we call 'play' is the printed text.

Here is the remedy:

1 For a period of thirty years, the proscription of every alien art. We shall replace the drawing-room setting with the setting of the theatre itself, our intention being solely to provide a background for all imaginable actions.

2 For the first ten years of this thirty year period: proscription of any elevation on stage, such as stools, staircases, terraces, balconies, etc. The actor will have to give the impression that he is higher and his partner lower, when in reality they are side by side.

Later, the authorization of certain forms of elevation on the condition that they create even greater challenges for the actor.

3 For the first twenty years of this thirty year period: the proscription of any vocal sound.

Later, the acceptance of inarticulate cries for five years.

Finally, words accepted for the last five years of the thirty year period, but invented by the actor.

4 After this period of war: stability. Plays shall be composed in the following order:

A Rough outline of the written action serving as a basis for work.

B The actor miming his action, then accompanying it with inarticulate sounds, then improvising his text.

C Introduction of a dramaturge to translate the text into choice language, without adding a word.

D Reappearance of alien arts, but practised by the actors. And when the actor is master in his own home he shall see to the employment of dancers, singers and musicians for indispensable and well-defined tasks.

But is this really the remedy? . . . It is a matter of cutting off the theatre's right hand. (1931)

This article, born thirty years ago, was my first proper piece of writing on art. And it was published!

In a review for fellow actors, roneotyped on grey, easily crumpled paper.

Its readers, young theatre people, used to spend all night talking in the street. It is for them that the article speaks – sitting, standing, stepping out. I must have written it while putting on my make-up.

Let us leave it with its needlessly risky formulas, on the edge of the question. When my past returns to me, I have no desire to amend it. I still believe in the main points, namely: that one must rehearse a play before writing it; and that the theatre is the actor art, which proves that, as an art of the beautiful, theatre does not exist (New York, March 10, 1962).

Regrets

In the French edition of this book, I did not pay tribute to the memories of the Frenchman, Noverre, nor to the German, Joss.

Was this regrettable omission caused by their belonging to the world of dance? Certainly. But in their case this cannot be considered a good reason.

Noverre, who was born in Paris in 1727 and died in 1810, was primarily a dancer. But he worked with both theory and practice to build up a type of pantomime the character of which had previously been unknown.

Joss, also a dancer, placed himself outside dance and old-style pantomime, and created the ballet known as 'The Green Table'. This play without words moves from satire to tragedy. Its success was great, and long-lived throughout the world; and it belongs to the period immediately after the First World War.

One day I hope to write further on the contribution made by these two 'brothers'.

Charlie Chaplin

Many books have been written about him.
If I were to undertake to write my own,
I would feel the full weight of the undertaking.
Yet this prospect would make me less afraid than that of giving, in passing, two or three opinions on one of the most eminent men of the time in which I have lived. I at least want this collection to end with the name of the gymnast, of the artist and of the citizen whose soul, assuredly, transcends his craft:

CHARLIE CHAPLIN
(New York, May 30, 1962)

CHAPTER 2

Ana Sánchez-Colberg

Altered states and subliminal spaces

Charting the road towards a physical theatre

IT HAS BEEN CRITICALLY ACKNOWLEDGED that the development of what has been loosely termed 'physical theatre' has marked one of the most significant trends in dance and theatre since the 1980s. At a surface level, the term has been collectively used to identify an eclectic production commonly understood to be one which focuses on the unfolding of a narrative through physicalized events and which relegates verbal narrative – if at all present – to a subordinate position. However, it is precisely on evaluating such eclecticism that one is faced with a problematic. To admit to the above mentioned generalization would allow us to equate productions as varied as a Christmas pantomime to the work of Grotowski, or, indeed, Bausch. The problems arising from this are obvious.

The term itself – 'physical theatre' – denotes a hybrid character and is testimony to its double legacy in both avant-garde theatre and dance. It is precisely this double current of influences which needs to be taken into consideration in any attempt to delineate specific parameters of the new genre.

This study proposes that the process of contextualizing physical theatre needs to take into consideration its location both within avant-garde theatre, particularly that production considered to be 'body-focused', and also within the context of avant-garde dance and its particular parameters which set the body as the centralizing unit within the theatrical space. In examining this double influence one must not forget that cross-references between the two forms of avant-garde production abound. The locating of physical theatre within the avant-garde means that attention must be given to issues of anti-establishment within the context of alienation and transgression common to both forms. However, this study does not aim to arrive at a reductive classification of physical theatre. Rather it aims to show that what the genre defines is not only a set of stylistic features of a production which is bodily based, but rather one which extends discursive practices within the relative and tense relationship between the body/text/theatre reality which goes beyond mere representation via the body.

I

The polemic created by the very notion of the body on stage . . . has once again opened basic ontological questions about the nature of theatre and its relationship to the larger reality which contains it or which it is deemed, in a classical sense, 'to mirror'. Garner (1990) describes this polemic as generated by

> the almost obsessive interest in the body as a political unit . . . and its role within the context of subjectivity and subjection. Exploiting the body's centrality within the theatrical medium, contemporary political dramatists have refigured the actor's body as a principal site of theatrical and political intervention, establishing in the process a 'body politic' rooted in the individual's sentient presence. (p. 146)

What Garner places in post-Brechtian theatre since 1956, Innes (1993) sees as part of a much longer process which can be traced to early primitivist avant-garde theatre . . . Irrespective of its precise historical birth . . . what becomes palpable is the unresolved controversy surrounding what can be defined (both semiotically and phenomenologically) as 'world-constitution' via the body as it

> interacts with the environment and the consequences upon this subject of an external infringement directed at the body and the personal world it serves to ground.
>
> (Garner, p. 148)

However, this body focus needs to be seen as arising from a progressive devaluation of language and a move towards a nonverbal idiom . . . This devaluation is based – and I simplify – on a mistrust of language to convey the condition of man-in-the-world, a language which aims to articulate, and thus contain, universal truths without questioning the material practices which gave rise to that language . . .

With Brecht one encounters a first attempt at a revolution of language both verbal and theatrical which will lead (in later generations) to a revolution of that language as it is embodied. Epic theatre techniques are geared to re-emphasize (and, therefore, defamiliarize) the process of language construction. It is also significant to remember that Brecht was among the first to leave the work of rearticulation to the audience . . .

Like Brecht, Ionesco shares in an attempt to use the theatre to shake the audiences from their passive acceptance of the world as given . . .

> Everything is permitted in the theatre; to bring the characters to life, but also to materialise states of anxiety, inner presences. . . . Just as the words are contained in gesture, action, mime, which, at the moment when words become inadequate, take their place, the material elements of the stage can in turn further intensify these.
>
> (Ionesco in Hayman, 1979: 132)

Language is used in a non-referential manner; it no longer carries any meaning nor does it provide the structures to organize world-experience. A direct sign–signifier relationship is broken. Objects, characters, scenes and events acquire a multiple, fluctuating, fragmented identity . . .

Any discussion of a physical theatre needs to consider the work of Artaud. His writings on the theatre, particularly those on the 'theatre of cruelty', have inspired generations of theatremakers. In fact, Innes (1993) discusses how Artaud, although commonly associated with the production of the Living Theatre, Grotowski and Brook, was also influential in the work of Ionesco. However, it is also agreed that there is a gap between Artaud's vision of the theatre and that which he was actually able to produce during his working life. His thoughts on theatre as expressed in *The Theatre and Its Double* (1938) clearly place him, together with Brecht and Ionesco, in an antagonist position to language – which he equates to culture/civilization – and its institutions:

> If confusion is the sign of the times, I see at the root of this confusion a rupture between things and words, between things and the ideas and signs that are their representation . . . A civilised man is regarded as a person instructed in systems, a person who thinks in forms, signs, representations – a monster whose faculty of deriving thoughts from acts, instead of identifying acts with thoughts, is developed to an absurdity.
>
> (Artaud, 1958: 12)

Artaud's theatre is one of the phenomenal body, not only because the body is the centre of the *mise en scène*, but also because the function of this body is not to identify layers of signification within operative cultures (i.e. the domain of semiotics) but to aim to discover 'language beyond words', a metaphysics of the theatre via an immersion in the physical. This state of being he equates to 'life', and it is this 'life' which he believes the theatre needs to rediscover . . . What becomes clear during the course of reading Artaud is the vision of a stage which is a 'concrete physical space' (ibid.: 37) to be filled by 'its own concrete language' . . . He summarizes by stating that 'the possibilities for realisation in the theatre relate entirely to the *mise en scène* considered as a language in space and in movement' (ibid.: 45) . . .

With this shift, the polemics of what constitutes the 'political' are drastically changed. There is no longer an objectified otherness (whether ideology, language, societal institutions, etc.) which serves to ground the discourse of the body as a battle between self and the world. The world (as in the work of Beckett) is the body, its limits the boundary of reality. Therefore, the process of alienation becomes self-referential. The body/self is no longer alienated from an external environment but becomes painfully aware of being alienated from itself. The degree of alienation is such that transgression is no longer directed towards an environment outside of oneself but is a transgression of self through actions created and directed towards the self. The act of transgression becomes the only avenue to establish consciousness of being. The body is no longer just a semiotic body 'conscious of signification' (Sue-Ellen Case in Erickson, 1990: 229) but becomes a 'zero-point' (Garner, 1990: 148) within a phenomenal world . . .

II

If we have identified the process of language devaluation in avant-garde theatre as a necessary first step in the process to contextualize physical theatre, a similar process can be traced within avant-garde dance. If the process of language devaluation in theatre production came as a result of a general mistrust of language's ability to convey the experience of self-in-the-world, a parallel mistrust of codified 'languages of the body' is present in the history of contemporary dance from Duncan to Bausch . . .

In Laban's work the principal guiding premise is that of the 'body in space'. Before there is movement, there is a body in space – a body that has orientation, dimensions, inclination, that by virtue of just existing occupies and produces space. Movement *follows* from this first principle. The experience of self is understood in relation to its approach to the space. It may seem like an incredibly simplistic statement, but to accept that dance is about the body, in space, through movement necessitates a significant shift from the common understanding of the body in movement through space.

Movement (and time) is a result of a first inner intention of the body – what Laban defined as inner motivation – as it desires to project itself into space. Movement is the effect, not the cause. The movement, however, is the mediator between two areas of experience: internal space, which he referred to as the land of silence, and the external world, the world of action (Laban, 1935) . . .

There are strong links between *Ausdruckstanz* and *Tanztheater* with respect to their shared attitude towards the understanding of the body/space relationship. The debate about what constitutes our inner and outer realities and how they are manifested on stage is central to production in both. Given that the focus is on the nexus of the body and space, movement becomes subordinate and intrinsically linked to the environment which contextualizes it. The generation of movement may be an important part of the body/space materialization, but not its main focus. Movement is relevant in as much as it may 'express' aspects of the body/space nexus. Therefore, the boundaries of what can constitute dance movement are opened and, consequently, so are the boundaries of what constitutes the dance medium. *Tanztheater*'s production extends this debate . . .

Two main features predominate. The first is what Birringer has summarized as an 'understanding of dance that formally transcends the limiting divisions into theatre of dance, voice or music' (Birringer, 1986: 96) but that at the same time remains firmly focused on the investigation of 'the specific dimensions of dance', and therefore has a distinct focus on the body – the second feature – and how it constitutes the subjective world of the stage . . .

The focus on the body is prevalent, particularly in wanting to explore what and how theatrical experiences are created with and through it in an attempt to question what is shared and what is specific within the human condition . . .

III

The establishment of 'physical theatre' as a distinct genre begins to take hold in the 1980s. In early writings the terms 'physical theatre' and 'dance-theatre' (the latter in quotation marks and hyphenated to associate it with the German production) were at times used interchangeably. The stylistic and aesthetic links between the two productions were evident. Critics and audiences alike pointed out that the work's powerful combination of design, text, dance, use of dancers/actors in production, was beginning to distinguish itself as a vital force in contemporary production . . .

The term 'physical theatre' began to identify the production in two ways. 'Theatre' implied a connection with narrative development via action – as distinct from the conventional choreographic structures from which it was wanting to dissociate itself . . . However, the term 'physical' – separate from theatre – implied a particular approach to its movement . . . What was at first regarded as another development in idiosyncratic movement style within dance (a comment that can be applied to the hundreds of dance companies who have adopted the movement style, but not the aesthetic complexity) soon was recognized as a distinct strategy of theatrical production which – as *Tanztheater* had done in the 1970s – existed in the intersection between theatre and dance. As discussed earlier, this intersection is inhabited by a body-focus which brings with it a double debate. First there is the role of language in the creation of subjects (a process which is social and ideological) and second the relationship between the body in space as *a priori* condition to the advent of this social body. The production arises from the interplay of these two conditions . . .

What has become evident is that physical theatre – whilst focusing on the issue of the body on stage – does not constitute a single proposition. Rather, a double perspective has been identified. Whilst admitting to the significance of a 'decoding' process of the body as a sign of discourse, it has also become significant to consider that the social body which is the focus of such structural analysis is also a spatial body which, although subject to social discourse, also has its own 'embodied' knowledge. This issue, together with the relevant shift to reexamining the body–space nexus, becomes increasingly necessary as we move into virtual worlds of constructed space where experience is defined in terms of location and not articulation.

References

Artaud, A. (1958) *The Theatre and Its Double*, New York: Grove Press.

Birringer, J. (1986) 'Pina Bausch dancing across borders', *Drama Review* 30(2) (Summer): 85–97.

Erickson, J. (1990) 'Appropriation and transgression in contemporary American performance: the Wooster Groups, Holly Hughes and Karen Finley', *Theatre Journal* 42(2) (May): 225–36.

Garner, S.B. (1990) 'Post Brechtian anatomies: Weiss, Bond and the politics of embodiment', *Theatre Journal* 42(2) (May): 145–64.

Hayman, R. (1979) *Theatre and Anti-theatre: New Movements since Beckett*, London: Secker & Warburg.

Innes, C. (1993) *Holy Theatre: Ritual and the Avant-Garde*, Cambridge: Cambridge University Press.

Laban, R. (1935) *A Life for Dance*, Bristol: Arrowsmith.

CHAPTER 3

David E.R. George

Performance epistemology

> We are such stuff as dreams are made on.
> William Shakespeare,
> *The Tempest*

THE TERM 'PERFORMANCE' has two primary meanings: a 'carrying out' or 'execution' (and hence implicit service to a preconceived task or set of orders) and a 'presentation'. The term appears in its first sense in *The Tempest* where Ariel puts on little plays both to deceive, and to reform, the other characters, under Prospero's instruction. Since then, performances have tended to be seen as the execution of someone else's orders, generally authors' and directors', but it was also in *The Tempest* that Shakespeare faced the problematic implications of performance as presentation, invoking the ephemerality and insubstantiality of the worlds it constructs:

> Our revels now are ended. These our actors,
> As I foretold you, were all spirits, and
> Are melted into air, into thin air:
> And, like the baseless fabric of this vision,
> The cloud-capp'd towers, the gorgeous palaces,
> The solemn temples, the great globe itself,
> Yea, all which it inherit, shall dissolve,
> And, like this insubstantial pageant faded,
> Leave not a rack behind.
> (Act IV, scene 1,148–56)

In 1995 the term is now regularly used as a criterion of evaluation, as a category of contemporary research and to refer to postmodern theatre. Even more profoundly, it has evolved as an emerging paradigm for describing a wide range of ideas.

In considering performance three critical but crucial problems remain, concerning terminology, methodology and epistemology. Taken together they point to significant gaps in current research. First, the term 'performance' is still often confused with 'theatre' . . .

The methodology for its investigation, however, is, to date, suspect and this is the second crucial problem in performance research . . . It is largely inductive-reductive, a form of positivism which extrapolates laws and common features from a range of cited phenomena. Typically, research into performance bases itself on lists of purportedly related phenomena followed by an attempt to identify their common denominators. As a methodology – in any discipline – this is suspect since it assumes that the list of phenomena is both comprehensive and internally coherent. The methodology itself is therefore trapped in a classic 'hermeneutic circle' in which the glimmering definition that has already been used to identify the items to be analysed is dependent on the prior existence of the list that is meant to provide the definition – with which it actually started . . . There is, however, a classical solution and alternative to this trap: a phenomenological epoche . . .

Phenomenology is especially useful to the present inquiry because it recognizes that we all construct and live in a variety of different realities, each one defined by certain conventions and specific cognitive operations and assumptions. As we step from one reality (the academic or professional world, for example) into others (reading, listening to music, watching or engaging in a play) we re-format our consciousness in the sense of altering radically our expectations of the kinds of experiences and knowledges we are turning from and to. As Husserl argued, the continuity of any cultural phenomenon, the praxis of any body of knowledge, involves a string of people not simply learning a set of axioms which someone invented in the past, but also themselves repeating the cognitive breakthrough of its 'inventor' and actually reinventing the institution itself each time . . .

As we walk into a performance, we make adjustments to fundamental cognitive assumptions. We know that the time, the place, the persons we will encounter will be radically different in kind from time, place and person in other social realities. It is not only our bodies which enter the world of performance; it is, even more significantly, our minds which step across a threshold from one set of assumptions about one kind of reality into another. Those realities consist both of implicit epistemologies – cognitive operations and assumptions – and their ontological implications – that is, the kind of reality they posit. Such a phenomenological reduction is attempted below; what it produces begins, it is hoped, to resolve the third problem in current research, namely that performance has, as yet, no developed theory as an epistemology/ontology in its own right.

What kind of a reality or knowledge performance is and what sorts of truths it provides remain to be fully analysed. Some epistemology and ontology are implicit, but inquiry into their being remains dispersed. While there have been statements about performance and these have noted its liminality, contingency and ephemerality, to my knowledge there has been no attempt to frame performance as a system or as an episte-mological 'map'. That is what is now needed: an attempt to identify how the elements of performance form an internal system, constructing a unique reality and providing a unique form of experience . . .

Conventionally, theatre is the translation of a written dramatic text into representation in space and time. A performance is then a one-off version of that transformation, since a dramatic text is 'performed' in and by the theatre . . . The priority of text over performance represents a brief phase in the recent history of western drama and has never presumed such a place in Asia. The Greeks, the medieval playwrights, Shakespeare and Molière all wrote as Zeami and Kuan Han-ching wrote: constructing scenarios and performance texts which were not intended to be works of literature but were written to provide learnable scripts for actors and to supply records for future possible performances. It was only within the last two hundred years that dramatic texts assumed the status they now have as the primary mode of being of the art-form in the west.

It is no accident that that same period is the one we now designate as the reign of modernity and the (meta)narrative. That modernist reversal of the priority of performance and its replacement by text represents more than just a logocentric bias; it is also an example of a compulsive tendency in western philosophy, namely to deduce from primary experiences a putative, prior source and a *post facto* effect and then rewrite the whole sequence as if the cause had really preceded the effect . . .

Performance was and is primary: before there was writing, before there was theatre, there were surely performances. However, this primacy of performance creates serious problems for the theorist. Texts can be returned to and reread, they have, for all their possibilities of reinterpretation, a certain ontological fixity. Performance, which is fundamentally ephemeral, has no such stability. The qualities of performances, their temporality, ephemerality, ambiguity, specificity, their restless improvisation, their haunting by shadowy options, make them events or at best processes. It is only now, when events and processes are being recognized as the fundamental data of experience, and experience as the foundation of knowledge, that serious attempts are being made to analyse performance as the primary reality . . . As an ontology, performance may be summarized as: temporal, transient, ephemeral; particular, singular; doubled; ambiguous and speculative.

A performance exists only and ever as a flux, in time. That flux is not at all like the linear time of modernism or its analogue in narrative. Linear time is constructed as rational, causal, teleological; by contrast, performance time is not only transient, it is also both doubled and ambiguous. It is a present which is somehow parallel to another present, a now which is not-now but also not-not-now . . .

No performance is ever the same as any other. Performances are singular and unrepeatable events, characterized by improvisation (the word means, literally, 'unforeseen'). Again theory stumbles, for it depends always on the reiterability of the phenomena it analyses: an experiment must be repeatable if it is to yield 'scientifically' valid results. Performance can do that only in the broadest terms; its secrets lie elsewhere – in the unrepeatable . . .

While theatre has always been shadowed by the text, and therefore by the author or the director, performances are shadowed only by their own other possibilities. They are exercises in restless semiosis, in which all meaning is derived from interdependent relations and not by ascription to some objective referent . . .

One of the major problems of performance research is to explain how spectators make judgements about the quality of what they are witnessing. In many performance modes, the apparent answer lies in the fact that spectators are often aficionados. In many performance forms – opera or Noh theatre, for example – most spectators have seen other performers perform the same part differently. Such performances are shadowed by their own ghosts. But what happens with a performance which we are seeing for the first time? When we witness a performance which we have not seen before, we see both what is done and what is not done. This itself becomes a criterion of evaluation. In this sense performances create their own alternatives . . .

A performance is 'present' in a spatial as well as a temporal sense, it is happening here. That 'here', however, is similarly doubled and ambiguous – it is a here which is not-here but also not-not-here. We shall need to examine the role of the spectator in all this very soon but one implication is already clear: spanning two different space-times, performances occur always and only in a liminal field. Performances occur neither on stage nor in the auditorium but in between the two; they are, in effect, exercises in the creation and occupation of thresholds . . .

To summarize: performance is distinguished as an ontological-epistemological system by a set of characteristics and experiences which reverse the generalizing and immobilizing metaphysics of language in favour of a retemporalization and reparticularization of experience, and a common pattern of doubling – time, space and person . . .

Theatre and performance are not necessarily different events; they are different perspectives on the same event, which can be seen as theatre, or experienced as performance. The 'same' event can be seen as re-presenting characters on quasi-real sets enacting authored scripts or as performers – generating multiple, particular significations in ambiguous time and space. The difference lies in where one starts. One can begin with the act, or one can begin with the assumption that it is only the end of a process, in which case one begins with its ghosts. Performance is not a new art-form so much as a new paradigm: it offers not so much a new phenomenon as a new way of looking at known phenomena with different ways of responding to them, experiencing them and thinking about them . . . The distinction between performance art and theatre is now at the level of the operations performed by the spectator.

The spectator as much as the performer is the originator of theatre. Traditionally the destination of the process, the spectator in fact stands at the very beginning, not only historically but praxiologically: all along the way towards a performance, the practitioners have been speculating on the spectator. Ever since Aristotle responded to Plato's condemnation of the supposed effect of theatre on its spectators with his alternative hypothesis of response, theorists have based their analyses of drama and theatre on teleological models. Masquerading as descriptions of how spectators respond, they were all really prescriptive. Only recently has any real work been done on what epistemological operations spectators actually perform. And yet speculation on their responses pervades not only the theory, it pervades the praxis too: directors have defined and legitimized their function as being both the voice of the author and the 'first spectator'.

Performance is spectator-orientated behaviour: it is the spectator who sits in the limen, steps into the threshold to perform the strange exercise of 'othering'. The concentration this requires has deceived some observers into accusing spectators of passivity. Those physically inert bodies are, however, only the necessary precondition of a cognitive and emotional intensity, an exercise in virtual experience . . .

Cognitively, then, performance returns its participants to the unique, singular, personal, immediate, direct and temporary encounters on which we construct our 'truths'. All too soon such moments pass as we construct from experiences both objective worlds and subjects cognizing them: experiences are always accompanied by an awareness of a 'self' having that experience and hence very rapidly shift from direct cognition to self-consciousness. Those cognitive operations performed by spectators are paralleled by emotional operations . . .

This is no place to engage in a detailed account of 'rasa' theory; its main arguments may, however, be briefly summarized: what distinguishes aesthetic sentiments from social emotions is that the former are always vicarious; that in turn means that, whereas an emotion is always accompanied by an urge to act, is always in some way motivational, aesthetic feeling is truncated at that point; aesthetic sentiments, 'rasas', are therefore desireless emotions – sensual impressions which do not generate want (George 1986) . . .

What is offered very schematically above is an alternative method derived from phenomenology, namely a series of reflections on the preconditions of the phenomenon, deductions of its epistemology from its ontology and vice versa.

Theatre in the west was always haunted by the word and the idea and thus by the metaphysical assumption that any representation must be a distortion of a transcendent truth. Only the wholesale jettisoning of that metaphysics could possibly emancipate the theatre from entrapment in its own metaphor. As an epistemology, performance offers a rediscovery of the now; relocation in the here; return to the primacy of experience, of the event; rediscovery that all knowledge exists on the threshold of and in the interaction between subject and object; a rediscovery of ambiguity, of contradiction, of difference; a reassertion that things – and people – are what they do . . .

To return to *The Tempest*: the masque which Prospero conjures up at the wedding of Miranda and Ferdinand contains no less truth than the world they usually inhabit, and probably more than the 'real' world which that, in turn, gestures at . . .

References

George, D. (1986) *India: Three Ritual Dance-Dramas*, Cambridge: Chadwick-Healey.
Husserl, E. (originally written in 1936, and published in 1939) 'Origin of Geometry', *Revue internationale de philosophie* 1:2.

CHAPTER 4

J.-J. Rousseau, Citizen of Geneva

Letter to M. d'Alembert on the theatre

To M. d'Alembert, of the French Academy, the Royal Academy of Sciences of Paris, the Prussian Academy, the Royal Society of London, the Royal Academy of Literature of Sweden, and the Institute of Bologna; on his article Geneva in the seventh volume of l'Encyclopédie and especially on the project of establishing a dramatic theatre in that city.

WHAT! OUGHT THERE to be no entertainments in a republic? On the contrary, there ought to be many. It is in republics that they were born, it is in their bosom that they are seen to flourish with a truly festive air. To what peoples is it more fitting to assemble often and form among themselves sweet bonds of pleasure and joy than to those who have so many reasons to like one another and remain forever united? We already have many of these public festivals; let us have even more; I will be only the more charmed for it. But let us not adopt these exclusive entertainments which close up a small number of people in melancholy fashion in a gloomy cavern, which keep them fearful and immobile in silence and inaction, which give them only prisons, lances, soldiers, and afflicting images of servitude and inequality to see. No, happy peoples, these are not your festivals. It is in the open air, under the sky, that you ought to gather and give yourselves to the sweet sentiment of your happiness. Let your pleasures not be effeminate or mercenary; let nothing that has an odour of constraint and selfishness poison them; let them be free and generous like you are, let the sun illuminate your innocent entertainments; you will constitute one yourselves, the worthiest it can illuminate.

But what then will be the objects of these entertainments? What will be shown in them? Nothing, if you please. With liberty, wherever abundance reigns, well-being also reigns. Plant a stake crowned with flowers in the middle of a square; gather the people together there, and you will have a festival. Do better yet; let the spectators become an entertainment to themselves; make them actors themselves; do it so that each sees and loves himself in the others so that all will be better united.

CHAPTER 5

Augusto Boal

Theatre, human beings

for Paulo Freire,
for the Workers'
Party of Brazil
For Grete Leutz
and
Zerka Moreno

1 Theatre, the first human invention

THEATRE IS THE FIRST HUMAN invention and also the invention which paves the way for all other inventions and discoveries.

Theatre is born when the human being discovers that it can observe itself; when it discovers that, in this act of seeing, it can see *itself* – see itself *in situ*: see itself seeing.

Observing itself, the human being perceives what it is, discovers what it is not and imagines what it could become. It perceives where it is and where it is not, and imagines where it could go. A triad comes into being. The observing-I, the I-*in-situ*, and the not-I, that is, the other. The human being alone possesses this faculty for self-observation in an imaginary mirror. (Doubtless it will have had prior experience of other mirrors – its mother's eyes, its reflection in water – but henceforward it is able to view itself by means of imagination alone.) The 'aesthetic space', which we will treat later, offers this imaginary mirror.

Therein resides the essence of theatre: in the human being observing itself. *The human being not only 'makes' theatre: it 'is' theatre.* And some human belngs, besides being theatre, also make theatre. We all of us are; some of us also do.

Theatre has nothing to do with buildings or other physical constructions. Theatre – or theatricality – is this capacity, this human property which allows man to observe himself in action, in activity. The self-knowledge thus acquired allows him to be the subject (the one who observes) of another subject (the one who acts). It allows him to imagine variations of his action, to study alternatives. Man can see himself in the act of seeing, in the act of acting, in the act of feeling, the act of thinking. Feel himself feeling, think himself thinking.

The cat chases the rat, the lion pursues its prey, but neither animal is capable of self-observation. When a man hunts a bison, he sees himself in the act of hunting; which is why he can paint a picture of the hunter – himself – hunting the bison. He can invent painting because he has invented theatre: he has seen himself in the act of seeing. An actor, acting, taking action, he has learnt to be his own spectator. This spectator (spect-actor) is not only an object; he is a subject because he can also act on the actor – the spect-actor is the actor, he can guide him, change him. A spect-actor acting on the actor who acts.

Birds sing, but know nothing about music. Singing forms part of their animal activity – along with eating, drinking, coupling – and their song never varies; a nightingale will never try to sing like a swallow, nor a thrush like a lark. But the human being is capable of singing and seeing itself in the act of singing. That is why it can imitate animals, discover variations of its own song, compose. Birds are not composers, they are not even interpreters of music. They sing, just as they eat, drink and couple. Only the human being is tri-dimensional (the I who observes, the I-*in-situ* and the not-I) because it alone is capable of dichotomy (seeing itself seeing). And as it places itself inside and outside its situation, actually there, potentially here, it needs to symbolise that distance which separates space and divides time, the distance from 'I am' to 'I can be', and from present to future; it needs to symbolise this potential, to create symbols which occupy the space of *what is, but does not exist* concretely, of what is possible and could one day exist. So it creates symbolic languages: painting, music, words. Animals have access only to a language of signals (signs made up of calls, grunts, grimaces). The alarm call of an African monkey will be understood perfectly by an Amazonian monkey of the same species. (We know that some big monkeys have a tribal language: they make specific references to 'this tree' or 'that tree'. But it remains a signaletic language; they are capable of talking about the danger of this tree (signal), but incapable of understanding the concept of tree (symbol).) But the word signifying alarm – *danger* – spoken in good Portuguese, will never be understood by a Swede or a Norwegian (who will, however, be able to understand the alarm signalled by the face of the person calling).

The being becomes human when it invents theatre.

In the beginning, actor and spectator coexisted in the same person; the point at which they were separated, when some specialised as actors and others as spectators, marks the birth of the theatrical forms we know today. Also born at this time were 'theatres', architectural constructions intended to make sacred this division, this specialisation. The profession of 'actor' takes its first bow.

The theatrical profession, which belongs to a few, should not hide the existence and permanence of the theatrical vocation, which belongs to all. Theatre is a vocation for all human beings: it is the true nature of humanity.

2   Human beings, a passion and a platform: the 'aesthetic space'

What is theatre?

Over the centuries theatre has been defined in thousands of ways. Of these definitions, to my mind the simplest and most essential is that provided by Lope de Vega, for whom 'theatre is two human beings, a passion and a platform'. Theatre is the *passionate combat of two human beings on a platform.*

Two beings – not just one – because theatre studies the multiple interrelations of men and women living in society, rather than limiting itself to the contemplation of each solitary individual taken in isolation. Theatre denotes conflict, contradiction, confrontation, defiance. And the dramatic action lies in the variation and movement of this equation, of these opposing forces. Monologues will not be 'theatre' unless the antagonist, though absent, is implied; unless her *absence* is *present.*

The passion is necessary: theatre, as an art, does not have as its object the commonplace and the trivial, the valueless. It attaches itself to actions in which the characters have an investment, situations in which they venture their lives and their feelings, their moral and their political choices: their passions! What is a passion? It is a feeling for someone or something, or an idea, that we prize more highly than our own life.

And where does the platform fit into all this? In his use of the word 'platform', Lope de Vega reduces all theatres, all existing forms of theatrical architecture, to their simplest equipment and their most elementary expression: a space set apart, a 'place of representation'. This can equally well be a few planks in a public square, an Italian rococo stage, an Elizabethan playhouse or a Spanish 'corral'; today it can be the arena, just as yesterday this was the Greek stage. Modern experiments have transformed lorries, boats, even swimming pools, into theatre stages, and even the stage/audience division has been fragmented in various ways. However, in all cases, separation remains a feature: one space (or more) is intended for the actors and another (or several others) for the spectators, whether these spaces are stationary or mobile.

What is theatre? Boal's expression of Lope de Vega's theatre as 'two human beings, a passion and a platform' (Figure 5.1).

2 human beings
1 passion
1 platform
= aesthetic space

Aesthetic space:
Penta-Dimensional: three dimensions of the physical space + a) Memory, b) Imagination
    Dychotomic and Dychotic
    Plastic
    Tele-microscopic

Like any space, these various dimensions possess, from a physical point of view, three dimensions: length, width and height – the objective dimensions.

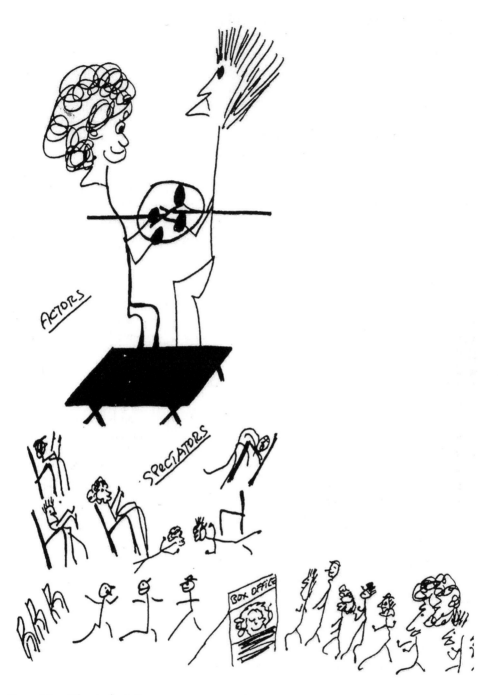

Figure 5.1   What is theatre?

Into this empty space, surrounded by things – this stage – other things can enter, other beings. Like the space itself, the things in this space (and the spaces which these things are, every thing being a space) possess these same three physical, objective and measurable dimensions, which are independent of the individuality of each observer. The same surface can seem big to me and small to someone else, but if we measure it we will always find the same square metreage. The same applies to time: an interval of time can seem long to me and short to another; but the number of minutes will be the same.

Spaces possess, then, subjective dimensions: an affective dimension and an oneiric – (of or belonging to dreams) – dimension, which we will study later.

The aesthetic space

The object which Lope de Vega calls the 'platform' has as its primary function the creation of a *separation*, a *division* between the space of the actor – the one who *acts* – and the space of the spectator – the one who *observes* (spectare = to see).

However, this separation becomes more important *per se* than the object which produces it. It can occur even without that object. The separation of spaces can occur without the 'platform' existing as an actual object. All that is required is that, within the bounds of a certain space, spectators and actors designate a more restricted space as 'stage': an aesthetic space – (in its Greek root 'aesthetic' means 'of or pertaining to things perceptible by the senses'). Whatever the process by which the bounds of this limited space have been determined, we then accept it as an aesthetic space, and it acquires all of the concomitant properties, even in the absence of a physical platform or any other object; it is a space within a space, a superposition of spaces. It can be a corner of the room, or a space around a tree in the open air. We simply decide that 'here' is 'the stage' and the rest of the room, or the rest of whatever space is being used, is 'the auditorium': a smaller space within a larger space. The interpenetration of these two spaces is the *aesthetic space* . . .

The aesthetic space thus comes into being because the combined attention of a whole audience converges upon it; it attracts, centripetally, like a black hole. This force of attraction is aided by the very structure of theatres and the positioning of stages, which oblige the spectators all to look in the same direction; and it is abetted by the simple presence of actors and spectators who connive in their acceptance of the theatrical codes and their participation in the celebration of the show. The 'theatre-platform' is a 'time-space'; it exists as such and will retain its particular properties as long as spectators are present or implied.

Thus we can say that not even the physical presence of spectators is necessary for the creation of this subjectively dimensioned space: it will suffice for actors – or a single actor, even a single person – to animate the real or virtual existence of that space and be aware of it. Anyone can designate and thereby create such a space, in their own front room, a space which occupies part or all of the room and immediately becomes, 'aesthetically', a 'stage': the 'platform'. The creator of such a space can then play for herself, without an audience – or with an imaginary audience – like an actor rehearsing alone in an empty theatre: in front of the future audience, absent at that moment, but present in the imagination.

So theatre does not exist in the objectivity of bricks and mortar, sets and costumes but in the subjectivity of those who practise it, at the moment when they practise it. It needs neither stage nor audience; the actor will suffice. With the actor is born the theatre. The actor is theatre. We are all actors: we are theatre!

Aesthetic space exists whenever there is either separation between the actor's space and the spectator's, or dissociation of two times – 'today I am here and yesterday I was here'. Or today and tomorrow; or now and before; or now and later. We coincide with ourselves when we integrate, into the present we are living, our memory of the past and our imagination of the future. (To coincide with ourselves is to be two in one, as we are on stage.)

The 'theatre' (or 'platform', at its simplest, or 'aesthetic space', at its purest) serves as a means of separating actor from spectator; the one who acts from the one who observes. Actor and spectator can be two different people; they can also *coincide in the same person*.

We have seen that, for theatre to exist, neither stage nor spectators are necessary. And we can affirm that even actors – in the professional, full-time sense – are not necessary to it, since aesthetic activity, which emanates from the aesthetic space, is 'vocational', it belongs to all human beings and manifests itself constantly in our relations with other people and other objects. This activity is concentrated a thousand times and made a thousandfold more intense in what we call theatre or performance.

Since the division between stage and audience is not only spatial and architectural, but also intensely subjective, it dampens, discourages, de-activates the 'audience' part and confers on the 'stage' part two subjective dimensions: the affective dimension and the oneiric dimension. The affective dimension is principally responsible for the introduction of memory into the aesthetic space, while the oneiric dimension brings imagination into play.

Characteristics and properties of the aesthetic space

The aesthetic space possesses gnoseological properties, that is, properties which stimulate knowledge and discovery, cognition and recognition: properties which stimulate the process of learning by experience. Theatre is a form of knowledge.

CHAPTER 6

Marcel Mauss

Body techniques

1   The notion of body techniques

A KIND OF REVELATION CAME TO me in hospital. I was ill in New York. I wondered where previously I had seen girls walking as my nurses walked. I had the time to think about it. At last I realized that it was at the cinema. Returning to France, I noticed how common this gait was, especially in Paris; the girls were French and they too were walking in this way. In fact, American walking fashions had begun to arrive over here, thanks to the cinema. This was an idea I could generalize. The positions of the arms and hands while walking form a social idiosyncrasy, they are not simply a product of some purely individual, almost completely psychical, arrangements and mechanisms. For example: I think I can also recognize a girl who has been raised in a convent. In general, she will walk with her fists closed. And I can still remember my third-form teacher shouting at me: 'Idiot! why do you walk around the whole time with your hands flapping wide open?' Thus there exists an education in walking, too.

Another example: there are polite and impolite *positions for the hands at rest*. Thus you can be certain that if a child at table keeps his elbows in when he is not eating, he is English. A young Frenchman has no idea how to sit up straight; his elbows stick out sideways; he puts them on the table, and so on.

Finally, in *running*, too, I have seen, you all have seen, the change in technique. Imagine, my gymnastics teacher, one of the top graduates of Joinville around 1860, taught me to run with my fists close to my chest: a movement completely contradictory to all running movements; I had to see the professional runners of 1890 before I realized the necessity of running in a different fashion.

Hence I have had this notion of the social nature of the 'habitus' for many years. Please note that I use the Latin word – it should be understood in France – *habitus*. The word translates infinitely better than '*habitude*' (habit or custom), the 'exis', the 'acquired ability' and 'faculty' of Aristotle (who was a psychologist). It does not designate those metaphysical *habitudes*, that mysterious 'memory', the subjects of volumes or short and famous theses. These 'habits' do not vary just with individuals and their imitations; they vary especially between societies, educations, proprieties and fashions, prestiges. In them we should see the techniques and work of collective and individual practical reason rather than, in the ordinary way, merely the soul and its repetitive faculties.

Thus everything moved me towards the position that we in this society are among those who have adopted, following [Auguste] Comte's example: the position of [Georges] Dumas, for example, who, in the constant relations between the biological and the sociological, leaves but little room for the psychological mediator. And I concluded that it was not possible to have a clear idea of all these facts about running, swimming, etc., unless one introduced a triple consideration instead of a single consideration, be it mechanical and physical, like an anatomical and physiological theory of walking, or on the contrary psychological or sociological. It is the triple viewpoint, that of the 'total man', that is needed . . .

4   General considerations

General considerations may perhaps be of more interest to you than these lists of techniques that I have paraded before you at rather too great a length.

What emerges very clearly from them is the fact that we are everwhere faced with physio-psycho-sociological assemblages of series of actions. These actions are more or less habitual and more or less ancient in the life of the individual and the history of the society.

Let us go further: one of the reasons why these series may more easily be assembled where the individual is concerned is precisely because they are assembled by and for social authority. As a corporal, this is how I taught the reason for exercise in close order, marching four abreast and in step. I ordered the soldiers not to march in step drawn up in ranks and in two files four abreast, and I obliged the squad to pass between two of the trees in the courtyard. They marched on top of one another. They realized that what they were being made to do was not so stupid. In group life as a whole there is a kind of education of movements in close order.

In every society, everyone knows and has to know and learn what he has to do in all conditions. Naturally, social life is not exempt from stupidity and abnormalities. Error may be a principle. The French navy only recently began to teach its sailors to swim. But example and order, that is the principle. Hence there is a strong sociological causality in all these facts. I hope you will accept that I am right.

On the other hand, since these are movements of the body, this all presupposes an enormous biological and physiological apparatus. What is the breadth of the linking psychological cog-wheel? I deliberately say cog-wheel. A Comtian would say that there is no gap between the social and the biological. What I can tell you is that here I see psychological facts as connecting cogs and not as causes, except in moments of creation or reform. Cases of invention, of laying down principles, are rare. Cases of adaptation are an individual psychological matter. But in general they are governed by education, and at least by the circumstances of life in common, of contact.

On the other hand there are two big questions on the agenda for psychology: the question of individual capacities, of technical orientation, and the question of salient features, of bio-typology, which may concur with the brief investigations I have just made. The great advances of psychology in the last few years have not, in my opinion, been made vis-à-vis each of the so-called faculties of psychology, but in psychotechnics, and in the analysis of psychological 'wholes'.

Here the ethnologist comes up against the big questions of the psychical possibilities of such a race and such a biology of such a people. These are fundamental questions. I believe that here, too, whatever the appearances, we are dealing with biologico-sociological phenomena. I think that the basic education in all these techniques consists of an adaptation of the body to their use. For example, the great tests of stoicism, etc., which constitute initiation for the majority of mankind, have as their aim to teach composure, resistance, seriousness, presence of mind, dignity, etc. The main utility I see in my erstwhile mountaineering was this education of my composure, which enabled me to sleep upright on the narrowest ledge overlooking an abyss.

I believe that this whole notion of the education of races that are selected on the basis of a determinate efficiency is one of the fundamental moments of history itself: education of the vision, education in walking – ascending, descending, running. It consists especially of education in composure. And the latter is above all a retarding mechanism, a mechanism inhibiting disorderly movements; this retardation subsequently allows a co-ordinated response of co-ordinated movements setting off in the direction of a chosen goal: this resistance to emotional seizure is something fundamental in social and mental life. It separates out, it even classifies the so-called primitive societies according to whether they display more brutal, unreflected, unconscious reactions or, on the contrary, more isolated, precise actions governed by a clear consciousness.

It is thanks to society that there is an intervention of consciousness. It is not thanks to unconsciousness that there is an intervention of society. It is thanks to society that there is the certainty of pre-prepared movements, domination of the conscious over emotion and unconsciousness. It is right that the French navy is now to make it obligatory for its sailors to learn to swim.

From here we easily move on to much more philosophical problems.

I don't know whether you have paid attention to what my friend Granet has already pointed out in his great investigations into the techniques of Taoism, its body techniques, and breathing techniques in particular (1929, 1930). I have studied the Sanskrit texts of Yoga enough to know that the same things occur in India. I believe precisely that at the bottom of all our mystical states there are body techniques which we have not studied, but which were studied fully in China and India, even in very remote periods. This socio-psycho-biological study should be made. I think that there are necessarily biological means of entering into 'communication with God'. Although in the end breath technique, etc., is only the basic aspect in India and China, I believe this technique is much more widespread. At any rate, on this point we have the methods to understand a great many facts which we have not understood hitherto. I even believe that all the recent discoveries in reflex therapy deserve our attention, ours, the sociologists', as well as that of biologists and psychologists . . . much more competent than ourselves.

References

Granet, Marcel (1929) *La Civilisation chinoise: la vie publique et la vie privée*, La Renaissance du Livre, Paris.

Granet, Marcel (1930) *Chinese Civilisation*, trans. Kathleen Innes and Mabel R. Brailsford, Kegan Paul, London.

CHAPTER 7

Terry Eagleton

Morality

THE BODY, THAT INCONVENIENT reminder of mortality, is plucked, pierced, etched, pummelled, pumped up, shrunk and remoulded. Flesh is converted into sign, staving off the moment when it will subside into the sheer pornographic meaninglessness of a corpse. Dead bodies are indecent: they proclaim with embarrassing candour the secret of all matter, that it has no obvious relation to meaning. The moment of death is the moment when meaning haemorrhages from us. What seems a celebration of the body, then, may also cloak a virulent anti-materialism – a desire to gather this raw, perishable stuff into the less corruptible forms of art or discourse. The resurrection of the body returns as the tattoo parlour and the cosmetic surgeon's consulting-room. To reduce this obstreperous stuff to so much clay in our hands is a fantasy of mastering the unmasterable. It is a disavowal of death, a refusal of the limit which is ourselves.

Capitalism, too, for all its crass materialism, is secretly allergic to matter. No individual object can fulfil its voracious appetite, as it hunts its way restlessly from one to the other, dissolving each of them to nothing in doomed pursuit of its ultimate desire. For all its love affair with matter, in the shape of Tuscan villas and double brandies, capitalist society harbours a secret hatred of the stuff. It is a culture shot through with fantasy, idealist to its core, powered by a disembodied will which dreams of pounding Nature to pieces. It makes an idol out of matter, but cannot stomach the resistance it offers to its grandiose schemes.

It is, to be sure, no crime to tattoo your biceps. The West has long believed in moulding Nature to its own desires; it is just that it used to be known as the pioneer spirit and is nowadays known as postmodernism. Taming the Mississippi and piercing your navel are just earlier and later versions of the same ideology. Having moulded the landscape to our own image and likeness, we have now begun to recraft ourselves. Civil engineering has been joined by cosmetic surgery. But there can be more and less creditable reasons for piercing your navel. The creditable reason is that it is fun; the discreditable reason is that it may involve the belief that your body, like your bank account, is yours to do what you like with. There may be excellent reasons to sport a vulture on your chest or a steel bolt through your nose, but this is not one of them.

'Personalizing' the body may be a way of denying its essential impersonality. Its impersonality lies in the fact that it belongs to the species before it belongs to me; and there are some aspects of the species-body – death, vulnerability, sickness and the like – that we may well prefer to thrust into oblivion. Even then, there is no very coherent sense in which my body belongs to me. It is not a possession, like a scarlet fez or a mobile phone. Who would be the possessor? It sounds odd to call a 'possession' something which I never acquired and could never give away. I am not the proprietor of my sensations. Having a painful twinge is not like having a tweed cap. I could give you my cap, but not my twinge. I can call my body 'mine', but this is to mark the distinction between my body and yours, not to indicate that I am the owner of it. There is no private entrepreneurship when it comes to flesh and blood.

The body is the most palpable sign we have of the givenness of human existence. It is not something we get to choose. My body is not something I decided to walk around in, like a toupée. It is not something I am 'in' at all. Having a body is not like being inside a tank. Who would be this disembodied 'I' inside it? It is more like having a language. Having a language, as we have seen, is not like being trapped in a tank or a prison house; it is a way of being in the midst of a world. To be on the 'inside' of a language is to have a world opened up to you, and thus to be on the 'outside' of it at the same time. The same is true of the human body. Having a body is a way of going to work on the world, not a way of being walled off from it. It would be odd to complain that I could come at things better if only I could shuck off my flesh. It would be like complaining that I could talk to you better if only this crude, ineffectual stuff called speech did not get in the way.

The fact that my body is not one of my possessions does not give you *carte blanche* to muscle in on it. You cannot possess it either. But this is not because I got there first, like a piece of lucrative land to which I staked the first claim. Part of the point of bodies is their anonymity. We are intimate with our bodies, but we cannot grasp them as a whole. There is always a kind of 'outside' to my body, which I can only ever squint at sideways. The body is my way of being present to others in ways which are bound in part to elude me. It slips through my grasp, just as it does when it asserts its own stubborn material logic in the face of my hubristic schemes. In all of these ways, its mortality is revealed – for nothing is at once more intimate and more alien to us than death. My death is my death, already secreted in my bones, stealthily at work in my body; yet it leaps upon my life and extinguishes it as though from some other dimension. It is always untimely.

SECTION 2

Roots:Routes

The human body itself

Aeschylus, the first great playwright of the Western world, was also a choreographer: one of the few facts known about him is that the movements of his chorus were meticulously devised and directed by the master himself. But physical theatre, over the centuries, has both flourished and languished, formed – at times – the backbone of a robust popular tradition – at other times – been almost forgotten. Today we see a vast and thrilling revival of interest in theatre which uses the full range of human expressiveness: shapes, sounds, silences, and this form; the human body itself.

Richard Eyre, in John Keefe (1994)
Moving Into Performance, Mime Action Group

Essay 2

Roots or routes; the technical traditions of contemporary physical theatre

■ Jonathan Pitches

Introduction

THE PUNNING OF 'ROUTES' AND 'ROOTS' is a favourite game for theatre practitioners. Jatinder Verma, Artistic Director of Tara Arts, and seasoned thinker on the migration of ideas and practices over time, is one of many contemporary thinkers to have enjoyed the verbal play of terms to illustrate his perspective on theatre making. Discussing his 2002 trilogy, *Journey to the West*, Verma makes the following distinction:

> Chris Arnot: So is this epic play an attempt to identify [your] roots?
> Jatinder Verma: It depends how you're spelling the word . . . I prefer to think of it as r-o-u-t-e-s. Roots lead backwards. Routes are more progressive, leading you to make connections with others. I'm not interested in the particular village in India where my grandfather came from. My identity is located on the road.[1]

An inveterate creator of epic theatre and, in his own words, 'always looking for the grand narratives' (Plastow 2004: 86), Verma is nevertheless suspicious of the regressive connotations associated with the word 'roots'. Instead, he sees himself on an advancing intercultural journey, one that, significantly, he locates 'on the road'.

Eugenio Barba, director of the ensemble Odin Teatret, sees things differently. Barba is actively seeking a line back to his grandfathers, in an effort to compensate for what he calls his professional orphaning:

> In my family of professional *ethos* there are no parents. There is an older brother, Jurek – Jerzy Grotowski. Many uncles and relatives: Vakhtangov, and Copeau,

Brecht, Decroux, Sulerzhitski, and Artaud. Ahead of them all, the two grandfathers: Stanislavsky and Meyerhold.

(Barba 2003: 108)

For Barba, there is real merit in looking back, in recognising and acknowledging the practices that have shaped his work, and in determining which figures ultimately are part of the tradition of Odin Teatret. Importantly, in this personal history, Stanislavsky and Meyerhold are not identified as 'masters', but as 'two small traditions' (ibid.), and as such their differing styles and approaches militate against the unilateral fixity of a single progenitor. It is roots Barba wants to unearth, not *the* root.

Taken together, these statements by Jatinder Verma and Eugenio Barba represent two poles on a continuum of physical theatre histories and their juxtaposition here raises a host of difficult questions. To identify just a few: what value do practitioners and critics place on past practices and how are these judgments made? What constitutes a tradition itself and how are these lineages agreed or disputed? What are the politics underlying the establishment of a tradition? How do traditions evolve and how are these evolutionary processes affected by specific cultural influences and contexts? In short, what are the mechanics, spoken or unspoken, underlying the construction of a tradition?

Physical theatre is fraught with its own terminological problems, partly because as a singular form it is borne out of a paradoxical mix of imprecision and pigeonholing. It is now a commonplace to bemoan the excessive inclusivity of the term, which shares with its recent colleague, the Creative and Cultural Industries, a remit too broad to be in any way meaningful. Yet at the same time, many of us are all too familiar with 'physical theatre' as a shorthand label, used by companies (and by the mid-scale British theatres which host them) to identify a particular set of techniques drawn mainly from contact improvisation and contemporary dance.

Both too confining and somehow not confining enough, the term 'physical theatre' is clearly problematic, not least because its ambivalence resists that key aspect of a tradition which allows for a reference point to be drawn between practices, that function which Eugenio Barba describes as the 'means of orientation for the conquest of one's *difference*' (Barba 2003: 115, his emphasis). It is helpful to be reminded that difference not sameness can often define a practitioner's place in a tradition and that the plotting of the *roots* of a given set of practices is always in tension with the examination of the potential *routes* those practices might navigate in the future.

This collection proposes a taxonomy of *physical theatres*, plural, and this is the first step towards delineating how a number of different traditions of corporeal performance have developed. The next step is to examine in more detail the technicalities of these practices and to assess this tension between difference and similarity. Two examples might suffice in the short space of this essay to illustrate the complexity of this exercise: Jacques Copeau (1879–1949) and the French tradition and Konstantin Stanislavsky (1863–1938) and the Russian tradition of physical theatres.

Copeau and the French tradition

For Copeau, there were two traditions of French theatre and both are expressed in rather polarised terms: the 'true' or 'original' tradition (Copeau 1990: 145), by which he meant the spirit of innovation and discovery embodied in Molière, and the false or 'supposed tradition' or what he called the 'mechanical habits of certain actors' (Rudlin 1986: 26) trained at the National Conservatoire and performing at the Comédie-Française after Molière's death. According to Copeau, truth is associated with something 'spiritual' and 'pure', falseness with routine and detachment, and he sought to rewrite the tradition of French acting accordingly, consciously effacing the work of generations of actors and placing his own project as a direct continuation of Molière's:

> I am seeking to bring works closer to the 'true tradition' by freeing them from the contributions loaded on them for three centuries by the official actors [of the Comédie-Française]. The important tradition is the original one.
>
> (Copeau 1990: 145)

In his quest to 'return to sincerity', Copeau dismissed much of his country's theatrical heritage as *cabotinage*, 'the total mechanisation of the person' as he called it in a lecture delivered in New York in 1917 (ibid.: 253). Where Meyerhold had turned to the *cabotin* as a model of popular, unabashed theatricality and the potential saviour of the Russian theatre tradition (Braun 1991: 122–3),[2] Copeau saw it as evidence of a moribund theatrical culture. Much of his writing is underpinned by this assumed polarity of the sincere versus the artificial and it becomes a touchstone for the construction of his own tradition: he venerates Aeschylus (and Greek drama in general), Noh theatre, Molière, *commedia dell'arte*, and his contemporaries Stanislavsky and Antoine; he abhors the National Conservatoire, the Comédie-Française, Dumas *fils* and the bourgeois comedy of the nineteenth century. Above all, he places huge emphasis on the revivifying potential of youth and on the importance of unfettered play:

> Children teach us authentic inventiveness. Enhance their games . . . Learn everything from children. Impose nothing on them.
>
> (Copeau 1990: 12)

From the Greek theatre, Copeau drew inspiration from the chorus as a model of collective energy, discipline and musicality; from his work in *commedia*, Copeau saw a vision of a bare stage, also inspired by the Spanish popular theatre and Lope de Rueda's 'four trestles and five planks' (ibid.: 83); from the Japanese Noh form, he imagined a theatre of simplicity and poetry; from his love of the medieval mysteries, he planned open-air theatre events, and from Antoine's early work at the Théâtre Libre, Copeau witnessed a director ostensibly pursuing the same goals: authenticity and sincerity, fuelled by the energies of the young.

Doubtless, such a short summary hardly does justice to the legacy of Copeau but my purpose is different here – to outline the intersection of a range of different theatre traditions in the construction of the Copeau tradition. The main source in English for his commentary on practice is Copeau's *Texts on Theatre* (spanning the years 1913–1945).[3] In these writings, Copeau locates his work in an evolutionary context of his own making, setting up 'reference points', as Barba puts it, which are both meaningful for the development of his own practice, as well as to the audience of his theoretical texts, an audience operating at one remove (at least) from the repertoire of the Vieux Colombier. As a member of this second level audience it is easy to see Copeau's concern for the popular theatre tradition and how this fascination intermingles with his love of the deep traditions, embodied in Aeschylus and Aristophanes. A reverence for antique forms is also reflected in his passion for Noh and the Japanese theatre's long tradition of performance characterised by formidable levels of technique and control.

But Copeau was not simply a nostalgic: he also looked to contemporary Europe and to his own native France for a means of orientating his work. The physiologist and educationalist, Georges Hébert's 'natural gymnastics' were one important source of inspiration, for example, and Hébert served for a brief period as a movement teacher at the Vieux Colombier (Evans 2006: 64). In an open letter to Antoine in 1913, Copeau indicated how cognisant he was of the way in which such contemporary reference points might be read. Celebrating Antoine's 'sincerity', Copeau made the following statement:

> In reaching out to take your hand we are conscious that this binds us to a beautiful tradition of labour and courage.
>
> (Copeau 1990: 212)

What is noticeable in this self-declared inter-praxis is the extent to which Copeau is *beginning* a tradition of body-based transmission, not working from learnt practices himself.[4] The traditions he calls upon in his own writings are often distant ones – his project is to *revive* the spirit of, say, Aristophanic comedy, given its historic demise, or to *become* a multi-skilled man of the theatre, à la Molière. Whilst Noh was a key research area for Copeau as early as 1916, he did not see any Japanese performance until 1930 and the playfulness and improvisation skills he derived, in part, from *commedia* were co-taught with his collaborator and actress Suzanne Bing. Bing came to the Vieux Colombier with previous acting experience in France and Germany and displayed a demonstrable talent as a teacher in her own right, something acknowledged by Copeau in a commendatory letter: 'through her experiments . . . she furnished me with the elements of a method of education for young actors' (Copeau 1990: 255). In many ways, then, it was the distinguished list of Copeau's actors and pupils who formed the new, living tradition, experimenting as they were on a day-to-day experiential basis with the techniques of the past: Bing herself, Charles Dullin and Louis Jouvet, Jean Dasté, Michel St Denis, and Étienne Decroux.

This final point raises a further question for our list: how do we value different modes of transmission in the development or delineation of a tradition? Physical theatres by their very nature tend to sustain themselves on body-based modes of transmission. This is most obviously true of the great traditions of East and South Asian theatre practice, based on the passing on of elaborate, codified gestures from master to pupil: the Noh theatre, again, or the Kathakali dance of southern India. Significantly, these practices often depend on the longer rhythms associated with training in a 'family' (Allain and Harvie 2006: 213), as with the *commedia* tradition in Europe, and it was precisely this dependence on the infrastructure of an acting family which Copeau was trying to revivify with the Vieux Colombier. In the absence of an immediate master, he had to become the father-figure and build up the family from scratch. He may have appealed to a rich set of traditions in the framing of his own practice but there is an unavoidable and significant lacuna in the journey back to his founding fathers.

Stanislavsky and the Russian tradition

Stanislavsky was also driven by the desire to revolutionise the stage and to combat artifice at every step. According to his collaborator Nemirovich-Danchenko, the roots of nineteenth-century Russian theatre practice were rotten and thus it was necessary to:

> Reconstruct [theatre's] whole life . . . to change *at the root* the whole order of rehearsals and the preparation of plays.
>
> (Carnicke in Hodge 2000: 12, my emphasis)

Where Copeau railed at *cabotinism*, Stanislavsky lamented the Russian star system and the extended histrionics of Romanticism. He too revered the *commedia dell'arte* as well as having his own contemporary models to draw on – Ludwig Chronegk from the Meiningen Troupe, Tommaso Salvini, the Italian actor. Like Copeau, Stanislavsky turned professional later in life – in fact both were thirty-four when they respectively launched the Vieux Colombier (in 1913) and the Moscow Arts Theatre (in 1897).

As founder of the modern Russian tradition, Stanislavsky's name is associated with an even longer list of luminary pupils and influences than Copeau's; having uprooted the old traditions, Stanislavsky forged himself a position as the progenitor of a new root of twentieth-century Russian actor training. For the American director, and co-founder of the Group Theatre, Harold Clurman, his influence was even greater:

> The Modern Theatre stems from Danchenko and Stanislavsky – and from their joint creation, the Moscow Art Theatre.
>
> (in Cole and Chinoy 1954: 421)

Unlike Copeau, though, and in spite of his position as the founder of a Russian (or even Western) Modern Theatre, Stanislavsky's direct connections to the living traditions of acting in Russia are clear and undisputed. These 'strong native roots', according to Toby Cole, underpin 'a straight line of development' (ibid.: 415–16) from Mikhail Shchepkin (1788–1863), through the playwright and director Ostrovsky (1823–1886), to Stanislavsky, a lineage Stanislavsky is happy to corroborate in *My Life in Art*. Shchepkin is:

> The pride of our national art, the man who re-created in himself all that the West could give and created the foundations of true Russian dramatic art and its traditions, our great lawgiver and artist.
>
> (Stanislavski 1980: 80)

We might add to this list Alexander Fedotov, who trained at the Imperial Maly Theatre, in the Shchepkin school of Realism, and then went on to direct Stanislavsky, before he turned professional, at the Society of Art and Literature. Fedotov took to Stanislavsky's imitative histrionics like a surgeon, seeding in the young actor the Shchepkinian principles of 'real life and stirring passions, in all their truth' (Cole and Chinoy 1954: 422). Interestingly, it is the fact that Shchepkin treated his pupils as a family which Stanislavsky highlights in his eulogy.

With Copeau working as a theatre critic and writer, and Stanislavsky operating as an actor and emergent director before both the Vieux Colombier and the MAT were launched, it is not surprising that their relationship to the French and Russian traditions, respectively, would be different. Put simply, the roots of Copeau's practice are more literary and historic than Stanislavsky's, even though the latter owes a clear debt to Aristotle and, more generally, to Enlightenment thinking. More contentiously, I have used the words 'living tradition' to define the embodied transmission of ideas experienced in the studio or laboratory, not as a means of criticising Copeau's declared roots but to highlight that his project was to *revivify* the dying connection between France's popular theatre tradition and the early twentieth-century French theatre movement, to forge a *new* evolutionary line.

What unites the two tradition-makers is the astonishing diversity of practice to emerge from their one starting point. If 'difference' defines a practitioner's place in a tradition, Stanislavsky's legacy is a living tradition *par excellence*. Some of the more notable names in that tradition read as a roll call of modern theatre innovators: Vsevolod Meyerhold, Eugene Vakhtangov, Michael Chekhov, Richard Boleslavsky, Maria Ouspenskaya, Alice Koonen, Maria Knebel. In turn, the *routes* of this tradition extend to America via Strasberg, Adler and Chaikin (even though the latter rejected his Method training outright). They develop further in Russia, touching Tovstonogov, Lyubimov, Yefremov, Dodin and Vasiliev. They branch off into Polish theatre in Grotowski's work and inform much of Barba's thinking in Denmark and Odin Teatret, as already noted. In short, the Stanislavsky tradition is in some way implicated in most of the key contributions to physical theatre practice in the last century. Indeed, it crosses over into the Copeau tradition as well, with the 1922 visit of the MAT to France, following a correspondence of some six years between the two directors (Copeau 1990: 215–19).

Conclusion

So we find ourselves back with the conundrum of imprecision first identified with the term 'physical theatre'. How to escape this, and is it possible to delineate precisely a tradition (or traditions) of physical theatre praxis?

I would like to suggest two means by which this problem might be reviewed, to offer a potential focus for the reader, in advance of sampling the many traditions identified in the following section.

The first is a call to remodel the image of a tradition in one's imagination. A tradition is often thought of in linear terms, indeed my own use of the verb 'delineate' trades off this metaphor: we talk of 'tracing the line back to *x*' and 'what is the lineage of *y*?'. Yet any botanist will confirm that root systems are anything but linear and, depending on the age of the organism, can spread over wide distances and form into complex configurations. In doing so, they characteristically cross over and tangle with other root systems and may surface in a location which is not easily related to the organism itself. The complexity of the multiple traditions evident in this essay clearly highlights a similar tangling of histories and practices, fuelled by political, cultural and rhetorical forces as well as by the practical demands of an efficacious training. Far better, perhaps, to imagine a forest rather than a line, where each influential practitioner is separated out at ground level but unavoidably intertwined below as their roots grow out to support their individual branches. Think, too, maybe, of these trees forming a canopy, which is similarly interleaved far above our heads, as the routes of those ideas are forced into contact with each other.

The second relates to this distinction between routes and roots, for evident also in this short essay is a strong sense of these two terms coexisting, on a continuum, rather than being in any way separable. It is more a question of roots *and* routes than roots *or* routes. Traditions of physical theatre, particularly, have to negotiate a balance between the past and the future, specific to the form in question, and this is nowhere more evident than in the work of Copeau, touched upon here. Consider, as a final thought, Copeau himself, evaluating the influence of the deep tradition begun by the Greeks:

> It is not a question of comparative history, where the past is compared to the present, like dead things to living ones. It is rather a close wedding of knowledge and practice, of renewing one's good faith in ancient traditions and rhythms, of reviving not the actual forms of the past but that spiritual bond which unfailingly puts us in contact with their principles.
>
> (Copeau 1990: 40)

Copeau's words offer us a telling formula for the interplay of roots and routes and capture compellingly the motivation for all of these traditions: the need for a sustainable forest . . .

Notes

1   From *The Guardian*: 'Staging a Survival', by Chris Arnot, Wednesday 13 March 2002.
2   Cf. Meyerhold's essay 'The Fairground Booth' (*c.*1912): 'It seems to me that we should apply ourselves to the study and restoration of those theatres of the past in which the cult of cabotinage once held sway', Braun 1991: 123.
3   Copeau's works have been posthumously edited and collated in French, currently in six volumes, entitled *Registres* (1974–2000).
4   See, for example, Maurice Kurtz: 'Jacques Copeau, the critic, editor, playwright, director, actor and founder of the Théâtre de Vieux-Colombier, could lay claim to no theatrical or literary tradition in his family', Kurtz 1999: 3.

References

Allain, Paul and Harvie, Jen (2006) *The Routledge Companion to Theatre and Performance*, London: Routledge.
Barba, Eugenio (2003) 'Grandfathers, Orphans, and the Family Saga of European Theatre', *New Theatre Quarterly*, 19 (2): 108–117.
Braun, Edward (ed. and trans.) (1991) *Meyerhold on Theatre*, London: Methuen.
Carnicke, Sharon (2000) 'Stanislavsky's System: Pathways for the Actor', *Twentieth Century Actor Training*, ed. Alison Hodge, London: Routledge.
Cole, Toby and Chinoy, Helen (1954) *Actors on Acting*, New York: Crown.

Copeau, Jacques (1990) *Texts on Theatre*, ed. and trans. John Rudlin and Norman H. Paul, London: Routledge.

Evans, Mark (2006) *Jacques Copeau*, London: Routledge.

Kurtz, Maurice (1999) *Jacques Copeau: Biography of a Theatre*, Carbondale and Edwardsville: Southern Illinois University Press.

Plastow, Jane (2004) 'Jatinder Verma: Encounters with the Epic – An Interview', *Contemporary Theatre Review*, 14 (2): 82–7.

Rudlin, John (1986) *Jacques Copeau*, Cambridge: Cambridge University Press.

—— (2000) 'Jacques Copeau: the Quest for Sincerity', *Twentieth Century Actor Training*, ed. Alison Hodge, London: Routledge.

Stanislavski, Constantin (1980) *My Life in Art*, trans. J.J. Robbins, London: Methuen.

A

Deep traditions: classical and popular

CHAPTER 8

Aristotle

The art of poetry

4

IT IS CLEAR THAT THE GENERAL ORIGIN of poetry was due to two causes, each of them part of human nature. Imitation is natural to man from childhood, one of his advantages over the lower animals being this, that he is the most imitative creature in the world, and learns at first by imitation. And it is also natural for all to delight in works of imitation. The truth of this second point is shown by experience: though the objects themselves may be painful to see, we delight to view the most realistic representations of them in art, the forms for example of the lowest animals and of dead bodies. The explanation is to be found in a further fact: to be learning something is the greatest of pleasures not only to the philosopher but also to the rest of mankind, however small their capacity for it; the reason of the delight in seeing the picture is that one is at the same time learning – gathering the meaning of things, e.g. that the man there is so-and-so; for if one has not seen the thing before, one's pleasure will not be in the picture as an imitation of it, but will be due to the execution or colouring or some similar cause. Imitation, then, being natural to us – as also the sense of harmony and rhythm, the metres being obviously species of rhythms – it was through their original aptitude, and by a series of improvements for the most part gradual on their first efforts, that they created poetry out of their improvisations . . .

It certainly began in improvisations – as did also Comedy; the one originating with the authors of the Dithyramb, the other with those of the phallic songs, which still survive as institutions in many of our cities . . .

6

Reserving hexameter poetry and Comedy for consideration hereafter, let us proceed now to the discussion of Tragedy; before doing so, however, we must gather up the definition resulting from what has been said. A tragedy, then, is the imitation of an action that is serious and also, as having magnitude, complete in itself; in language with pleasurable accessories, each kind brought in separately in the parts of the work; in a dramatic, not in a narrative form; with incidents arousing pity and fear, wherewith to accomplish its catharsis of such emotions. Here by 'language with pleasurable accessories' I mean that with rhythm and harmony or song superadded; and by 'the kinds separately' I mean that some portions are worked out with verse only, and others in turn with song.

I. As they act the stories, it follows that in the first place the Spectacle (or stage-appearance of the actors) must be some part of the whole; and in the second Melody and Diction, these two being the means of their imitation. Here by 'Diction' I mean merely this, the composition of the verses; and by 'Melody', what is too completely understood to require explanation. But further: the subject represented also is an action; and the action involves agents, who must necessarily have their distinctive qualities both of character and thought, since it is from these that we ascribe certain qualities to their actions. There are in the natural order of things, therefore, two causes, Character and Thought, of their actions, and consequently of their success or failure in their lives. Now the action (that which was done) is represented in the play by the Fable or Plot. The Fable, in our present sense of the term, is simply this, the combination of the incidents, or things done in the story; whereas Character is what makes us ascribe certain moral qualities to the agents; and Thought is shown in all they say when proving a particular point or, it may be, enunciating a general truth. There are six parts consequently of every tragedy, as a whole, that is, of such or such quality, viz. a Fable or Plot, Characters, Diction, Thought, Spectacle and Melody; two of them arising from the means, one from the manner, and three from the objects of the dramatic imitation; and there is nothing else besides these six. Of these, its formative elements, then, not a few of the dramatists have made due use, as every play, one may say, admits of Spectacle, Character, Fable, Diction, Melody and Thought.

II. The most important of the six is the combination of the incidents of the story.

Tragedy is essentially an imitation not of persons but of action and life, of happiness and misery. All human happiness or misery takes the form of action; the end for which we live is a certain kind of activity, not a quality. Character gives us qualities, but it is in our actions – what we do – that we are happy or the reverse. In a play accordingly they do not act in order to portray the Characters; they include the Characters for the sake of the action. So that it is the action in it, i.e. its Fable or Plot, that is the end and purpose of the tragedy; and the end is everywhere the chief thing. Besides this, a tragedy is impossible without action, but there may be one without Character . . .

We maintain, therefore, that the first essential, the life and soul, so to speak, of Tragedy is the Plot; and that the Characters come second . . . We maintain that Tragedy is primarily an imitation of action, and that it is mainly for the sake of the action that it imitates the personal agents. Third comes the element of Thought, i.e. the power of saying whatever can be said, or what is appropriate to the occasion . . . One must not confuse it with Character. Character in a play is that which reveals the moral purpose

of the agents, i.e. the sort of thing they seek or avoid, where that is not obvious . . .
Fourth among the literary elements is the Diction of the personages, i.e. as before explained,
the expression of their thoughts in words, which is practically the same thing with verse
as with prose. As for the two remaining parts, the Melody is the greatest of the pleasurable
accessories of Tragedy. The Spectacle, though an attraction, is the least artistic of all the
parts, and has least to do with the art of poetry. The tragic effect is quite possible without
a public performance and actors; and besides, the getting-up of the Spectacle is more
a matter for the costumier than the poet.

CHAPTER 9

David Wiles

The performer

The choral dancers of tragedy

ARISTOTLE RECORDS THE HISTORICAL consensus that drama originated in improvisations by the leaders of choral dances dedicated to Dionysos. However, the classical historian Herodotus mentions that 'tragic choruses' in the town of Sikyon were transferred in pre-classical times from the worship of the hero Adrastus to the god Dionysos,[1] so we should beware of postulating an essence of tragedy identified with the spirit of a single god. Only one thing is entirely clear: tragedy is a logical extension of choral dance, which was the most important form of cultural expression in the pre-classical period. Choral dances honoured the gods, they demarcated and drew together the component groups of the community such as unmarried girls or warriors, and they had an educational function in physical training, in transmitting the traditions of the community and in teaching individuals to subordinate self to the collective . . .

The earliest fragments of dramatic dialogue from the Greek world were probably written to be performed as an interchange between Sappho as chorus leader and the chorus of girls for whom she bore responsibility. The circular dance around the altar allowed the leader either to lead and set movements for the procession, or else to stand in the centre and establish her or his difference[2] . . .

In the time of Aeschylus there were twelve in the tragic chorus, the number twelve signifying the complete cosmic circle,[3] and the function of chorus leader still belonged, effectively, to the lead actor. In Aeschylus' earliest play, *The Persians*, the lead actor – presumably Aeschylus himself – must have taken the two major tragic roles of the Persian Queen and her son Xerxes . . .

In the time of Euripides and Sophocles the number increased to fifteen, a number which lends itself to the rectangle or triangle rather than the circle, and generates a strategic position for the leader, now known as the *coryphaeus* (indicated below by X; Figure 9.1).

The function of actor has now separated itself decisively from that of chorus leader. The emphasis of the choreography must have shifted from performing a circular ritual around the altar towards a more frontal form of delivery.

In the twentieth century, Jacques Lecoq has been the most systematic researcher into choral movement. He stresses the importance of flexibility in the chorus:

> It can be a bearer of contradictions: its members can sometimes oppose each other in sub-groups, or alternatively unite to address the audience together. I cannot imagine a tragedy without a chorus. But how do we group these figures? How do we bring life to this collective body? How to make it breathe, and move like a living organism, while avoiding aestheticized choreography and militarist geometry?[4]

In later times, when chorus and actors occupied different spaces, the militaristic rectangle became established as the standard formation, but in the classical period the choreography would have been more fluid.[5] Though opposed to regimentation, Lecoq personally finds more flexibility in the rectangle than in the ritual circle, and Greeks of the classical period must have gone through similar processes of experimentation.

An inscription from the classical period relating to a tragedy by Euripides lists fourteen members of a chorus by name, and it may well be that the 'Socrates' who set up the monument took on both the financial role of choregos and the performance role of *coryphaeus* in order to maximize his prestige.[6] This may have been quite common. Post-classical references to the famous 'chorus-trainer' Sannio indicate that his role extended to performing and thus taking the *coryphaeus* role.[7] The *coryphaeus* was both leader and teacher, and in performance played a crux role in setting the time that the other dancers followed. However, there is no evidence to support the common idea that the *coryphaeus* alone spoke the short passages of dialogue which were allocated to the chorus but not designated for dancing. Because actors were masked, a single anonymous voice emanating from a crowd would not have been identifiable as the speech of any one individual; but unison speech is equally plausible, even though it seems an alien convention to individualistic modern performers.

Or:

Figure 9.1   The chorus

Notes

1   Herodotus, v.67. See Richard Seaford (1994) *Reciprocity and Ritual*, Oxford: OUP.
2   See Claude Calame (1997) *Choruses of Young Women in Ancient Greece*, Lanham: Rowman & Littlefield.
3   David Wiles (1997) *Tragedy in Athens*, Cambridge: CUP.
4   Jacques Lecoq (1997) *Le Corps Poétique*, Actes Sud-Papiers 10, see David Bradby (2000) *The Moving Body*, p. 130, London: Methuen.
5   See text in *NTDWD*, 20–62, and *COAD*, 360–4.
6   See text in *COAD*, 360–1.
7   See text in *COAD*, 13, 154–5.

Editors' Note

NTDWD   *Nothing To Do With Dionysos? Athenian drama in its social context*, ed. John J. Winkler and Froma Zeitlin (Princeton University Press, 1992)
COAD   *Contexts of Ancient Drama*, ed. Eric Csapo and William J. Slater (University of Michigan Press, 1995)

CHAPTER 10

Alan S. Downer

Irving

I RVING SUMS UP IN HIS STYLE all that the Victorian theater had learned about the art of acting. The treatment of high tragedy by the Macready school he modified by character acting in the manner of Fechter and, to a lesser extent, the new English school . . .

Yet even in this early role, Irving's performance was marked by those singularities, those oddities of by-play which became his trademark. 'Such, for example, was the act, simple in itself, of carefully, yet as it were unconsciously, testing the fragrance of the cork drawn from the generous bagman's present of a bottle of old port – a movement full of subtle suggestions of habitual self-indulgence'.[162] This kind of character business, outside of the author's text, is inseparable from the new school manner . . . Irving's performance was a kaleidoscope of business. 'His usage, in each performance, is to stud the work with indications of the physical as well as the mental peculiarities of the man whom he has undertaken to embody.' . . .[164]

Gordon Craig's description of Irving's first entrance as Matthias in *The Bells* indicates clearly how the entire production was built about the characterization of the leading player, and how his command of the audience in what is after all a trivial role was largely due to his mastery of by-play – or at least to his ability to convince the audience of the significance of his by-play.

> The storm raging outside the house; the sudden blowing open of a window in the next room, which smashed a whole trayful of crockery and glass as it swung open – the looking at the clock which told of the long overdue traveller – the slow, quiet talk which mumbled on – and above all, the queer 'hurry music', as it is called, which was astonishingly dramatic: all these things led up to the first point to be made, and made with decision: 'Here

is the man!' [A perfect example of the shrewd building of the entrance of the star] . . .

Irving once on, the shout of applause going up, he lowers his arms, he lowers his head, he relaxes his force all over, seems to turn it off to an almost dead calm, while the applause rolls on and up. Twice, maybe three times, he, as it were, shifts on one foot (his right I think it was), and by this slight and meaningless gesture a limit is being reckoned to the applause which goes on and on – no other motion, except that the foot in shifting sends a slight vibration also without significance, through the whole person before us – and then as the applause dies away, at the first sign of it dying, the actor clips it off by a sudden gesture of awakening from his long and patiently-endured ordeal – flings cap and whip to right and left, and begins to shed his coat, his muffler, as his wife and daughter run to help him off with them.

The process of getting rid of his coat, and brushing off the snow as he stands on the mat by the door being over, he works his way down to a chair in the centre (Irving was always in the centre – he had no inferiority complex), and there, taking off his boots, he begins to put on and buckle his shoes.

While he is taking off the boots and pulling on the shoes the men at the table, who are smoking and drinking lazily, are telling in drawling tones that just before he came in they were saying that they did not remember a night like this . . .

By the time the speaker had got this slowly out – and it was dragged purposely – Irving was buckling on his second shoe, seated, and leaning over it with his two long hands stretched down over the buckles. We suddenly saw these fingers stop their work; the crown of the head suddenly seemed to glitter and become frozen – and then, at the pace of the slowest and most terrified snail, the two long hands, still motionless and dead, were seen to be coming up the side of the leg.[166]

The description continues, but enough has been quoted to show in what Irving's interpretation of a character role consisted: shaking the snow from his coat while standing on the mat, a natural touch unheard of in the older theater where actors went indifferently bareheaded or hatted whether outdoors or in a drawing room; revelation of character by a simple gesture of the hands; using the fostered applause of the audience as a springboard – all the result of ingenuity and study. 'I don't,' said Irving, 'chance very much in my performances. No – not much. One has to know what one's doing, why one's doing it, and exactly what effect it is certain to have upon an audience'[167] . . .

All this character business was rapturously received by audiences, and by many of the critics . . .

But when the King and Queen start from their chairs, Hamlet springs from the ground, darts with a shrill scream to the seats from which they vanished like ghosts, flings himself – a happy thought – into the chair which the King has vacated, his body swaying the while from side to side in irrepressible excitement, and recites there – though the roar of applause into which the audience is surprised renders it barely audible – the well-known stanza, 'Why let the stricken deer go limp.'[171]

A less favorable critic describes the same business:

> he shows his emotion by falling upstairs into the throne, where he lies sunk together in a bundle so fearfully and wonderfully verveless as to remind one painfully of the puppet Punch when not engaged in his stirring drama, but reposing in his box. . . .[172]

To sum up, it may be said that the development of the style of serious acting in England in the nineteenth century was a continuous process of narrowing down. From the majesty of Kemble and the violence of Kean, we pass almost immediately to the naturalistic touches of Macready and the increasing attention to naturalism in the staging of comic and domestic drama. As this naturalism is applied more and more to the staging of romantic drama, the personality of an Irving is required to keep the old plays alive. For the most part, the new school of acting is suited only to the new school of playwrighting as it develops from Robertson to Pinero. The player was prevented from utilizing the full resources of his art by the dramatist who was too much interested in the finicky details of reality. It was Yeats who confessed, for the whole period, in *The Circus Animals' Desertion*,

> Players and painted stage took all my love,
> And not those things that they were emblems of.

Notes

162   *The Bill of the Play*, ed. J. H. Thornhill (London, 1882), p. 115.
164   William Winter, *Henry Irving* (New York, 1885), p. 35.
166   Edward Gordon Craig, *Henry Irving* (London, 1930), pp. 55–9.
167   *We Saw Him Act*, ed. H. A. Saintsbury and Cecil Palmer (London, 1939), p. 167.
171   L. R. Russell, *Irving as Hamlet* (London, 1875), p. 46.
172   W. Archer and R. W. Lowe, *The Fashionable Tragedian* (London, 1877), p. 10.

CHAPTER 11

Jeff Pressing

Improvisation

Methods and models

Introduction

HOW DO PEOPLE IMPROVISE? How is improvisational skill learned and taught? These questions are the subject of this chapter. They are difficult questions, for behind them are long-standing philosophical quandaries such as the origins of novelty and the nature of expertise, which trouble psychologists and artificial intelligence workers today almost as much as they did Plato and Socrates in the fourth and fifth centuries BC.

In a previous article (Pressing 1984a) I summarized a number of general properties of the improvisation process on the basis of the diverse historical writings of artists, teachers, and musicologists. This material was integrated with precepts from cognitive psychology to sketch out the beginnings of a general theory of improvisation.

In this article a much more explicit cognitive formulation is presented, the first proper (though by no means necessarily correct) theory of improvised behaviour in music. The building of this theory has required input from many disparate fields with which the general musical reader may not be familiar. For this reason I begin with the survey of appropriate background research and its relation to improvisation. Some of these areas may initially seem distant from the topic at hand.

A survey of pertinent research

Some physiology and neuropsychology

Although our state of knowledge in these areas is far too meagre to have any definite repercussions for improvisation, there are a few facts which are at least strongly suggestive.

To begin with, improvisation (or any type of music performance) includes the following components, roughly in the following order:

(1)   complex electrochemical signals are passed between parts of the nervous system and on to endocrine and muscle systems;
(2)   muscles, bones, and connective tissues execute a complex sequence of actions;
(3)   rapid visual, tactile, and proprioceptive monitoring of actions takes place;
(4)   music is produced by the instrument or voice;
(5)   self-produced sounds, and other auditory input, are sensed;
(6)   sensed sounds are set into cognitive representations and evaluated as music;
(7)   further cognitive processing in the central nervous system generates the design of the next action sequence and triggers it.
– return to step (1) and repeat –

It seems apparent that the most starkly drawn distinctions between improvisation and fixed performance lie in steps (6) and (7), with possibly important differences in step (3). This chapter therefore inevitably focuses on these aspects.

The given steps are often collapsed into a three-component information-processing model of human behaviour which has ready physiological analogies: input (sense organs), processing and decision-making (central nervous system, abbreviated CNS), and motor output (muscle systems and glands).

Control of movement by the CNS is complex: the cerebral cortex sends signals to both the cerebellum and the basal ganglia, which process the information and send a new set of signals back to the motor cortex. The brainstem nuclei are also involved in details of motor co-ordination. It has been suggested that the basal ganglia and cerebellum have complementary roles, with the basal ganglia initiating and controlling slow movements while the cerebellum is active in the co-ordination of fast, ballistic movements (Sage 1977).

Motor signals from the cortex pass to the spinal cord and motor nuclei of the cranial nerves via two separate channels: the pyramidal and extrapyramidal systems. These two nerve tracts illustrate the simultaneously hierarchical and parallel-processing aspects of CNS control, for they run in parallel but interconnect at all main levels: cortex, brainstem, and spinal cord. Hence while each tract has some separate functions there is a redundancy that can be used to facilitate error correction and motor refinement. Similar redundancy and parallel processing is found at lower levels of motor control. Alpha-gamma coactivation, for example, describes the partial redundancy of neural information sent to two distinct types of motoneurons, alpha and gamma, whose axons and collaterals terminate on the main skeletal muscles and the intrafusal muscle fibres, respectively.

The organization of behaviour has often been linked with the existence of motor action units (or equivalent concepts), and their aggregation into long chains to develop more complex movements. The validity of the concept of motor action units can be seen mirrored physiologically in the existence of command neurons, single nerve cells in invertebrates whose activation alone suffices to elicit a recognizable fragment of behaviour. The effect is achieved by excitation and/or inhibition of a constellation of motoneurons (Bentley and Konishi 1978; Shepherd 1983). While there are no known single cells that fully trigger complex behaviour in mammals, populations of neurons in the brains of higher animals are strongly suspected of serving a similar function (Beatty 1975). It is therefore possible to speculate that skilled improvisers would, through practice, develop general patterns of neural connections specific to improvisational motor control.

Finally, it is of interest that neurological correlates have recently been discovered for a division of knowledge and memory into two separate categories: declarative and procedural. A degree of independence of these two types of memory (for facts or procedures) has been reported among amnesic and post-encephalitic patients for some time (for example Milner 1962; Brooks and Baddeley 1976). Typically, patients cannot remember new facts, but are able to learn new motor skills over a period of time, yet without any awareness on successive days of having performed the tasks before . . .

Motor control and skilled performance . . .

The starting point for nearly all the existing theories is the three-stage information-processing model mentioned earlier, based on sensory input, cognitive processing, and motor output. To this must be added the notion of feedback (auditory, visual, tactile, or proprioceptive). Traditional 'open-loop' theories include no feedback, and hence no mechanisms for error correction. In its starkest form this theory is clearly inappropriate for improvisation; however, there is persistent evidence, dating back to the medical work of Lashley (1917), and including studies of insect behaviour and de-afferentiation techniques in monkeys, that points to the existence of motor programmes that can run off actions in open-loop fashion.

In contrast stand 'closed-loop' theories, which contain feedback, and hence allow for the intuitively natural possibilities of error detection and correction. The closed-loop negative feedback (CLNF) model is one of the oldest. In this model the feedback (primarily auditory in the case of musical improvisation) is sent back to an earlier stage in the control system which compares actual output with intended output, producing a correction based on the difference between the two (see for example Bernstein 1967). Such closed-loop models have their historical roots in engineering models of servomechanisms, control theory, and cybernetics . . .

By the late 1970s the consensus was that both open- and closed-loop control must occur in skilled performance (see Summers 1981 for a review). That is, movements are both centrally stored as motor programmes, and susceptible to tuning (adjustment) on the basis of feedback. Coupled with the well-established concept of *flexibility* characteristic of skilled (but not rote) performance (Welford 1976), this promoted approaches based on more abstract programming notions that brought the field closer to artificial intelligence (and made it more germane to improvisation) . . .

This convergence of theory is useful in constructing a model of improvisation (see below). However, it remains rather unspecific, and has run far ahead of experiment. But as of this writing there seems only one alternative in the area of motor behaviour. This is the organizational invariant approach of Turvey, Kugler, Kelso, and others (see Kelso 1982 for further references) . . .

Skill classification

Various dimensions of skill classification have been proposed and improvisation can be placed within these. Two possible categories are 'open' skills, which require extensive interaction with external stimuli, and 'closed' skills, which may be run off without reference to the environment (Poulton 1957). Solo improvisation is basically a closed skill, as it relies only on self-produced stimuli, whereas ensemble improvisation is more open . . . Improvisation is a fine, complex skill, with both perceptual and motor components; continuous actions predominate, although there are also discrete and serial motor aspects. This last point varies somewhat with the nature of the instrument played.

It is important to also emphasize the contrast between unskilled and highly skilled performance. A vast majority of reported skill studies treat simple motor tasks like tracking, under an implicitly reductionistic scientific methodology. It is increasingly acknowledged, however, that highly developed skills have distinctive emergent properties missed in these earlier short-term studies, properties such as adaptability, efficiency, fluency, flexibility, and expressiveness (Welford 1976; Shaffer 1980; Sparrow 1983). These are vital components of improvisatory skill.

Feedback and error correction

Feedback is a vital component in improvisation for it enables error correction and adaptation – a narrowing of the gap between intended and actual motor and musical effects. But feedback is also important for its motivational (Gibbs and Brown 1956) and attention-focusing effects (Pressing 1984a) . . .

Feedback can also be considered to operate over different time scales. Thus short-term feedback guides ongoing movements, while longer term feedback is used in decision-making and response selection. Still longer term feedback exists in the form of knowledge of results (KR) for skills where external evaluation is present or result perception is not sufficiently precise or immediate. The importance of this for improvisation has been demonstrated by Partchey (1973), who compared the effects of feedback, models, and repetition on students' ability to improvise melodies. Feedback, in the form of playbacks of recordings of the students' own improvisations, was clearly superior to listening to pre-composed model melodies, or repetition, as an improvisation learning technique. In group improvisation, feedback loops would also operate between performers (Pressing 1980).

In view of the interconnectedness of the parts of the central nervous system, it is also clear that there exist internal feedback (and feedforward) loops not based on sensory processing (Brooks 1978). That is, if higher cognitive levels set the design of motor programmes while movement fine structure is specified in closed-loop fashion by lower levels of the CNS, notably the spinal cord, then copies of these lower level motor instructions are almost certainly sent directly back up to higher centres. In other words, there is some kind of central monitoring of efference. This would serve to increase overall processing speed and accuracy.

The role of errors in improvisation has been discussed previously (Pressing 1984a). It will simply be pointed out here that errors may accrue at all stages of the human information processing system: perception, movement/musical gesture selection and design, and execution. Minor errors typically demand no compensation in following actions, whereas major errors typically do.

Anticipation, preselection, and feedforward . . .

The idea of preparation is very important for improvisation, where real-time cognitive processing is often pushed up near its attentional limits. It can be formally proved, for example, that only a control system with a model of disturbances and predictive power can become error free. For improvised performance that aims at artistic presentation, where discrepancies between intention and result must be kept within strict bounds, practice must attempt to explore the full range of possible motor actions and musical effects, to enable both finer control and the internal modelling of discrepancies and correction procedures, including feedforward . . .

Time scales for the control of movement

This is a subject with an enormous and complex literature. For background purposes in modelling improvisation a few points only seem sufficient.

Actual neural transmission times are of the order of tens of milliseconds. According to Davis (1957; see also Sage 1977), auditory stimulus activity reaches the cerebral cortex 8–9 ms after stimulation while visual stimulation involves a longer latency of 20–40 ms. Since the two neural pathways are of comparable length, this difference points to a greater transmission speed for audition than vision. It should, however, be noted that the auditory system contains both ipsilateral and contralateral pathways, while the pathways of the visual system are exclusively crossed. The cortical response time for a movement stimulus appears to be of the order of 10–20 ms (Adams 1976).

Reaction time is the time taken for a sense stimulus to travel to the CNS and return to initiate and execute a largely pre-programmed motor response. Simple reaction time (RT) with only one chosen motor response typically falls in the range 100–250 ms, depending on conditions and sensory modality (Summers 1981) . . .

Timing and movement invariants

Up to this point very little has been said about the timing of skilled performance, yet it is obviously a vital point. . . . Such performance rhythm, or 'hometetic' behaviour, as some have termed it, shows great tuneability: over wide variations in distance and overall time constraints, invariance of phasing and accelerations (equivalently, forces) can be observed (Schmidt 1983). By phasing is meant the relative timings of component parts of the entire movement sequence.

But it is also true that the relative timings of movement components can be changed intentionally, at least to a considerable degree. Hence the improviser has access to generalized action programmes (in both motor and music representation), which allow overall parametric control (time, space, force) *and* subprogram tuneability. This may well be responsible for the flexibility of conception characteristic of experienced improvisation.

Motor memory

It has often been suggested that a distinct form of memory for action, called motor memory, exists. The subjective impression of improvisers (and other performers) is certainly that potentially separate yet often interconnected motor, symbolic, and aural forms of memory do exist. For a review of this extensive topic and its relationship to verbal memory the reader may wish to consult Laabs and Simmons (1981) . . .

Studies and theories of musical improvisation . . .

Musical improvisation has also been considered as a vehicle for consciousness expansion and the tapping of deep intuitions. A full history of this 'transpersonal' approach would go back thousands of years to the sacred texts of many religions. Here I only survey recent Western opinion. Hamel (1979) has intelligently chronicled music of the avant-garde (for example Riley, Stockhausen) from this perspective. Laneri (1975) has developed a philosophy of improvisation based on different states of consciousness, featuring the concepts of synchronicity and introversion. The resultant music is primarily vocal, since the voice is considered the primal instrument. A powerful system of sonic meditation most applicable to local improvisation groups has been developed by Oliveros (1971). 'Sensing' compositions have been published by Gaburo (1968). An attempt to connect music, altered states of consciousness, and research in parapsychology has been given by Pressing (1980), while Galas (1981/82) has created a primal vocal music based on obsession, excessive behaviour, and trance states of severe concentration.

The approaches in the literature to the teaching of improvisation may be broadly grouped as follows. First, there is the perspective overwhelmingly found in historical Western texts, that improvisation is real-time composition and that no fundamental distinction need be drawn between the two. This philosophy was dominant in pre-Baroque times but had become rare by the eighteenth century. In practice this results in a nuts-and-bolts approach with few implications for the modelling of improvisation beyond basic ideas of variation, embellishment, and other traditional processes of musical development. A second approach, which historically took over as the first one waned, sets out patterns, models, and procedures specific to the improvisational situation, which, if followed by those possessing a solid enough level of musicianship, will produce stylistically appropriate music. In this category fall the many figured bass and melodic embellishment texts of the seventeenth and eighteenth centuries (for example Mersenne 1635; Quantz 1752/1966; Bach 1778/1949; Arnold 1965), as well as the riff compendia and how-to-do-it books in the field of jazz (such as Coker *et al.* 1970; Slonimsky 1975; Nelson 1966).

A third technique is the setting of a spectrum of improvisational problems or constraints. The philosophy behind this technique shows a clear contrast with the second approach above, as described by Doerschuk (1984), referring to the Dalcroze system.

> The art of improvisation rests on . . . a developed awareness of one's expressive individuality. This knowledge grows through interactive exercises with a teacher, whose function is not to present models for imitation, but to pose problems intended to provoke personal responses. (p. 52)

Jaques-Dalcroze (1921) seems to have pioneered this approach in our century with a revealing series of improvisation exercises for piano. These include composition-like problems in rhythm, melody, expressive nuance, and harmony; muscular exercises; imitation of a teacher; exercises in hand independence; the notation of improvisation just after performing it; and what may be termed an 'interrupt' technique. In this last technique the word 'hopp' is recited by the teacher, as a cue for the student to perform pre-set operations such as transposition or change of tempo during the performance. This technique is reminiscent of a much later suggestion by Roads (1979) that musical grammars used in improvisation might be 'interrupt-driven'. This idea is developed in the model below.

Parsons (1978) has made effective use of this third technique in a collection of short pieces by many different composers defined largely by improvisational instruction sets; he also presents a taxonomy of psycho-improvisational faults and recommended exercises for correcting them. A shorter multi-author collection of improvisational exercises is found in Armbruster (1984). Jazz fake books like the *Real book* (no listed authors or dates) or *The world's greatest fake book* (Sher 1983) may also be considered to act along the lines of this technique.

A fourth approach is the presentation of multiple versions of important musical entities (most commonly motives) by the teacher, leaving the student to infer completely on his or her own the ways in which improvisation or variation may occur by an appreciation of the intrinsic 'fuzziness' of the musical concept. This imitative self-discovery approach is found in the Persian *radif*, which is a repository of musical material learned in a series of increasingly complex versions by the aspiring performer (Nettl and Foltin 1972), and in Ghanaian traditions (K. Ladzekpo, personal communication), for example. A related procedure made possible by the use of recording technology in the twentieth century is for the student to directly copy a number of improvised solos by repeated listening to recordings, and from this extract common elements and variation procedures. Song-form based improvisations, in which solos consist of a number of choruses which repeat the same underlying chord progression, are particularly suitable. This method has been widely used in jazz and blues since the end of the First World War.

A fifth approach is allied to the self-realization ideas of humanistic psychology. It is based on concepts of creativity and expressive individuality which go back in music explicitly at least to Coleman (1922), implicitly certainly to Czerny (1829/1983), and probably in a general sense at least to the Enlightenment. In the words of Jaques-Dalcroze:

> Improvisation is the study of direct relations between cerebral commands and muscular interpretations in order to express one's own musical feelings . . . Performance is propelled by developing the students' powers of sensation, imagination, and memory.
>
> (Abramson 1980: 64)

Intuition and creativity

These are two related concepts, each with a vast literature. Their connection with improvisation is undeniable, yet explicit mention of them in either field is rare. On the other hand, 'free' musicians and many music educators commonly use the two terms, but often without a very clear notion of just what is being discussed. This section attempts to bridge that gap.

The concept of intuition is much older than creativity, and it has separate philosophical and psychological traditions. Westcott (1968) has provided an excellent general survey, enumerating three historical approaches to philosophies of intuition. First comes Classical Intuition (for example Spinoza, Croce, Bergson), which views intuition as a special kind of contact with a prime reality, a glimpse of ultimate truth unclouded by the machinations of reason or the compulsions of instinct. Knowledge gained through this kind of intuition is unique, immediate, personal, unverifiable. The second approach, called by Westcott Contemporary Intuitionism (for example Stocks 1939; Ewing 1941; Bahm 1960), takes the more restricted view that intuition is the immediate apprehension of certain basic truths (of deduction, mathematical axioms, causality, etc.). This immediate knowing stands outside logic or reason and yet is the only foundation upon which they can be built. Knowledge gained through intuition constitutes a set of 'justifiable beliefs', which are nevertheless subject to the possibility of error. A third approach is positivistic (for example Bunge 1962) in that it rejects as illusory both the notions of immediacy and ultimate truth found in some earlier views. Rather, an intuition is simply a rapid inference which produces a hypothesis.

Of all these views, it is perhaps that of French philosopher Henri Bergson (1859–1941) which shows the greatest affinities with the common metaphors of improvisation. Bergson saw intuition as a way to attain direct contact with a prime reality ordinarily masked from human knowledge. This prime reality is an ongoing movement, an evolving dynamic flux which proceeds along a definite but unpredictable course.

> The prime reality is referred to as 'the perpetual happening' or 'duration'. The mind of man, according to Bergson, is shielded from the perpetual happening by the intellect, which imposes 'patterned immobility' on prime reality, distorting, inmobilizing, and separating it into discrete objects, events and processes. In the perpetual happening itself, all events, objects, and processes are unified.
>
> (Westcott 1968: 8)

In Bergson's view, the intellect can freely interact with the fruits of intuition (special knowledge and experience) to develop an enriched personal perspective.

The notion of tapping a prime reality is very similar to the improviser's aesthetic of tapping the flow of the music, as mentioned above. The same apparent process has been eloquently described with regard to the origins of folk-tales from many cultures by English writer Richard Adams:

> I have a vision of – the world as the astronauts saw it – a shining globe, poised in space and rotating on its polar axis. Round it, enveloping it entirely, as one Chinese carved ivory ball encloses another within it, is a second . . .

gossamer-like sphere . . . rotating freely and independently of the rotation of the earth.

Within this outer web we live. It soaks up, transmutes and is charged with human experience, exuded from the world within like steam or an aroma from cooking food. The story-teller is he who reaches up, grasps that part of the web which happens to be above his head at the moment and draws it down – it is, of course, elastic and unbreakable – to touch the earth. When he has told his story – its story – he releases it and it springs back and continues in rotation. The web moves continually above us, so that in time every point on its interior surface passes directly above every point on the surface of the world. This is why the same stories are found all over the world, among different people who can have had little or no communication with each other.

(Adams 1980: 12)

There is a clear convergence of imagery in this and other descriptions that points to a likely transpersonal component to improvisation.

The psychological perspectives on intuition are many and varied, but only two seem relevant here. The first is the widely occurring idea that intuition is a special case of inference which draws on cues and associations not ordinarily used (Westcott 1968). A similarity with certain theories of skill learning mentioned above is apparent. A second and wide-ranging approach is found in the recent work by Bastick (1982), which includes a search of over 2.5 million sources for common properties underlying intuition. After the identification and detailed analysis of some 20 of these properties, Bastick ends up describing intuition as a combinatorial process operating over pre-existing connections among elements of different 'emotional sets'. These emotional sets apparently contain encodings, often redundant, of many different life events (intellectual activities, movement, emotion, etc.). By giving strong emphasis to the role of dynamics, bodily experience, and the maximizing of redundancy in encoding, and by a series of suggestive diagrams of intuitive processing, Bastick seems to be on an important track parallel to emerging ideas of improvisation.

Research in creativity is probably more extensive than that in intuition, for intuition is most commonly considered a subcategory of creativity. Creativity research in music education has been recently surveyed by Richardson (1983). The only clear relations to improvisation she found were in specialized educational methods and a growing tendency to use improvisation tests in assessing musical creativity. Vaughan (1971), Gorder (1976), and Webster (1977) have designed and implemented such tests, but results show uneven patterns of correlation between general intelligence, creativity, musicality, composition, and improvisation, and seem to have no clear consequences for improvisation modelling.

General studies of creativity abound, and follow many divergent paths. Two alone seem relevant here. Guildford's Structure-of-Intellect (SI) model proposed a taxonomy of factors of intelligence (Guildford and Hoepfner 1971 (and earlier references mentioned therein); Guildford 1977). These intelligence factors, which number 120, are classified along three dimensions:

thought content: visual, auditory figural, semantic, symbolic, and behavioural information;
kinds of operation performed on the content: cognition, memory, convergent production, divergent production, evaluation;

products (the results of applying operations to content): units, classes, relations, systems, transformations, and implications.

These classifications are related to improvisation in a general way, but despite their intuitive appeal they have so far been fairly resistant to empirical verification.

Guildford further defined a set of six aptitudes for creative thinking: fluency, flexibility, originality, elaboration, redefinition, and sensitivity to problems. Torrance (1966) used this same set in designing a more open-ended approach to the testing and definition of creativity. Some of these six aptitudes are identical to the ones found in skilled performance above; they are considered here to be further guidelines for testing the plausibility of improvisational modelling.

Finally, Guildford and Hoepfner classified techniques of evaluation (in problem-solving), which they held to be due to appeals to logical consistency, past experiences, feeling of rightness, or aesthetic principles. Such a classification also has implications for improvisation . . .

The development of improvisational skill . . .

There are at least two additional components of improvisational skill: inventiveness and the achievement of coherence. In more fixed skills these are less important, since inventiveness provides few tangible advantages, and coherence is built in by the rigidity of the task demands.*

The specific cognitive changes that allow these properties to develop in improvised musical behaviour are considered to be:

(1) an increase in the memory store of objects, features, and processes in musical, acoustic, motor (and other) aspects;
(2) an increase in accessibility of this memory store due to the build-up of redundant relationships between its constituents and the aggregation of these constituents into larger cognitive assemblies;
(3) an increasingly refined attunement to subtle and contextually relevant perceptual information.

The build-up and improved access to memory of points (1) and (2) is presumably central to any learning process. In the language of the model of this chapter this involves the use of extensive redundancy, and also the aggregation of memory constituents (objects, features, processes) into new cognitive assemblies which may be accessed autonomously. Because such a procedure can presumably be nested to arbitrary depth, very complicated interconnected knowledge structures may develop . . .

Conclusions

This chapter has attempted to illuminate the process of musical improvisation by first examining the modelling tools available from a number of different disciplines. Based on this examination, a cognitive model has then been presented for the process itself, followed by a brief discussion of its relation to improvisational skill acquisition. The central features of the model are as follows. It is reductionist, in that cognitive structures of processing and control are considered to be broken down into aspects (acoustic, musical, movement, etc.), each of these into types of analytical representation (objects, features, processes), and each of these into characterizing elements (array components). At the same time the model is synergistic and capable of behavioural novelty, due to the extensive redundancy of the cognitive representations and the distributed and non-linear character of the outlined control processes. The extensive presence of feedback and feedforward contributes to this. The fundamental nature of the improvisation process is considered to be the stringing together of a series of 'event clusters' during each of which a continuation is chosen, based upon either the continuing of some existing stream of musical development (called here an event-cluster class) by association of array entries, or the interruption of that stream by the choosing of a new set of array entries that act as constraints in the generation of a new stream (new event-cluster class).

Acknowledgement

I am indebted to John Sloboda, Margot Prior, Geoff Cumming, Geoff Webb, Denis Glencross, and Glynda Kinsella for helpful criticism.

Note

* It is interesting to note that these two skills push in opposite directions, for inventiveness comes from the commitment to avoid repetition as much as possible, while coherence is only achieved by some degree of structural unity, which is only possible with repetition.

References

Abramson, R. M. (1980) 'Dalcroze-based improvisation', *Music Educator's Journal* 66 (5), 62–8.

Adams, J. A. (1976) 'Issues for a closed-loop theory of motor learning', in *Motor control: issues and trends* (ed. G. E. Stelmach), New York: Academic Press.

Adams, R. (1980) *The iron wolf*, Reading: Penguin.

Armbruster, G. (1984) 'First steps in improvisation', *Keyboard* 10 (Oct.), 37–44.

Arnold, F. T. (1965) *The art of accompaniment from a thoroughbass as practised in the XVIIth and XVIIIth centuries*, New York: Dover.

Bach, C. P. E. (1778/1949) *Essay on the true art of playing keyboard instruments*, New York: Norton.

Bahm, A. (1960) 'Types of intuition', *University of New Mexico Publications in Social Sciences and Philosophy*, No. 3.

Bastick, T. (1982) *Intuition: how we think and act*, Chichester: Wiley.

Beatty, J. (1975) *Introduction to physiological psychology*, Monterey, CA: Brooks/Cole.

Bentley, D. and Konishi, M. (1978) 'Neural control of behaviour', *Annual Review of Neurosciences* 1, 35–59.

Bernstein, N. (1967) *The coordination and regulation of movements*, London: Pergamon.

Brooks, D. N. and Baddeley, A. (1976) 'What can amnesic patients learn?', *Neuropsychologia* 14, 111–22.

Brooks, V. B. (1978) 'Motor programs revisited', in *Posture and movement: perspectives for integrating sensory and motor research on the mammalian nervous system*, New York: Raven.

Bunge, M. (1962) *Intuition and science*, Englewood Cliffs, NJ: Prentice-Hall.

Coker J., Casale, J., Campbell, G., and Greene, J. (1970) *Patterns for jazz*, Lebanon, IN: Studio Productions

Coleman, S. N. (1922) *Creative music for children*, New York: G. P. Putnam's Sons.

Czerny, C. (1829/1983) *Systematic introduction to improvisation on the piano* (trans. A. L. Mitchell), New York: Longman.

Davis, R. (1957) 'The human operator as a single channel information system', *Quarterly Journal of Experimental Psychology* 9, 119–29.

Doerschuk, B. (1984) 'The literature of improvisation', *Keyboard* 10 (Oct.), 48–52.

Ewing, A. (1941) 'Reason and intuition', *Proceedings of the British Academy* 27, 67–107.

Gaburo, K. (1968) *Twenty sensing compositions*, La Jolla, CA: Lingua Press.

Galas, D. (1981/82) 'Intravenal song', *Perspectives of New Music*, Fall-Winter 1981/Spring-Summer 1982, 59–62.

Gibbs, C. B. and Brown, I. C. (1956) 'Increased production from information incentives in an uninteresting repetitive task', *Manager* 24, 374–9.

Gorder, W. D. (1976) 'An investigation of divergent production abilities as constructs of musical creativity'. Unpublished EdD thesis. University of Illinois at Urbana-Champaign.

Guildford, J. P. (1977) *Way beyond the IQ*, New York: Creative Education Foundation.

Guildford, J. P. and Hoepfner, R. (1971) *The analysis of intelligence*, New York: McGraw Hill.

Hamel, P. M. (1979) *Through music to the self*, Boulder, CO: Shambhala.

Jaques-Dalcroze, E. (1921/1976) *Rhythm, music and education*, New York: B. Blom.

Kelso, J. A. S. (1982) 'Two strategies for investigating action', in *Human motor behaviour* (ed. J. A. S. Kelso), Hillsdale, NJ: Lawrence Erlbaum.

Laabs, G. J. and Simmons, R. W. (1981) 'Motor memory', in *Human skills* (ed. D. Holding), New York: Wiley.

Laneri, Roberto (1975) 'Prima materia: an opus in progress. The "natural" dimension of music'. Unpublished PhD thesis. University of California at San Diego.

Mersenne, M. (1635) *Harmonie Universelle*.

Milner, B. (1962) 'Les troubles de la memoire accompagnant des lesions hippocampiques bilaterales', *Phsyiologie de l'Hippocampe*, Paris: Centre National de la Recherche Scientifique.

Nelson, O. (1966) *Patterns for improvisation*, Hollywood: Nelson Music.

Nettl, B. and Foltin, B. Jr (1972) *Daramad of Chahargah*, Detroit: Information Coordinators.

Oliveros, P. (1971) *Sonic meditations*, Baltimore, MD: Smith Publications/Sonic Art Editions.

Parsons, W. (1978) *Music for citizen's band*, La Jolla, CA: W. Parsons.

Partchey, K. C. (1973) 'The effects of feedback, models, and repetition on the ability to improvise melodies'. Unpublished DEd thesis. Pennsylvania State University.

Poulton, E. C. (1957) 'On the stimulus and response in pursuit tracking', *Journal of Experimental Psychology* 53, 57–65.

Pressing, J. (1980) 'Music, altered states of consciousness, and psi', *Proceedings of the Psychic Orientation Conference* (ed. A. Gabay), Melbourne: La Trobe University.

Pressing, J. (1984a) 'Cognitive processes in improvisation', *Cognitive processes in the perception of art* (ed. W. R. Crozier and A. J. Chapman), pp. 345–63, Amsterdam: North Holland.

Quantz, J. J. (1752/1966) *On playing the flute* (trans. E. Reilley), New York: Free Press.

Richardson, C. P. (1983) 'Creativity research in music education: a review', *Council for Research in Music Education* 74 (Spring 1983), 1–21.

Roads, C. (1979) 'Grammars as representations for music', *Computer Music Journal* 3, 48–55.

Sage, G. S. (1977) *Introduction to motor behaviour: a neuropsychological approach*, Reading, MA: Addison-Wesley.

Schmidt, R. A. (1983) 'On the underlying response structure of well-learned motor responses: a discussion of Namikas and Schneider and Fisk', *Memory and control of action* (ed. R. A. Magill), Amsterdam: North Holland.

Shaffer, L. H. (1980) 'Analysing piano performance: a study of concert pianists', *Tutorials in motor behaviour* (ed. G. E. Stelmach and J. Requin), Amsterdam: North Holland.

Shepherd, G. M. (1983) *Neurobiology*, New York: Oxford University Press.

Sher, C. (1983) *The world's greatest fake book*, San Francisco: Sher Music.

Slonimsky, N. (1975) *Thesaurus of scales and melodic patterns*, London: Duckworth.

Sparrow, W. A. (1983) 'The efficiency of skilled performance', *Journal of Motor Behaviour* 15, 237–61.

Stocks, J. (1939) *Reason and intuition* (ed. D. M. Emmett), New York: Oxford University Press.

Summers, J. J. (1981) 'Motor programs', in *Human skills* (ed. D. Holding), Chichester: Wiley.

Torrance, E. P. (1966) *Guiding creative talent*, Englewood Cliffs, NJ: Prentice-Hall.

Vaughan, M. M. (1971) 'Music as model and metaphor in the cultivation and measurement of creative behaviour in children'. Unpublished EdD thesis. University of Georgia.

Webster, R. P. (1977) 'A factor of intellect approach to creative thinking in music'. Unpublished PhD thesis. University of Rochester, Eastman School of Music.

Welford, A. T. (1976) *Skilled performance*, Scott, Glenview, IL: Foresman.

Westcott, M. R. (1968) *Towards a contemporary psychology of intuition*, New York: Holt, Reinhart and Winston.

CHAPTER 12

Mel Gordon

Lazzi

The comic routines of the Commedia dell'Arte

I**T WOULD BE DIFFICULT TO THINK** of an historical style that has affected twentieth-century performance more than the Italian Commedia dell'Arte. For avant-garde directors in the 1910s – people like Vsevolod Meyerhold, Nikolai Evreinov, Max Reinhardt, Jacques Copeau, and Gordon Craig – the Commedia, with its reliance on stereotyped characters, masks, broad physical gestures, improvised dialogue and clowning, represented the very theatricality of the theatre. While performing across Europe and elsewhere from 1550 to 1750, often on informal stages and without dramatic texts as such, Commedia troupes developed large audiences composed of all social classes. It was this last feature that made Commedia so attractive to the avant-garde directors. The most popular entertainments of the first part of the twentieth century – motion picture comedy, both silent and sound, and radio comedy – seem closely related to the Commedia. Indeed, it is hard to conjure images of the Commedia without seeing Charlie Chaplin, W. C. Fields, Bert Lahr, the Marx Brothers, Jack Benny, or Laurel and Hardy . . .

If the reader looks carefully at the rich iconography in those books, he will find drawings, mezzotints, and paintings of perverse sexual play, nudity, vomiting, defecation, and all sorts of activities involving enemas and chamberpots – images of actions that are almost never described in the texts. For instance, in the authoritative Duchartre book, where captions accompany most of the pictures, a drawing of the Doctor administering an enema to Arlecchino's exposed buttocks is described as showing an 'injection' with a 'syringe'. In other books, the authors completely ignore this visual documentation. In fact, the Commedia's celebrated *lazzi*, or comic bits, are rarely discussed in more than a couple of paragraphs. Certainly these seldom even refer to the obscene *lazzi* which make up a good portion of the whole. It is as if these scholars, publishing in the early twentieth century, were psychologically or morally inhibited from accurately documenting the Commedia's best-known performance innovation, *lazzi*.

Definition of *lazzi*

From the beginning of Commedia scholarship, there has been a heavy concern with the derivation of the word *lazzi*. Luigi Riccoboni in his *Histoire du Théâtre Italien* . . . (Paris, 1728) wrote that it was a Lombard corruption of the Tuscan word *lacci*, which meant cord or ribbon. The term *lazzi*, Riccoboni reasoned, alluded to the comic business that tied together the performance. Of course, the practical reality was quite different; *lazzi* functioned as independent routines that more often than not interrupted or unravelled the Commedia plots or performance unity. Possibly the metaphor of an extraneous ribbon or the actual use of ropes and ribbons in the comic routines was the origin of the word.

Another, more widely accepted, etymological theory was proposed by A. Valeri in a series of articles published in the 1890s. *Lazzi*, according to Valeri, was only the simple corruption of *l'azione*, or the action, referring to the activities between the plotted scenes. Still other linguistic theories suggest parallels between the word *lazzi* and the Hebrew *latzon*, trick; the Swedish *lat*, gesture; and the Latin *lax*, fraud.

Whatever the origins of the word, the definition of *lazzi* is relatively standard; 'We give the name lazzi to the actions of Arlecchino or other masked characters when they interrupt a scene by their expressions of terror or by their fooleries', declared Riccoboni. In 1699, Andrea Perrucci simply defined the *lazzo*, a single *lazzi*, as 'some thing foolish, witty, or metaphorical in word or action'. Later scholars have described *lazzi* as 'stage tricks' or 'comic stage business'.

Clearly, the word had a multiplicity of meanings, even for the Commedia performers themselves. It co-existed with the Roman expression *trionfi*, triumphs; *azzi*, actions; *burla*, joke; and the French *jeu*, or play. Generally, *lazzi* refers to comic routines that were planned or unplanned and that could be performed in any one of dozens of plays. Put another way, *lazzi* allude to any discrete, or independent, comic and repeatable activity that guaranteed laughs, for its participants.

Function of *lazzi*

Although the *lazzi* were frequently thought of as occurring spontaneously or off-the-cuff, most were rigorously rehearsed and their insertion in performance sometimes preplanned. Constant Mic felt that the use of *lazzi* fell into three categories: (1) when, in fact, they arose out of the scenic occasion – for instance, when the audience became restless or bored during the performance, when the actors tried to comically cover dropped lines or cues, when the performers attempted to inject new and irrelevant amusements at the conclusion of a scene; (2) when the *lazzi* were an expected and welcome event for the spectators, who came to see the *lazzi* as high points or speciality acts in the performance; and (3) when the *lazzi* were actually written into the Commedia texts as contrived business . . .

How the *lazzi* were initiated on the stage seems to be a point of contention among historians, but again the answer may lie in a variety of approaches. Some were obviously used whenever a scene appeared to drag on too long and were totally improvised by one actor. Others, involving stage properties and several actors, had to be intricately preplanned.

Some *lazzi* could be instigated by a single performer, forcing his unsuspecting partners to improvise around him.

Sources of *lazzi*

Although several thousand performers enacted Commedia scenarios during its heyday, except for a single manuscript deposited at the library of Perugia, no detailed lists of *lazzi* are extant. Most of what is known of *lazzi* is from descriptions, performers' autobiographical statements, and notations of *lazzi* sequences – sometimes no more than titles – in Commedia plot outlines or scenarios that were posted on the wings of the stage or appeared in the Commedia texts that were intended for publication.

Why the *lazzi* were never made public can be explained in several ways. While the Commedia troupes could not patent their routines, they were not anxious to have their best work copied or read by a theatre-going public. If much of the Commedia was obscene, judging from the visual and fragmented written evidence, then writing down the explicit details could only jeopardize the troupes, who, like many itinerant performers, were sometimes only a step or so ahead of the legal authorities. Finally, it is possible that it never occurred to many Commedia troupes, like so many popular performers, to write out and preserve their *lazzi* . . .

Lazzi titles that are italicized are the actual names given to them by the Commedia practioners. *Lazzi* titles in quotes are descriptive names given by later historians . . .

Stage properties as *lazzi*

E06 'Lazzo of the tables' *(Paris 1670)*

Just as Pulcinella and Mezzettino are about to indulge in an elaborate feast, the tables suddenly arise and walk away. Or, part of the table settings arise and chase Arlecchino from the table.

E07 Lazzo of Arlecchino's portrait *(Paris 1685)*

In the flaps behind Arlecchino's portrait, Columbine (or Mezzettino) places her face.

E08 Lazzo of the zig-zag *(Paris 1688)*

Arlecchino (or Scaramouche) uses an expanding hinged apparatus to deliver a letter across the stage, or to pick the Doctor's pocket.

E09 Lazzo of putting the bell on his arse *(Paris 1688)*

Arlecchino breaks into Scaramouche's house at night. To warn himself when Scaramouche awakes, Arlecchino attempts to place a big bell on Scaramouche's arse.

Figure 12.1 VII. *Lazzo of the zig-zag* (E08) from *The Go-Between* in the *Grevenbroch Album*, Civic Museum, Venice, circa 1700.

E10 Lazzo of the disappearing fruit (Naples 1700)

Coviello and Lattanzio go to grab fruit, which disappears and changes into water and flames.

E11 Lazzo of the puppet (Naples 1700)

Pascale scares Pulcinella by dangling a marionette before his eyes as Pulcinella studies the darkness around him.

E12 Lazzo of the New World (Naples 1700)

Arlecchino (or Coviello) shows Pantalone (or the Doctor) his magic lantern or peep-show machine of 'The New World'. When Pantalone places his head inside the machine, Arlecchino passes a love-message or ring to Celia. This *lazzo* ends with the machine being broken over Pantalone's head.

Sexual/scatological *lazzi*

The sexual/scatological *lazzi*, the so-called 'stage crudities' of the Commedia, were among the most popular routines, although they remain the least analysed by scholars. The infantile and adolescent aggressions of shit and urine throwing, humiliation through exposure, of mixing food and faeces, of placing one's arse in another's face, and the telling of dirty jokes all remain the domain of the zanni characters. Despite the severity of the practical jokes, Arlecchino's intentions seem without undue malice.

F01 Lazzo of the enema (Rome 1560)

A widely-performed lazzo, this involved one of a number of actions: (a) thinking the Doctor will pay him the money owed to him, Gratiano has his pulse felt by the Doctor, who attempts to administer an enema. (b) Arlecchino (or the Captain) gives an enema to Pantalone's mule as Pantalone rides it. (c) Analyzing Arlecchino's urine, the Doctor declares that Arlecchino needs an enema, which leaves him pregnant. (d) Held by a servant with his posterior exposed, Pantalone is unwillingly given an enema by Zanni.

F02 'Lazzo of the chamber-pot' (Bavaria 1568)

The servant-girl (or Franceschina) empties a chamber pot out the window. It hits Pantalone (or the Captain) as he serenades Isabella.

F03 'Lazzo of vomit' (Venice 1611)

At the beginning of a performance, or just after drinking some of the Doctor's medicine, Arlecchino vomits.

Figure 12.2 IX. *Lazzo of the enema* (F01) from *A Third of the Time* in the Corsini MSS., Rome, circa 1610.

F04 'Lazzo of the rising dagger' *(Florence 1612)*

Hearing about the physical perfections of a certain woman, Pantalone's (or the Captain's) dagger begins to rise between his legs.

F05 'Lazzo of burying the urine' *(Rome 1618)*

Told that burying his urine and that of his wife would produce a son, Zanni procures a urinal that contains both liquids. Before spilling it on the soil, Zanni treats the urine as precious fluids.

Stupidity/inappropriate behaviour

I16 Lazzo of the pigs *(Perugia 1734)*

Pulcinella explains that, to avoid paying a tax, he hid a pig in his carriage. When he arrived at the city gate, the tax collectors asked him what was in the carriage. Pulcinella replied, 'That pig of my master.' So they let him go, but the pig cried out, and the tax collectors found it. Pulcinella maintains that the fault wasn't his, but with the pig who wouldn't be quiet.

117 Lazzo of paying homage to all of their names (Perugia 1734)

Pulcinella meets a number of characters. In an attempt to ingratiate himself with them, Pulcinella begins to praise their names in ridiculously insulting and long-winded fashion.

118 Lazzi of searching in his pants and pockets (Perugia 1734)

Gabba and Tristizia praise Pulcinella, saying, 'You're a man filled with virtue.' Confused, Pulcinella looks frantically in his pants and pockets.

119 Lazzo of the unanswered question (Perugia 1734)

Gabba and Tristizia ask Pulcinella if the daughter of the Captain is pregnant. Pulcinella replies, 'What are you having for breakfast?' They repeat their question and Pulcinella repeats his. They ask again and Pulcinella repeats his reply. Gabba and Tristizia run out to get sticks and beat him.

120 Lazzi of putting on and taking off their hats (Perugia 1734)

Gabba and Tristizia approach Pulcinella. Silently bowing to him, they continue to put on their hats and take them off according to Pulcinella's reactions.

121 Lazzi of delight (Perugia 1734)

Hearing good news, Pulcinella goes into a crazy dance, laughing in a ridiculous manner, kissing everyone.

Transformation *lazzi*

L07 Lazzo of each other's name (Perugia 1734)

Malizia, Gabba, and Tristizia meet and joke about each other's names. Respectively, they mean 'malice', 'he cheats', and 'wickedness'.

Scenario

From 'Pulcinella, the physician by force' (Act 1, sc.5–10) in the *Collection of Adriani di Lucca* in the library of Perugia, 1734, translated by Claudio Vicentini.

Scene five: (Roberto and the Captain)

Roberto tells the Captain that he is ready to conclude their recent agreement to marry his daughter. The Captain confesses that his daughter has just been injured in an accident and has lost the power to speak. Roberto replies that this is even preferable since a dumb wife is less gossipy than other wives. They leave in order to draw up a contract.

Scene six: (Pulcinella, alone)

Frustrated, Pulcinella enters (here he can show up without his stick and hat) and complains that the pest Malizia spoiled his speech. Pulcinella explains that he went to his master's farm but could not find the master. He decides to return again to the farm.

Scene seven: (Malizia, Gabba, and Tristizia)

Malizia, Gabba, and Tristizia have their *lazzo of each other's name* (L07). They complain about their masters. Gabba asks if any of them know a physician, who is needed to cure the Captain's daughter of her dumbness. In an aside, Malizia reveals that this might be an opportunity to avenge himself against Pulcinella by declaring Pulcinella a seasoned physician. Malizia then tells Gabba that he knows a great physician who wears a white sackcloth and always conceals his real skills. This physician is always alone, pretends to be clumsy and ridiculous in speech, and never admits his greatness unless he is soundly beaten; in this way, he has given wonderful treatments. Now, if they want this miracle-worker, he will deny that he is a doctor; but, after a thrashing, he will admit that he is a physician and cure the patient. Gabba and Tristizia are amazed at the physician's modesty. They thank Malizia and all go off looking for the physician.

Scene eight: (Orazio and Lelio)

Orazio complains that the old man, Roberto, has promised his daughter to the Captain. Lelio enters separately and complains that the Captain has promised his daughter to Roberto. Orazio and Lelio notice each other and embrace. They each explain their love problems and promise to help one another. They decide that they will need their servants in order to plan a strategy. They exit.

Scene nine: (Pulcinella, alone)

Offstage, Pulcinella sings this song:

> Leave the hunting, and fish.
> The hunter [sic], to catch anything,
> Wastes his time and wears out the hook and bait.
> If he is lucky, he catches a worthless fish.

After the song, Pulcinella repeats it on the stage.

Scene ten: (the same with Gabba and Tristizia)

Watching Pulcinella sing, Gabba and Tristizia are amazed. Pulcinella tells himself that he is a collection of virtues. The servants whisper to each other that this must be the great physician. While Pulcinella is praising himself, Gabba and Tristizia surround him and deeply bow. They have their silent *lazzi of putting on and taking off their hats* (I20). This is repeated three times. Then Pulcinella suggests that they leave on their hats lest they catch cold. Aside, the servants marvel that he really is a physician since he knows about colds. They move closer to Pulcinella. He shouts that they should keep their distance. They remark that it is a shame that a man of his qualities should hide his own virtues. Pulcinella has his *lazzi of searching his pants and pockets* (I18). After which, Pulcinella announces that he is not hiding anything. They speak of his great virtue in medicine. Pulcinella has his different laughes [sic]. They ask him to come cure the Captain's daughter. Pulcinella has his laughes [sic] again. He asks them if they have had lunch in reply to their questions (I19). This *lazzo* is repeated three times. One of them goes to get sticks. The servants apologize for being so rude. Pulcinella has his laughes [sic]. Then the servants beat him, while asking if he is a physician. He shouts yes and then denies it. This *lazzo* (D16) is repeated three times. Pulcinella pleads that he does not yet want to go to hell and begs them to stop. Finally he admits that he is a physician. The servants then want to dress him like 'one of his peers'. Pulcinella maintains that he already is dressed like one of his peers. The servants raise their sticks, and Pulcinella replies that if the devil wants it this way, so be it. They all go and laugh on the way out.

References and selected further reading

Beaumont, Cyril W. (1926) *The History of Harlequin*, reprint 1967, New York: Benjamin Bloom.

Duchartre, Pierre L., trans. Randolph T. Weaver (1929) *The Italian Comedy*, New York: The John Day Co.

Mic, Constant (1927) *La Commedia dell'Arte*, Paris: Éditions de la Pléiade.

Nicoll, Allardyce (1931) *Masks, Mimes and Miracles*, reprint 1963, New York: Cooper Square.

Smith, Winifred (1912) *The Commedia Dell'Arte*, reprint 1964, New York: Benjamin Blom.

Editors' Note

See also Rudlin, John (1994) *Commedia Dell'Arte: An Actor's Handbook*, London: Routledge.

CHAPTER 13

Jeff Nuttall

A jewel on the nation's arse

. . . ALTHOUGH RANDLE IS PROGRAMMED TO appear in the first half, it is left to the king's heralds to tickle the audience's expectations . . . Curtain. Then the safety drop . . . More waving. The expectation intensifies.

Then, halfway through the second half (opening scenario a Deep South amalgam of *Showboat* and *Porgy and Bess* with a bit of Jolson thrown in . . .), as the stand-up comic Sonny Roy the Funny Boy is winding up his act with a shaggy-dog story, a terrible head appears for a moment through the curtains. It is like the cuckoo from the cuckoo clock, the court jester in the guillotine, wild of eye and manic of demeanour, wrought from spiritual elements of the hen-run and the madhouse, a strutting, crowing geriatric, an eminence gone boneless with bubbling libido from which controlling sanity has been for ever lifted. And . . . the family groups and the neighbourhood knots, throughout the amphitheatre, explode with a sustained roar fit to crack the heavens.

The laughter dies but, an infinitesimal shade of a second before the theatre has completely settled to rest, the head waggles as though jolted by some violent impulse of randiness injected from whatever fabulous forms of animated decrepitude are concealed by the drapes. The eyes roll like pickled eggs loose in brine and one precipitate menopausal cackle from somewhere around the fourth row of the stalls sends the whole cloud up again, billowing and bellowing, discharging small side-explosions of recognition and solidarity – 'Nathen, Frank, coom on y'owd bugger'.

And then the head freezes (Sonny Roy the Funny Boy become straight-man is still suspended in mid-narrative under the mike), completely inactive. The theatre awaits its next tremor with the breathless anticipation a trapeze act normally commands. What will he do? What will he say?

The head is taken by a second convulsion as though shaking off the residue of the first, and this lifts the laughter-cloud again. Then the head is gone, leaving the cloud inflated, echoing and booming.

Sonny Roy the Funny Boy lets it settle. He finishes his story cleverly, using Randle's unforgivable upstaging as a piece of suspense in his own long joke. Telescoping the narrative cleverly he winds up in two short sentences and a monosyllabic punch-line that makes use of the laughter Randle has left on the boil . . .

The front curtain goes up amidst dense silence on a backdrop where a Sunny Scene complete with village inn and signpost has been baldly painted. Where is he? Will he really enter? What will he do when he appears?

The hero's coming is announced by a slow, steady thump, something like the knocking of a malevolent ghost. Each blow is spaced with crafty irregularity so that it bangs out just before or slightly after it's expected, teasing, rib-tickling, warming the expectations once again to unbearable intensity.

And he appears CLUMP. Decrepit, revolting, irrepressible CLUMP. Clinging to a rough-cut tree branch higher than his own head CLUMP. A pair of khaki shorts as baggy and decrepit as a wet bell tent, hung over a pair of knees like billiard balls. Ragged muffler. Baggy jacket. Hair standing up from his bald pate in a kind of cock's comb. *Pince-nez* perilous on his nose. A rucksack as inflated as the balloon of humour with which he so skilfully juggles. From a pocket like a sack juts the black screw-cap of a beer flagon. On his boneless face he wears an audible smile, his mouth stretched under his nose to emit a constant octogenarian gurgle which acts as a bridge from gag to gag like the drone knits the phrases of a bagpipe . . . A randy pawing of the ground is indicated, a chortling faith in one's own unkillable spirit – 'Eeee, I'll gi'e 'em some stick!'

And his rolling eye, his out-thrown torso, his bandy, stomping deportment say: 'Here I am. What do you think of me? Aren't I amazing?'

'Eeeeee Oswaldtwistle,' he exults through the rising laughter. The name of the town that is present in force is something of a gift for Randle. The resounding 's's and 't's bring those gurgling juices to his flabby lips where they spray out like sparklers into the stage lights. He is full of subtle foretastes of the excess everyone knows is to come. There he stands, as abominable and hilarious as everybody's wildest imaginings, extravagant, unbelievable, but plain as a toper's nose for all to see. His first gag then is about this audacious display. 'Baghum, A seez a kid up theer, come runnin' to 'iz mother. "Come 'ere mother, thur'z a monkey up a stick!"' . . .

The throat gurgle finds somewhere in its stave a dying whine of resignation . . . 'Me feet are reddott! But baghum A've just 'ad a bit of a narra squeak.' The 'e' sound allows him to stretch his lips near to the back of his neck. The 'k' clacks out. The orchestration of his patter is gurgle, against sudden shouted statement, dying into an innuendo that is kicked out of the way by savagely emphasised syllables. 'A wozz goon' across a *field*. Thur woz a bull innit. It wozn't Barney's bull neither . . . aye . . .' dying into a complicity with the audience who acknowledge the reference to a mutual myth by sending the cloud up to the ceiling again. 'In fact it woz an 'ell of a long way from bein' Barney's bull!' Voice dies again, 'Aye . . .', into the laughter. 'Ooooooo it woz a fierce un! It 'ad a coupla prongs on it az long az this stick.' The sudden angle of the displayed tree tickles that surprised female shriek from the stalls. He teases her response with a mock-threatening jab. Woman stifles her helpless giggles for very shame but the ripples spread. '. . . only they were a damn sight sharper ner this, I'll tell yer. It come tuppin' away . . .', gurgle into sigh again, giving the word 'away' a curious *double entendre*. 'A thowt it woz apologizin', the way it woz bowfin' and scrapin' away . . .' rides the laughter with an extended 'Aye . . . Aye, A shooed it away wi' me 'andkerchief . . .', brandishes huge red spotted bandana, rides laugh with a knowing, grinding 'Aye . . .'. By now the theatre has difficulty restraining its laughter sufficiently to hear the next line. Each emphasised syllable is underlined with a pawing of the ground with his great boot which he wears on the wrong foot, by a spasm of the knees; each dying drone is accompanied by a 360 degrees survey of the auditorium, manipulating the direction and the warmth of the rapport.

Randle plays his visual tricks with a restraint that subtly contradicts his obvious extravagance. There is the power in him to precipitate total hysteria. He has plenty of margin to play with and he deploys it sparingly. 'It med it a damn sight wuss . . . aye . . . aye . . . It come, but did I pick 'em up? A furly sizzled!' 'Z's buzz waspishly. The immediate picture of this bag of impudent senility haring across a field pursued by a bull with clouds of wrath snorting from either nostril, a simple image straight from the pen of the Film Fun cartoonist who, at that time, had Randle as a strip character, keeps the cloud up and bouncing . . . 'I'll be 82 in a few more days. Eighty-two and A'm as full of vim az a butcher'z dog . . . A'm as livelagh' – last syllable of 'lively' is a belch carefully supressed and used to change the tone of the vowel – 'az a cricket. Why, A'll tek anybody hon at me age and weight – dead or alive . . .' The laughter balloon, let to rest a bit, gets a prod. 'An' A'll run 'em, walk 'em, jump 'em, fight 'em . . . aaaa – a – aghye . . .' An extended sighing drone implies the missing alliterative syllable and the laughter cloud is inflated to the full again.

There is little point to what the hero is saying now . . . The verbal structure of the act is gradually being discarded. The balloon is sustained increasingly by underlining of character, by visuals and aurals. It is a subtle reassurance for the bottom levels of the working class, the heavy manual labourers who are uncomfortable with words most of the time. It is a warm collective return to the infantile with all the consonant dropping of taboos – 'Baghum, thur'z another hurr comin' 'ere' – seizes it between finger and thumb and pulls the hair out straight so that a tiny peak of stretched flesh is visible. The sight is simultaneously outrageous and relieving. The owd bugger is actually playing with his body like a child, and so, we feel, might we. The implications are obvious but never stated . . . His hand explores the awful regions of his thigh, overhung by his vast shorts. How far will the exploration extend? Will he? Dare he? He meets the challenge with a saucy, quizzical glare. 'Thur's a hurr 'ere wi' a knot in it . . . aye . . . aye . . . It'z surprisin' wur thi keep comin' from. Eighty two an' look at this for a thick 'urr . . .' High enough now for dangerous *double entendre*. The lady in the stalls obliges. Turns towards the poor shrieking creature, displays the distended growth with all the phallic air of a bantam. 'Straight as a bulrush!' – biblical use of rhetoric, driving the *double entendre* ruthlessly home. And now that sex has been filtered into the range of reference Randle knows that he has activated a whole new set of raw nerves. Like Max Miller he has a thorough knowledge of, and to some extent shares, all the repressions and double standards of a class whose sex is severely discoloured by large families in two-room terrace houses, by the systematic guilt-policies of the Methodist and Baptist movements, by the incapacity following fatigue after ten- and twelve-hour shifts. Each nerve in this new category is swollen to hypersensitivity by hot compression of guilt and the longing for release. He is further into the region of the seaside postcard. He approaches the 'saucy' . . .

'Well A woz 'evvin' a bit o' fun wi' these youngunz. A took one of 'em for a walk. We walked about five miles. Neither of us spoke a word. A sed, "A penny for yer thoughts." Ooo she gimme such a clout across t' lug. A sed, "Wot's t'do wi' yi? I only sed a penny for yer thoughts." "Ee," she said. "A thowt yi sed a penny for me shorts."' The gurgle in full spate carries through the huge gust of laughter. And now to the bottle: 'A think A'll 'ev a sup. Aye . . .' He gargles. Here come the great inevitables of every Randle performance. 'All slops!' he pronounces – play on brewery trade name Allsops – and then he belches formidably. 'Baghum, yi'll 'ave to excuse . . .' but he's overtaken by another eruption and now, at its most gastric, simple, alimentary, explicit point, Randle's style is at its purest. Now the audience knows that the spoken word may be abandoned . . .

A vast belch: 'A don't like this ale but A'll sup it if it keeps me up all neet' – back in the filth, working up to the finish. 'Thur'z about thirty-six burps in this bottle' – another catch phrase that gets a huge recognition . . .

Even a serious note now? – A moral? – 'A'm owd enough t' mek most of yerz grandfather – Get plenty of exercise, plenty of fresh urr and ale. Look at me. A'm 82. A could jump a five-bar gate – if it woz laid ont' floor like . . .' – the fading note – 'It woz only t'other dee. A went to a funeral. A woz comin' awee from t' graveside. A chap looks at me, 'e sez, "'Ow old are you?" A sed, "82." 'E sed, "A don't think it's much use you goin' 'ome at all . . ."'

The applause fills the theatre like white sound. The clumping stick punctuates his exit and he leaves us well fed, replete . . .

CHAPTER 14

Peter J. Arnold

Sport, the aesthetic and art

Further thoughts

OVER THE PAST FEW YEARS the relationship of sport to art has been a matter of some considerable controversy. It centres not on whether sport can be a subject of art, which is clearly possible, but whether or not sport itself can be regarded as an art. Put more specifically the question is: are there any sports that are so constituted that they may be regarded as a form of art? It is a further attempt to look at this question that is the main concern of this paper . . .

Three categories of activities in relation to sport and dance

(a) Non-aesthetic sports

In an effort to clear up some of the confusions endemic in the literature to do with aesthetics and sports, Best[1] made a distinction between 'purposive' sports and 'aesthetic' sports. Purposive sports, he maintains, are characterised by the fact that each of these sports can be specified independently of the manner of achieving it, as long as it conforms to the rules or norms which govern it . . . e.g. football, rugby, track and field . . .

(b) Partially aesthetic sports

Aesthetic sports are so called because 'the aim cannot intelligibly be specified independently of the means of achieving it'.[2] Included in this smaller category are such activities as gymnastics . . . and surfing. Inherent in all these sports is a concern for the way or manner in which they are performed . . . As one reference on gymnastics states:

A perfect exercise with a maximum rating is one that is presented with elegance, ease, precision and in a style and rhythm well adapted to the nature of the aesthetic performance with no faults in execution. The faults in execution or style are penalized by a deduction in points or fraction of points according to the following direction.

Defects in elegance in general. An exercise, although executed without fault, but presented in a rhythm too quick or too slow, or with an ill-proportioned display of force, counts less than a perfect exercise as described . . .[3]

An example of the way in which gymnastics can be both technically commented upon as well as aesthetically perceived by a knowledgeable onlooker is conveyed by the following descriptions of Ludmilla Tourischeva's floor exercise sequence in the 1972 Munich Olympics, where she won a Gold Medal. *Technically* it was said:

This sequence demonstrates a very high level of Olympic Gymnastic proficiency, combining difficult techniques with a high level of originality.

Her sequence required only two superior difficulties in order to obtain the maximum marks of four points and for these she chose a double twisting back-somersault and a half-twisting back somersault; these she executed with mechanical perfection, with amplitude and with virtuoso integration of parts.

In addition to the minimum requirements in superior difficulty exercises, she elaborated her composition with a full twist and an aerial cartwheel as well as an aerial walk-over.

The sequence as a whole has precision, continuity, climax and a total integration of elements, her movements skilfully matching the music.

But *qualitatively* it was possible to say of Tourisheva's performance that:

She commanded the restricted and circumscribed floor space with illusory ease and elegance; her floor patterns, aerial designs and dynamics were integrated into a composition of contrasts, complexity and completeness.

Of qualities of form, she displayed poise, controlled balance, cleanness of line, and each in turn – an arched, curled, twisted and extended torso; her long supple limbs described sinuous and circular movements and her shapely flexible fingers made florid gestures in space. Her footwork had a precision at times forceful and firm and yet again dainty with impeccably shaped and patterned placings.

Of sensory qualities there were combined in this sequence a softness of movement, a sharp crispness, and again a great delicacy together with smoothness, flowing continuity, resilience and elasticity.

Of intensity qualities there were evidenced: a disguised power, an ease and effortlessness in flight, a freedom to fly, float and soar and a seeming denial of natural inertia and gravity.

Qualities of complexity drew forth the crowd's ecstatic applause – intricate revolutions with speed, deft and devious trunk rotations – and always landing with the same secure precision and control.

> Her sequence was above all expressive with a medley of qualities from nonchalance, playful arrogance and pride to coyness, piquancy and at times cool dignity. Even dramatic qualities emerged with tension, climax and resolution; but perhaps dominantly characteristic were her rhythmical lyricism and closely integrated movements with the accelerandos, rubatos and rallentandos of the music.[4]

Interesting though these two quotes are, the point they help bring out is that with an 'aesthetic sport' its purpose can only be specified in terms of the aesthetic manner of achieving it. Put the other way round *the aesthetic sport is one in which the purpose cannot be specified without reference to the aesthetic manner of achieving it.*

(c) Artistic activities

What marks out a work of art is that its meaning cannot be expressed in any way other than the way it is . . . a work of art is a unique presentation of embodied meaning.

Notes

1   D. Best (1985) 'Sport is not art', *Journal of the Philosophy of Sport* 12, pp. 25–40.
2   D. Best, (1978) *Philosophy and Human Movement*, George Allen and Unwin: London, p. 105.
3   J. R. White (ed.) (1966) 'Gymnastics', *Sports Rules Encyclopaedia*, Palo Alto: National Press, p. 61.
4   G. F. Curl (1980) Commentary given at a lecture at Dunfermline College, Edinburgh, Scotland.

CHAPTER 15

Joan Littlewood

Goodbye note from Joan

I N 1961, AFTER SEVERAL highly successful West End transfers, Joan Littlewood announced that, after the production of James Goldman's *They Might Be Giants*, she was leaving England and Theatre Workshop.

Dear ENCORE

Such a lot of nonsense has been talked about my reasons for leaving England that I wanted to write to you before I went. You have always given serious consideration to the problems facing people working in the English theatre.

It is not unusual for someone to leave a situation in which they cannot do the work for which they are qualified. That is my case.

My objective in life has not changed; it is to work with other artists – actors, writers, designers, composers – and in collaboration with them, and by means of argument, experiment and research, to help to keep the English theatre alive and contemporary.

I do not believe in the supremacy of the director, designer, actor or even of the writer. It is through collaboration that this knockabout art of theatre survives and kicks. It was true at The Globe, The Curtain, The Crown, and in the 'illustrious theatre' of Molière and it can work here, today.

No one mind or imagination can foresee what a play will become until all the physical and intellectual stimuli, which are crystallized in the poetry of the author, have been understood by a company, and then tried out in terms of mime, discussion and the precise music of grammar; words and movement allied and integrated. The smallest contact between characters in a remote corner of the stage must become objectively true and relevant. The actor must be freed from the necessity of making effective generalizations.

I could go on but you too know how the theatre must function if it is to reflect the genius of a people, in a complex day and age. Only a company of artists can do this. It is no use the critics proclaiming overnight the genius of the individual writer; these writers must graft in company with other artists if we are to get what we want and what our people need, a great theatre.

This does not depend on buildings, nor do we need even a fraction of the money they are spending on their bomb. Each community should have a theatre; the West End has plundered our talent and diluted our ideas; cannot each district afford to support a few artists who will give them back some entertainment, laughter and love of mankind?

Young actors and actresses, don't be puppets any longer! The directors and the critics won't help you; in television, film or theatre they ask for the dregs of the old acting, mere 'expression', exploitation of your 'type'. In Shaftesbury Avenue or in the Brecht theatre, it's all the same. The theatre should be made up of individuals, not pawns. Keep your wits, develop your talent, take over the theatre which now belongs to the managers or the landlords. Let's stop this waste of human ability. I have tried, for nearly twenty seven years. I've had my nose to the grindstone and I'm still, comparatively speaking, alive. I'll be back, I'll be more help.[1]

JOAN LITTLEWOOD [SEPTEMBER 1961]

Note

1 Two years later, Joan returned to direct a re-assembled company in *Oh What a Lovely War*, one of her finest productions and the most decorated production ever staged by Theatre Workshop.

B

Hybrid pathways

CHAPTER 16

Mel Gordon

German Expressionist acting

The New Man possesses even greater, more direct feelings. He stands there grasping his heart. And from the surge welling up in his blood, he is in an absolutely impulsive state. It is as if he would wear his heart painted onto his chest. Now he is not an image anymore – he is actually MAN. Completely entangled in the Cosmos, but with cosmic perceptions. Not counterfeit thoughts, but his emotions alone lead him and guide him. Only then can he advance and approach absolute Rapture, where the tremendous ecstasies soar from his soul . . . Yet, these New Men are in no way crazy or foolish. Their thought-processes work according to a different nature. They are untouched. They reflect upon nothing. They live not in circles nor through echoes. They experience *directly*. And that is the greatest secret of their artifice: it is without psychology.

(Kasimir Edschmid, *On Poetic Expressionism*, 1917)

L IKE OTHER AVANT-GARDE MOVEMENTS Expressionism developed both a dramatic literature and a theatrical style. Although they shared a similar philosophical underpinning, the Expressionist drama and theatre evolved separately, being created by different people, at different times. Occasionally, theatre scholars have analyzed one in terms of the other, producing a number of misconceptions. To be sure, the earlier Expressionist dramatic literature inspired the development of the Expressionist styles of performance. Yet, some of theatrical Expressionism's roots and influences came from sources that were antithetical to literary Expressionism. More often than not, however, theatrical Expressionism, particularly in the acting, advanced modes of performance that were uniquely its own . . .

Theory and roots of Expressionist acting

For the Expressionists, the new, untested Expressionist actor was not just a symbol or the physical rendering of the New Man: his abilities to transform himself from one soul-state to another, to emote the broadest range of feelings, to express the ecstasy of the playwright, and to guide the audience made him the New Man incarnate. The failure of Expressionist performance, they thought, would doom Expressionism as an artistic movement and philosophy.

Most of the important Expressionist statements on acting were prescriptive, coming months and years before the heyday of the Expressionist theatre . . .

First and best-known of these statements, 'Epilog to the Actor', was written by the Expressionist playwright Paul Kornfeld in May 1916 as an afterword to his play *The Seduction* (1913), a year and a half before it was produced at the Schauspielhaus in Frankfurt by Gustav Hartung on 8 December 1917 . . . Kornfeld exhorted the Expressionist actor not to behave

> as though the thoughts and words he has to express have only arisen in him at the very moment in which he recites them. If he has to die on the stage, let him not pay a visit to the hospital beforehand in order to learn how to die; . . . Let him dare to stretch his arms out wide and with a sense of soaring speak as he has never spoken in life; let him not be an imitator or seek his models alien to the actor. In short, let him not be ashamed of the fact that he is acting.
>
> (in Sokel, 1963)

Only this sort of non-reality imitating actor could embody the single, pristine, emotional essence of the new drama, Kornfeld claimed. Through careful selection and avoidance of complex Naturalism, the new actor could be the necessary 'representative of thought, feeling, or Fate'. Despite the heavy Expressionist rhetoric, Kornfeld's model for the Expressionist actor was operatic – 'The dying singer (who) still gives forth a high C' – and in some ways did not significantly differ from the conception of the Reinhardt or pantomimic actor . . .

At the earliest stage, Expressionist directors and actors were most strongly affected by the proto-Expressionist (Strindberg, Wedekind, Kokoschka, Alfred Doblin, and Carl Sternheim) and Expressionist dramas themselves. The majority of these texts provided detailed, almost operatic instructions as to the performers' movement and voice: 'inside, breathing heavily, laboriously raises his head, later moves a hand, then both hands, raising himself slowly, singing, withdrawing into a trance', 'seeking each other's eyes – swing arms – gradually all rising – bursting out in a joint cry', 'suddenly weak in one arm', etc. Even the speaking parts were relatively clear and simplistic; the telegraphic or lyric dialog frequently was keyed to unchanging stereotyped characters. Still, it was evident to the Expressionists that even the most descriptive stage directions and simple characterizations could not furnish the essential creative basis for their performances. Other stimuli were needed . . .

For example, Fritz Kortner, one of the two most celebrated Expressionist actors, trained as a choral leader in Reinhardt's production of *Oedipus Rex* (1912). There he was taught not only a particular choral voice and diction but also the appropriate statuesque gestures that were meant to project across gigantic staging areas. As Kortner was later to discover, the very same movements when applied to a much smaller stage and auditorium were to have a completely different effect on the spectator and the speaker. However, in no other field of performance does one find a stronger, if relatively unexplored, similarity with Expressionist acting than in the Middle-European dance and cabaret of the 1910s. Not only did the German and Swiss dancers and choreographers influence the early theatrical Expressionists in the areas of movement-philosophy and technique, they were also largely responsible for the evolution of a new critical understanding and journalistic analysis that explained the performer's craft in terms of self-motivation and private expression.

Before the outbreak of the First World War, two distinct dance styles evolved from the revolt against classicism in Central Europe. The first was an off-shoot of the imitative Greek, individually expressive, and earth-bound style of Isadora Duncan . . .

Also, at this time, the Swiss composer Emile Jaques-Dalcroze began to teach his concept of *eurhythmics* at Hellerau, outside Dresden . . . Later, the theatrical Expressionists would compress and join these two ways of moving and working – the lyrical, unrestrained, emotive flow of Duncanism with the musically symbolic, muscular posturings of Dalcroze – to form an abrupt series of gesture-combinations that were begun in one kind of tempo and intensity and completed in another. These movement-hybrids were executed from one style to the next without any transitional gestures. Frequently, the movements were initiated in a monumental, intense, laboriously slow, Dalcroze-like tempo and then suddenly exploded into a string of disjointed, separate, staccato emotional-gestures that resembled the projection of minute flashes of Duncan's counterparts.

A third modern force in the pre-war Central European dance was that of the Hungarian-born Rudolf von Laban. According to Laban, all human movement could be divided into centrifugal movements, radiating from the center (i.e. in the arms: 'scattering') or peripheral movements, inward from the extremities (i.e. 'scooping'). To distinguish it from the more static *eurhythmics*, Laban called his system *eukinetics*. Like Dalcroze, he developed movement-choirs to realize his theories, but Laban's dancers performed in a music-less, plastic environment . . .

Another non-theatrical source of inspiration for the Expressionists were the German solo and cabaret dancers of the time . . . But among the cabaret performers, none excited the theatrical Expressionists more – nor served as a more common acting model – than Frank Wedekind (1864–1918) . . . In Max Krell's anthology *German Theatre of the Present* (Munich, 1923), Kasimir Edschmid recalled Wedekind's animal-like, tortured presence as the greatest acting experience that he ever witnessed. It is also noteworthy that the other most lauded Expressionist actor – along with Fritz Kortner – Werner Krauss, worked with Wedekind before entering the Expressionist stage.

Possibly the most coherent and detailed analysis of the philosophical/technical aspects of theatrical Expressionism was published in a book that appeared long after the Expressionists' apogee, Felix Emmel's *The Ecstatic Theatre* (Prien, 1924). In his chapter on Expressionist, or ecstatic, acting, Emmel differentiated and described two kinds of actors: (1) the actor of nerves – as exemplified by the Neo-Romantic actor Albert Bassermann, and (2) the actor of blood – as exemplified by Friedrich Kayssler, also a Neo-Romantic actor. Although both performers essentially came out of the same Reinhardt tradition, they worked and acted from theoretically opposed points of view. Bassermann generally created his stage-characters from the study of other men. His final presentation would be based on a combination of many individual characteristics that he observed in scores of people. His character-performances revealed a finely-drawn, psychological mosaic of many types that were bound together after much practice until his nerves were automatically capable of reproducing the illusion of a new, single character. Kayssler, on the contrary, always played himself. He allowed his changing stage personas to grow from the character-emotions rooted in his 'soul', or from the flood and unity of his 'blood'. His acting rhythms and character motivations always came directly from his own internal experiences and essence . . .

Modes of Expressionist acting and performance

At the center of the Expressionist universe was Man. All other objective or conceptual phenomena – every physical property, theory, idea, formal grammar, science, or methodology – that precluded Man was eliminated or diminished. This emphasis on Man, and Man alone, produced a variety of different performance and acting styles since the theatrical Expressionists themselves strongly disagreed as to the concept or mode of presentation of their Man-centered art; once the curtains were drawn and the stage-space revealed, the post-war German audiences could expect to viscerally experience one of several kinds of Expressionist utopias.

Borrowing some of the terminology from Bernhard Diebold's influential study *Anarchy in the Drama* (Frankfurt, 1921) that was used to describe models of pre-Expressionist and Expressionist dramas, German Expressionist performances can be sub-divided into three general styles based on their expressive relationship to the audience – the creation of ecstasy through induction, association, or identification – and their overall approach to acting. These three categories are:

1   the *Geist* (purely spiritual or abstract) *performance*, which could be viewed as an ultimate vision of pure expression without the conventional intervention of dramatic characters or intricate plot – a sort of absolute communication between the playwright/director's *Seele* (mind), and his audience;

2   the *Schrei* (scream or ecstatic) *performance*, which could be likened to an actual, if hazy, intense dream-state where movement, exteriors, language, motivation, and inner logic were uniformly and bizarrely warped;

3   the *Ich* (I or ego) *performance*, which resembled the second type in certain ways, but focused upon a central performer who acted less – *or more* – grotesquely than the other, often stereotypical, characters and who was the subject of the playwright's and audience's identification – a kind of dream told to another person or a dream remembered.

References

Sokel, Walter (1963) *An Anthology of German Expressionist Drama: A Prelude to the Absurd*, New York: Garden City.

CHAPTER 17

Anaïs Nin

The theatre and the plague

S CHOOLROOM OF THE SORBONNE, a Thurdsay evening in Paris.

Allendy and Artaud were sitting at the big desk. Allendy introduced Artaud.
The room was crowded.
The blackboard made a strange backdrop.
There were people of all ages, followers of Allendy's lectures on New Ideas.
The light was crude. It made Artaud's eyes shrink into darkness, as they are deepset.
This brought into relief the intensity of his gestures.
He looked tormented. His hair, rather long, fell at times over his forehead. He has
the actor's nimbleness and quickness of gestures. His face is lean, as if ravaged by fevers.
His eyes do not seem to see the people. They are the eyes of a visionary.
His hands are long, long-fingered. Beside him Allendy looks earthy, heavy, gray. He
sits at the desk, massive, brooding. Artaud steps out on the platform, and begins to talk
about *The Theater and the Plague*.
He asked me to sit in the front row. It seems to me that all he is asking for is
intensity, a more heightened form of feeling and living. Is he trying to remind us that it
was during the Plague that so many marvelous works of art and theater came to be,
because, whipped by the fear of death, man seeks immortality, or to escape, or to surpass
himself.
But then, imperceptibly almost, he let go of the thread we were following and began
to act out dying by plague.

NO ONE QUITE KNEW WHEN IT BEGAN. TO ILLUSTRATE HIS
CONFERENCE, HE WAS ACTING OUT AN AGONY.

'LA PESTE' IN FRENCH IS SO MUCH MORE TERRIBLE THAN 'THE PLAGUE' IN ENGLISH.

BUT NO WORD COULD DESCRIBE WHAT ARTAUD ACTED OUT ON THE PLATFORM OF THE SORBONNE.

HE FORGOT ABOUT HIS CONFERENCE, THE THEATER, HIS IDEAS, DR. ALLENDY SITTING THERE, THE PUBLIC, THE YOUNG STUDENTS, PROFESSORS, AND DIRECTORS.

HIS FACE WAS CONTORTED WITH ANGUISH, ONE COULD SEE THE PERSPIRATION DAMPENING HIS HAIR. HIS EYES DILATED, HIS MUSCLES BECAME CRAMPED, HIS FINGERS STRUGGLED TO RETAIN THEIR FLEXIBILITY.

HE MADE ONE FEEL THE PARCHED AND BURNING THROAT, THE PAINS, THE FEAR, THE FIRE IN THE GUTS.

HE WAS IN AGONY.

HE WAS SCREAMING. HE WAS DELIRIOUS.

HE WAS ENACTING HIS OWN DEATH,

HIS OWN CRUCIFIXION.

At first people gasped.

And then they began to laugh.
Everyone was laughing.

They hissed.

Then one by one, they began to leave, noisily, talking, protesting.

They banged the door as they left.

The only ones who did not move were Allendy, his wife, the Lalous and Marguerite.

More protestations.
More jeering.
But Artaud went on, until the last gasp.

HE STAYED ON THE FLOOR.

Then when the hall had emptied of all but his small group of friends, he walked straight up to me and kissed my hand. He asked me to go to the café with him. Everyone else had something to do. We all parted at the door of the Sorbonne, and Artaud and I walked out in a fine mist. We walked, walked through the dark streets.

HE WAS HURT, WOUNDED, BAFFLED BY THE JEERING.
HE SPAT OUT HIS ANGER.

'THEY ALWAYS WANT TO HEAR ABOUT;

THEY WANT TO HEAR AN OBJECTIVE CONFERENCE ON
THE THEATER AND THE PLAGUE,
I WANT TO GIVE THEM THE EXPERIENCE ITSELF,
THE PLAGUE ITSELF,
SO THEY WILL BE TERRIFIED,
AND AWAKEN.'

'I WANT TO AWAKEN THEM.
BECAUSE THEY DO NOT REALIZE THEY ARE DEAD.
THEIR DEATH IS TOTAL, LIKE DEAFNESS AND BLINDNESS.
THIS IS AGONY I PORTRAYED.
MINE YES,
AND EVERYONE WHO IS ALIVE.'

The mist fell on his face, he pushed his hair away from his forehead. He looked taut and obsessed, but now he spoke quietly. We sat in the Coupole. He forgot the conference.

'I HAVE NEVER FOUND ANYONE WHO FELT AS I DID. I HAVE BEEN
AN OPIUM ADDICT FOR FIFTEEN YEARS.
IT WAS FIRST GIVEN TO ME WHEN I WAS VERY YOUNG,
TO CALM SOME TERRIBLE PAINS IN MY HEAD.'

'I FEEL SOMETIMES THAT I AM NOT WRITING,
BUT DESCRIBING THE STRUGGLES WITH WRITING,
THE STRUGGLES OF BIRTH.'

He recited poetry. We talked about form, the theater, his work.

'YOU HAVE GREEN, AND SOMETIMES VIOLET EYES.'

HE GREW GENTLE AND CALM.

WE WALKED AGAIN, IN THE RAIN.

FOR HIM THE PLAGUE WAS NO WORSE THAN

DEATH BY MEDIOCRITY

DEATH BY COMMERCIALISM

AND DEATH BY THE CORRUPTION WHICH SURROUNDED US.

HE WANTED TO MAKE PEOPLE AWARE THAT THEY WERE DYING.
TO FORCE THEM INTO A POETIC STATE.

'THE HOSTILITY ONLY PROVED THAT YOU DISTURBED THEM',
I SAID.

BUT WHAT A SHOCK TO SEE A SENSITIVE POET CONFRONTING A
HOSTILE PUBLIC.

WHAT BRUTALITY, WHAT UGLINESS IN THE PUBLIC.

CHAPTER 18

Allan Kaprow

A statement

(rewritten from a recorded interview)

IN MY SHOW AT THE Hansa Gallery in 1952 were paintings in a variety of styles, but the variety was expressive of different kinds of interests. I now realize that I was not just casting around for a way to paint, but was casting around for a way to include all the levels of meaning that I was intending. For, in addition to paintings, there were also constructions, or what we would call today 'assemblages'. Some were suspended on the wall, others from the ceiling.

I had begun to clarify what I felt, even then, was a multilevelled attitude toward painting . . .

Soon afterward I developed a kind of action-collage technique, following my interest in Pollock. These action-collages, unlike my constructions, were done as rapidly as possible by grasping up great hunks of varied matter: tinfoil, straw, canvas, photos, newspaper, etc. I also cut up pictures which I had made previously, and these counted as autobiographical fragments, as much as they were an intended formal arrangement . . .

The next exhibition was an extension of these single works. Now I just simply filled the whole gallery up, starting from one wall and ending with the other. When you opened the door, you found yourself in the midst of an entire Environment. I made its parts in my studio in New Jersey according to a floor plan of the gallery, and what I thought would be able to fill it properly. I then hung the parts in an overlapping planar arrangement along the dominant axis of the room . . .

But I complained immediately about the fact that there was a sense of mystery until your eye reached a wall. Then there was a dead end. At that point my disagreement with the gallery space began. I thought how much better it would be if you could just go out of doors and float an Environment into the rest of life so that such a caesura would not be there . . . I immediately saw that every visitor to the Environment was part of it. I had not really thought of it before. And so I gave him occupations like moving something, turning switches on — just a few things. Increasingly during 1957 and 1958, this suggested a more 'scored' responsibility for that visitor. I offered him more and more to do, until there developed the Happening. My first Happenings were performed elsewhere, in lofts, stores, classrooms, gymnasiums, a friend's farm and so forth. The integration of all elements — environment, constructed sections, time, space, and people — has been my main technical problem ever since. Only now am I beginning to see results.

The name 'Happening' is unfortunate. It was not intended to stand for an art form, originally. It was merely a neutral word that was part of a title of one of my projected ideas in 1958–59. It was the word which I thought would get me out of the trouble of calling it a 'theatre piece', a 'performance', a 'game', a 'total art', or whatever, that would evoke associations with known sports, theatre, and so on. But then it was taken up by other artists and the press to the point where now all over the world it is used in conversation by people unaware of me, and who do not know what a Happening is. Used in an offhand fashion, the word suggests something rather spontaneous that 'just happens to happen' . . . 'Oh, isn't that a Happening?' . . .

But there is also the question of whether people are not just relating them to show that they suspect every authored Happening of being no more than a casual and indifferent event, or that, at best, it is a 'performance' to release inhibitions. It is one thing to look acutely at moments that just happen in one's life. It is quite another to pay no attention to these moments ordinarily but then invoke them as evidence of the foolishness of the Happening as an art form. This hostile sense of the 'Happening' is unfortunate.

In another sense it is unfortunate because the word still has those implications of light indifference which such people pick up on. It conveys not only a neutral meaning of 'event' or 'occurrence', but it implies something unforeseen, something casual, perhaps — unintended, undirected. And if I try to impress everyone with the fact that I really direct a Happening inside out, as most of us do, they do not believe it. They say, 'It's not spontaneous? We don't do what we want to do?' I say, 'No, not at all', and they say, 'Well, why do you call it a Happening?' It is hard to give an answer to such questions . . . so for a while we shall be stuck with the implication of Happening-as-happenstance.

In first doing Happenings, I looked for friends to perform, anybody who would help me out, and they tended to be the artists, poets, musicians that I knew. Since I knew very few actors, I did not go to them except when Julian Beck recommended a few, who immediately turned out to be useless to me because they wanted to act. They wanted to have stellar roles. They wanted to *speak* for the most part, and I utilized little verbiage in my work. And all the things which I suggested were quite contrary to their background . . .

I found an alternative. This was to make deliberate use, simply, of what was available — the people as well as the environment . . . So the next thing was to find a method to do a performance without rehearsal — to make use of available people on the spot as quickly as possible. Which meant the development of new techniques, new forms, and new thoughts about my whole purpose. Especially since I wanted people involved rather than as spectators, I had to find a practical way to do this. So I thought of the simplest situations, the simplest images — the ones having the least complicated mechanics or implications on the surface. Written down on a sheet of paper sent in advance, these actions could be learned by anyone. Those who wished to participate could decide for themselves . . .

My works are conceived on, generally, four levels. One is the direct 'suchness' of every action, whether with others, or by themselves, with no more meaning than the sheer immediacy of what is going on. This physical, sensible, tangible being is to me very important. The second is that they are performed fantasies not exactly like life, though derived from it. The third is that they are an organized structure of events. And the fourth level, no less important, is their 'meaning' in a symbolical or suggestive sense.

For example, regarding this last, if I call for a single female in a work, whether it be a twist dancer or the dream girl in *The Courtyard*, she is usually the embodiment of a number of old, archetypal symbols. She is the nature goddess (Mother Nature) . . .

It is not that such symbols are esoteric: they are not. They are so general and so archetypical that actually almost everyone knows vaguely about these things. This is just the opposite from what I call 'private' symbols – the sort where a teacup stands for Grandma's house; as, for example, the cookie in Proust. In my case I try to keep the symbols universal, simple, and basic . . .

The structure of my recent Happenings (the earlier ones were somewhat different) is that which I find typical of most classical arts. They tend to be simple in outline, very often threefold and circular; that is to say, the conclusion is very often an inversion of, a variation of, or a continuation of, the beginning – a kind of resolution, if you want. And so the work tends to have an introductory statement of the thematic possibilities. It amplifies, builds up – often with strong implications of climax in it – and then, in one way or another, either rapidly or slowly, diminishes, and returns upon itself. However, if this is classical, it is not because I have derived the structure from the classical arts, but rather because I have seen these movements in nature, such as in the seasons, the circling of the stars, and in the cycle of a man's life . . .

Ideally it should be possible to do a mail-order Happening. But responsibility for its proper execution still remains. Someone has to be in charge. And thus far there is no one besides myself who can speak to the participants (as a football coach speaks to his players beforehand) and, by such a talk, convey something of the levels of meaning and the cohesiveness of the whole. I intend to continue this since it has had good results. But on the other hand, I like the idea of letting others execute a scenario according to their own directorship . . . I am working on ways to make this possible.

CHAPTER 19

Patrick Campbell and Helen Spackman

Surviving the performance

An interview with Franko B.

FRANKO B.: I only work with people I trust. I watch out for people from the gay press – my work has fuck all to do with AIDS – I like hospital imagery, but it's not a 'gay' piece.

SPACKMAN: Yes, we felt your work went well beyond any simplistic reading of the hospital imagery. As soon as you say no to obvious readings, it becomes weird, uncanny.

FRANKO B.: Some people read my images as solely about power politics – they're not, it's about passion. I'm not a sadomasochist. My work's to do with visual associations.

CAMPBELL: We noticed in the program you say nothing about yourself.

FRANKO B.: No, because it's shit, pretension. Sometimes people want me to write pretty words, 'explain' my work, but I chose not to have any notes included. It doesn't matter.

CAMPBELL: You want the audience to make their own meaning?

FRANKO B.: Yeah, right, if they like it or not, if people think you are a wanker or not, it doesn't matter. I don't want people pigeon-holing, categorizing according to their own agenda . . . I have this fetish for hospital things, but I also – I was actually partly brought up by the Red Cross. But as soon as you know this information, it's shit, it changes things.

SPACKMAN: So would you prefer us not to reference your personal associations in our analysis?

FRANKO B.: No, no I don't mind. But that [my childhood] doesn't explain everything about my work . . . There is this thing about the individual, the self, something which people overrate – we're all desperate souls and we try to get on. Life is short and I've got nothing to lose, I just want to make work matter, images that are memorable – and the images are memorable! I become an object, that's why I paint myself (Franko B., like butoh performers, whites-up his naked body for performance) . . . What I'm trying to create, is what is unbearable to look at – I want to make it bearable; whether you like it or not, you're going to go away with that image in your memory.

CAMPBELL: For me, it became almost unbearable, especially when you began to bleed.

SPACKMAN: But why shouldn't we see them? The images are beautiful. Why are they unbearable?

FRANKO B.: Probably because people are frightened of their own feelings and it's prohibited to find them beautiful. Like images of war, people find they have a political problem with them, but some war images I find very beautiful – somebody getting their head blown off like that very famous image from the Vietnam War, with the kid running – although I find it startling, it's one of the most powerful images I've ever seen and one of the most beautiful. But it's a record and not the same as talking about a beautiful painting or a posed . . . but it *is* a beautiful photo. I'm not anymore interested in what happened to the girl, I'm not – I see the image, I forget it's about Vietnam because it's beautiful. Some people might think this is sick, that I like to see images of people suffering, but to me, you forget the suffering, and in a way, that's what I mean in my work, that what is seen to be unbearable becomes bearable – as you become used to it, it becomes bearable . . . To me getting off on those images is S/M. You pay to be entertained, you send money – bang, bang, bang: you're paying to take away your fucking sorrow, your miserable life, your loneliness at the end of the day. So you focus on somebody else's misery.

SPACKMAN: In your performances you project these feelings of pain and hurt?

FRANKO B.: Well, in a way, yes. But the contradiction is I get off on them, with a syringe I do get off; I *do* love syringes but –

CAMPBELL: you also find a way of counteracting the pain, of coping?

FRANKO B.: – but the point is, my attitude is, you've got to see – in a way, even when I'm in a performance, the point is surviving it . . .

SPACKMAN: Do you find yourself coming up with recurring images?

FRANKO B.: In the paintings and ceramics the subject matter is very consistent – the water bottle (a prop in both *MICS* and *INYB*) was in a film I did in 1991. It's to do with love, or lack of love. The sink – the fluid, it's the same thing – to do with memory, the domestic.

SPACKMAN: Water bottle?! Sorry, I saw a teddy bear, it's such a poignant image.

FRANKO B.: That image for me is really desperate.

CAMPBELL: And the pain in the performance, you have to feel the pain, it has to be authentic?

FRANKO B.: Yes, for me, the pain is inevitable. I think whatever you're like you're going to get hurt, physical or mental, whenever you have a relationship with somebody. The idea of slapping me is the idea of assault, but even that is about . . . I have to express it physically, but it's almost light, it's not heroic. The value of the performance for me is surviving the performance. Once it's over, freedom: I've done what I set out to do. I achieved it. But it's not a macho thing.

CAMPBELL: And the cutting, the wounding?

FRANKO B.: The wounding has to do with covering up the things that come out of your body, with everyday shame; censorship is not a phantom – it's not to do with articulate action, it's difficult, it's impossible I think to articulate anger, grief, fear, loss. The wound is like showing my insides, my guts. It's a violation . . .

CAMPBELL: Is it to do with shaming?

FRANKO B.: Why are we ashamed? Again it comes down to the body, it's like wanking in a sense – something you're not supposed to do. I did a performance in a club with the blood enema; I was bleeding – it wasn't deliberate, it was really nice, though people thought it was disgusting. But I don't have a problem – I think it's funny. I'm not ashamed or embarrassed about what I do, otherwise I wouldn't do it.

SPACKMAN: Yes, this whole thing about sensuality, enjoying the sensations of the body, and how when we see our kids enjoying their bodies. You have to tell them 'You shouldn't do that' – that wonderful childlike fascination is not socially acceptable.

FRANKO B.: The thing is that I want to feel unashamed and uninhibited when I do stuff. The main thing is to be honest, I can't pretend . . .

CAMPBELL: It's very interesting how you've moved from installations to using yourself as an installation.

FRANKO B.: I don't know where I'm going. It works on more than one level: where I'm going is where I am at, but at the end of the day, there's always this line I'm crossing. That's why I cross the line and carry on – I want to push my limits.

CHAPTER 20

Enrique Pardo

The angel's hideout

Between dance and theatre

> Molti parlano di ispirazione di anima e nessuno di cultura.
> Quando io parlo del corpo alludo alla cultura, perché la cultura è un
> corpo. Se il cibo modella l'anima, la cultura modella i trati somatici,
> rende viscerale o no it nostro sentire. (Merini, 1995)
>
> Many speak of the soul's inspiration, no one of culture.
> When I speak of body, I am referring to culture, because culture is a
> body. If food shapes the soul, culture shapes the somatic traits,
> makes our capacity to feel visceral or not.

O UR CENTURY HAS SEEN A succession of artistic expeditions towards a promised land somewhere between dance and theatre, a performance geography where literature and the physical body might meet, enhance each other's possibilities, and yield more complex images than they would if they were staged as protagonists in their own domain. This article is about one such expedition, a piece created in 1995/6 with five dancers; it addresses specific strategies of an approach to dance-theatre – I will tend to speak of *choreographic theatre* – and includes mythological reflections on dance as seen by an outsider. It also presents a militant view of emotion in performance, one that brings in angelology: the 'angel's hideout' as the possible place referred to by Alda Merini, where 'our capacity to feel visceral(ly) or not' is shaped, educated, per-formed: emotion as an *'ange qui dérange'*, as a disturbing angel.

The search for dance-theatre hybrids gets attacked by purists on both sides . . . From my point of view, if dance-theatre wishes to confront language, the spoken word, and connect to its metaphorical and emotional implications, it cannot stop at movement with some voice effects, or at the exploration of aleatoric juxtapositions of gesture and word . . .

1   Diana's bath: dance and virginity

Contemporary dance studios are often temples of 'feeling', pervaded by a mystique of sensitivity. The mood in them can be quintessentially Artemisian (Artemis, the Roman Diana): private, feminine, soft, delicate, pure, devoted to febrile and sometimes fanatical listening to inner sensations. The atmosphere is that of Diana at her bath: clear water and pristine wilderness, protected groves, untainted by any hint of specularity or seduction (except of course for the narcissism of mirrors when they appear – but that is another matter; here I am referring to the gaze of the spectator) . . . We are as far as can be from one of the original words for 'actor': *hypokritos*.

Karine Saporta, a leading and spectacular choreographer . . . accuses Artemisian devotees of reaching degrees of sensitivity where they can no longer bear the gaze of a spectator – the ultimate withdrawal of dance from show . . .

But, if transparency is resented and you sense a refusal of your gaze and of your presence as a spectator, if there is a protective reaction of privacy (what has been called the goddess's 'vicious shyness'), then one is confronting a dangerous Artemis, one that must not be drawn into theatre but left to celebrate her private rituals. One also encounters, as in all closed mythological schools, something that could be called 'Artemisian proselytism': the righteousness of those who are not interested in your performance, but who want to put your bodies 'right' . . .

Choreographic theatre

Two working principles: conversion and contradiction

No single label can do justice to the fullness or complexity of an artistic research. My own reason for preferring 'choreographic theatre' to other terms such as 'dance-theatre' or 'physical theatre' is because it contains chorus, graphics and theatre. It implies bodies in image, and the 'theatre' between them – which, again, includes the spoken word, language, text, as one of its fundamental components. The other components of image are: the visual (all *graphia*: gestural, choral, pictorial), language (literary images), the voice (which, like dance, can be separate from or even contradict language, and trigger its own realm of music and images), and music.

I wish to focus on two working principles particularly concerned with the dynamic between dance and language. The aim is to be able to move back and forth between dance and language, to alternate between the two, to juxtapose and intermingle them, and above all to metamorphose them into each other. The first principle is that of 'conversion' – conversion from dance to text, and back again . . . This implies the capacity to radically change one's driving faith, styles and systems of expression. It speaks for versatility and casuistics (an adult, adulterous and adulterating process), the capacity for alternation and change. Secondly, conversion as in thermodynamics, where heat is turned into movement and vice versa: waterfalls into electricity, fuels exploding into speed, or imploding into diamonds . . .

Third, conversion as in the early days of psychiatry, where the 'syndrome of conversion' was played out in the great nineteenth-century amphitheatres, and key words yielded extraordinary feats of 'physical theatre': histrionics, *logos* spectacularly transformed into *soma*, psychosomatic drama, what came to be called hysteria . . .

The second working principle is the notion of 'contradiction'. In theatre, language can be 'the enemy', usurping the body's autonomous expressivity, subduing dance, for instance, into a secondary illustrative or decorative mode . . . In training, at least, I treat texts as enemies, paying them a higher tribute, and giving interpreters a chance to live up to them, to face up to them. The strategy is one of *contra-diction* (against-diction) and *inter-diction*: inhibiting and making the delivery of words a prohibiting affair, coming under an interdict, repressing, arresting any naive approach to speech. This might sound forbidding, but the aim is actually to deliver the performer from the tyrannical power of language . . .

Choreographic theatre: the sex of angels

Choreography, from this particular bias, is a mythography of sorts; it writes and reads patterns of relationships in a figurative cosmology. It transforms abstract space into places, revealing the potential exchanges between characters within mythological dramaturgies, and exploding, like dance, one-dimensional naturalism. It lets imagination breed in the angelic interstices . . .

A striking psychological definition of body once put forward by James Hillman in the context of theatre was that there is body wherever there is resistance. With provocative conciseness, and elegance, it sums up Psyche's perspective on body, caught in the double bind of desire and resistance of her relationship with Eros . . .

I tend to place my working definition of body in territories similar to Hillman's. It is a semantic approach that finds body every time it encounters *the angel of meaning*: making sense, sensual meaning. There is body when associations coagulate; when persons, objects and the air around them are visited and animated by presences, memories, spirits – epiphanies, manifestations; when metaphors rise, run and rain – body as sustained revelation, giving 'body' to our own physical bodies . . . matter awakened, quickened, set into motion by ideas . . . meaning as movement, movement as meaning . . . metamorphoses . . . objects, muscles, bones, skin, alive, transmuted, inhabited, moved . . . metaphoric animals, angels, and the flow of understandings . . . realizations, poetical harvests . . .

Underlying such a litany, especially one invoking angelology, is a basic philosophical bias; it requires the move from motion to emotion, and it says that there is body wherever there is emotion . . .

References

Hillman, James (1972) 'Pan and the Nightmare', Connecticut: Spring Publications.
Hillman, James (1996) *The Soul's Code*, New York: Random House.
Merini, Alda (1995) *La pazza delta porta accanto*, Milan: Bompiani.

Contemporary Practices

Jerome Bel's theatre of physical presence

The uniqueness of Jerome Bel is that he finds his inspiration in semioticians such as Ferdinand Saussure or Roland Barthes, rather than in the traditions of dance which he knows very well: the result is not dance, but a theatre of physical presence, in which Bel abruptly offers his actors the audience, and lets their bodies or the objects linked to them tell their own story.

Peter Anthonisson De Morgan, 1997:
http:/dance4.co.uk/nottdancesite04/Artists/
Jerome Bel

Essay 3

Gesturing towards post-physical performance

■ Franc Chamberlain

NOT LONG AGO I STARTED referring to my work as 'post-physical' (Smart, 2004). Previously I would simply refer to it as 'performance', but that began in the 1980s before that term became conflated with Live Art. Physical theatre was a term I would use to describe others' work and occasionally my own, but it had become theoretically problematic for me from the late 1980s.

Callery considers physical theatre 'not codifiable' (2001: 5) and to apply to such a diversity of practices that it is 'virtually undefinable'. Nevertheless she attempts to isolate some key features: the importance of the actor as a creator rather than as an interpreter; collaborative and somatic working processes; the 'live-ness' of the theatre and an open 'stage-spectator relationship' (2001: 5). It's virtually indefinable, yet we know what it is.

Or rather there was a moment, around 1985, when I felt pretty clear what physical theatre was: Peta Lily, Nola Rae, Animate Theatre, Avner the Eccentric, Théâtre de Complicité, Moving Picture Mime Show, Plexus, Footsbarn, David Glass, John Mowat, Ra Ra Zoo, Dario Fo, Trestle, Théâtre du Mouvement, Trickster, Geoffrey Buckley, Geoff Hoyle meets Keith Terry, and I understood where Steven Berkoff fitted in. By 1987, I'd also seen, *inter alia*, the Wissel Theatre, John Lee, Bim Mason, Mime Theatre Project, Les Bubb, and Black Mime. I had participated in training workshops with a number of Lecoq graduates and was making my own pieces of 'physical theatre'; I had a sense of being part of something that was making a difference in the theatre. But Ben Keaton's *Intimate Memoirs of an Irish Taxidermist* tipped something off-balance for me and drew attention to an implicit definition I was carrying around with me.

I can't really remember Keaton's piece. Nothing left except for a vague memory that this was a performance that disturbed something. What I remember is Keaton's performance being mostly a stand-up narrative without the physical virtuosity that I associated with mime and physical theatre. There were great differences between the work of other practitioners, between

Animate Theatre and Trestle, for example, where the former practised a very strict and formalist approach to mime and the latter a populist approach to mask, but there was something that seemed to be 'along the same lines', or a 'family resemblance'. The question raised for me by Keaton's show was: 'If this is mime, or physical theatre, then what isn't?'

There were several possibilities around at the time: mime, physical, physically-based, movement-based, and visual theatre,[1] but none of these, for me, would have accounted for the distinctiveness of Keaton's performance, which emphasized speech. This was also a period when I was working as a storyteller, so it wasn't the case that I expected mime to be a silent art, or that any performance had to have lots of movement in to be interesting. As practitioners we may label our work in response to funding categories, or to ally ourselves with the work of others, as scholars we may draw lines through the field whilst attempting to articulate particular characteristics at work. It was as an academic with an interest in description, analysis, and categorization that I was puzzled. I was also an audience member, a position supplementing the other two.

The problem I was having with classification is perhaps caught in a review I wrote of Ra Ra Zoo:

> A woman dancing on a trapeze accompanied by a live violin and guitar music, the flashy skills of the circus transformed into an expressive dance of mesmerizing intensity. No sequins, no big top and no safety net. A breath-stopping atmosphere [. . .] Describing themselves as 'neo-circus' [. . .] Ra Ra Zoo unleashed their skills under the guise of Mime '85. Whether their performance, which combined a variety of circus skills, can be described as 'mime' or not is a problem for academics [. . .] I felt the heat of naked flame on my face as two plates of fire connected by a cord were spun round like blazing rotor blades. My attention was heightened in the knowledge that one slip by the performer could cover herself or the front row with fire.
>
> (*UEA Phoenix*, 7 February 1985)

What strikes me as I read this through is the physicality of the experience, both the use of the body in performance and my own sensations of heat and intensity. As the writer, I'm not really concerned with categorization, I'm interested in the work and its effects and it seems to me that, at that time, I didn't think that this was the kind of thing that 'academics' were interested in.

I also notice my use of 'mime' and the first evidence I have for deploying 'physical theatre' is later in 1985 whilst considering the relationship between the work of David Gaines and Extemporary Dance Theatre. I don't remember connecting it to the work of Grotowski, although I was familiar with his writings and had some training with Rena Mirecka. Nor do I recall connecting it to Barba, Schechner, or Clive Barker. I was pretty ignorant of the use of the term in the early 1970s, by Nancy Meckler and Freehold, Triple Action Theatre and RAT, seeing it more as an attempt to define what was emerging under the contemporary mime umbrella to mark it out from both dance and theatre. There were still plenty of alternative and experimental theatre groups included under 'theatre' by the Arts Council, but the location of mime within 'dance' meant it wasn't recognized as an art form in its own right. Physical theatre became a way of laying out a line of flight for mime in the mid-1980s, taking it away from both dance and a simple reduction to the work of Marceau. The presence of a growing number of Lecoq graduates, still regarded by mainstream companies such as the RSC as 'mimes' rather than 'actors', was an important factor in this movement. My own company was called Hidden Risk Performance (1986–89) in an attempt to avoid the problems of the terms 'mime', 'physical theatre' or 'physical-based theatre'.

In 1994, Enrique Pardo asked whether the European Mime and Physical Theatre Workshop Symposium (also known as *Moving into Performance*) was a Decroux/Lecoq club. Where was the work of Barba and Odin, or Grotowski? These were interesting questions because my experience with Grotowski-based work had increased over the decade, including participation in Gardzienice's residency at Druidstone in Wales (1989) and Barba's ISTA at Brecon (1992).[2] I would have called this work 'third theatre' rather than 'physical theatre' in the 1980s because I reserved the latter for work inspired by Decroux/Lecoq. There was also a sense of Grotowski, Staniewski, and Barba as belonging to a tradition of 'director-led theatre' rather than that of a creative ensemble of performers (an 'actor-led theatre').[3]

DV8 were another significant absence at Moving into Performance (MIP). In 1986, Lloyd Newson formed DV8 Physical Theatre, a company plotting their own exit from dance and, by 1994, their style of work was rapidly becoming what most of the general public, and many academics, thought of as physical theatre (see Sánchez-Colberg, 1996). In 1993 Mime Action Group, formed in 1984 to 'advocate for greater recognition and status for Mime and Physical Theatre', published the *UK Mime and Physical Theatre Training Directory*. Funded by the Arts Council of Great Britain, the directory was the first guide to physical theatre training in the UK and contained over 200 listings. One thing that's striking about the list of companies and practitioners is the absence of DV8 Physical Theatre or performers associated with the company such as Newson or Nigel Charnock.[4]

By 1996, then, 'physical theatre' had become a contested term in which two main lines were identified: a mime lineage stemming from Copeau through to Decroux and Lecoq (and including Dario Fo), and a dance background where physical theatre 'meant' DV8. Added to these was a third line, stemming from Meyerhold, Artaud, and Grotowski, which had been obscured during the 1980s but was clearly part of the field. These lines open the possibility for multiple crossings and in 1991 the European Mime Federation had established a working group to examine questions of transversality. The working group's report, which was delivered at the MIP symposium, suggested that gesture might be the transversal which connected new developments in contemporary theatre. Whilst this attempts to mark a number of exits from a situation where different approaches could end up becoming fixed, or ghettoized, the use of 'gesture' as the starting point is too redolent of Lecoq's 'théâtre du geste', commonly translated into English as 'physical theatre', which brings us full circle.

In 1996, Mime Action Group, taking further some of the questions that had been raised at MIP, published a vision statement: *MAG – The Next Five Years 1997–2002*, and invited a creative response from members (see Chamberlain, this volume). One suggestion was to replace mime with 'physically-based theatre', but this was rejected and MAG mutated into Total Theatre Network with the aim to represent as wide a spectrum of performance practice as possible, whilst emphasizing 'Physical and Visual Performance' in particular.

By the mid-1990s *Total Theatre Magazine* included articles on companies such as Odin Teatret (Chamberlain, 1995) and extended its area of coverage to Live Art/Performance. Berghaus (2005: 133) mentions that 1960s Body Art mutated into 1980s 'performance art' and 'physical theatre' and, whilst Berghaus' use of 'physical theatre' here seems more backwards projection than evidence of contemporary usage, it does point to another line of creative work that became included under the Total Theatre umbrella. At MIP, the Adèle Myers Company presented *CORR-I-ADOR* which I described as 'more a Live Art installation' than a piece of mime or physical theatre (Chamberlain, 1997: 88). I was trying to find a working definition for physical theatre that operated on the basis of inclusions and exclusions, keeping work in neat categories whilst enjoying the hybrids that emerged through their intermixing. Live Art, then, is another emergent line of flight from an established practice that became part of the Total Theatre constituency.

The first issue of *Hybrid* (November/December 1992) was a foreshadowing of where *Total Theatre Magazine* was heading. There were connections to the Lecoq-based companies, through an obituary for Celia Gore-Booth, a former member of Complicité; the Grotowski line (Gardzienice, Mike Pearson); the dance line (Motionhouse, de Keersmaeker, Man Act); and the Live Art/Performance line (Jan Fabre, Station House Opera, Bobby Baker). In a 2005 issue of *Total Theatre*, we find coverage of the London International Mime Festival, which included some of the same artists involved either directly or indirectly in the first issue of the MAG Newsletter (1984) but also articles/reviews on The People Show, New York Performance Art, Jan Fabre, Phil Smith (Wrights & Sites), Teatr Piesn Kozla (ex-Gardzienice), Ansuman Biswas, and Marina Abramovic. One line of work that appears to be absent in all of this is that of Boal and those inspired by him. If a somatic training is central to physical theatre (Callery, 2001: 4), then we surely ought to pay attention to Boal's notion that the actor's body needs to be de-mechanized and re-sensitized (Boal, 2002: 29).

By 2005, Total Theatre Network covered a wide diversity of styles and approaches, all of which could be seen to have some connection to 'physical theatre' as a movement of breaking away from established practices and from categorization by critics, academics and/or funding bodies. But the breadth of work covered effectively signals the end of the term's usefulness both for thinking about contemporary performance and for gaining funding. There are virtually no references to physical theatre (or mime), except in links to a few companies such as DV8, Trestle, Yellow Earth, Kompany Malakhi and Vincent Dance Theatre, on the Arts Council of England website.

There are numerous courses on physical theatre at UK universities and a demand for academic texts on the topic, a sure sign that it's reached a point of exhaustion.

It no longer describes a movement of renewal in British theatre and performance, nor an innovative way of teaching or making performance, nor even a particularly useful critical term. Physical theatre was a heuristic term, useful for getting out of the gravitational pull of certain normalizing fields, but after the breakout the term becomes unnecessary, even burdensome, and Callery notes that 'many current practitioners resent the way their work is categorized as physical theatre' (2001: 6). What we need now is a new term that catches the diversity of what's happening in the performance world in the wake of the physical theatre adventure; a term that doesn't repeat something that was already there, as total theatre itself does. Visual theatre isn't sufficiently distinctive. I propose the term post-physical performance for a number of reasons.

First, post-physical performance takes heed of the resentment identified by Callery whilst acknowledging the route that such practitioners have taken. So, post-physical performance is what comes after physical theatre, and is 'performance' rather than simply 'theatre' to acknowledge the diversity of work that has emerged from these movements whilst paying attention to those who, like Franko B, 'hate theatre'.[5] It offers a descriptive opening rather than a closure.

Second, whilst physical theatre sets up a number of generic expectations, the post-physical implies their suspension. Complicité's use of technology in *The Elephant Vanishes* (2003), for example, wouldn't have fitted with my generic expectations of physical theatre in the 1980s, nor could I have predicted it from performances such as *A Minute Too Late* (1984) or *The Street of Crocodiles* (1992). Post-physical performance is full of unexpected hybrids but is always marked by its ancestry.

Third, the post-physical can encompass the current explorations of Stelarc, whose earlier work such as *Suspension* (1980) was quite easy to assimilate into an expanded notion of physical theatre. Stelarc recently declared the body 'obsolete'[6] and, whilst he has always used various technologies in his performance, he has become interested in biotechnology. Faith Wilding is another practitioner who has developed a recent interest in biotechnology and there is also the SymbioticA laboratory at the University of Western Australia that enables artists to work with 'wet biology practices'.[7] To use post-physical in relation to this work, however, brings us into contact with terms such as the post-organic and the post-human (Giannachi, 2004; Berghaus, 2005) which would be applicable to some but not all of the work that would come under the umbrella of post-physical performance.

Fourth, post-physical also takes us beyond the dualism that is often contained within discussions of physical theatre. Callery is a case in point:

> At its simplest, physical-theatre is theatre where the primary means of creation occurs through the body rather than through the mind.
>
> (2001: 4)

There are two issues here: (a) the opposition of mind and body here replicates a Cartesian dualism which regulary haunts the use of the term 'physical'. Even the use of 'psycho-physical' (Callery, 2001: 148) seems to keep the dualism. The aim of the term post-physical is to go beyond the physical/non-physical binary in order to better understand the work that's happening now and to re-think its predecessors. (b) A close study of working practices of physical theatre companies would reveal that different activities occur in various relationships rather than one always being primary and that there is a more fluid relationship between image and action and conversation. A post-physical perspective can help us think through the myths of physical theatre.

Fifth, post-physical performance offers us a way of describing our work to escape the confines of the physical theatre label whilst at the same time offering food for thought.

Post-physical performance is not synonymous with Lehmann's notion of postdramatic theatre. At a very basic level there is no fundamental rejection of the dramatic in either physical or post-physical performance, although some practitioners pursue a postdramatic agenda either in general or on particular occasions.

Notes

1   Each of these terms, except physical theatre, is used in Nigel Jamison's draft letter to the Arts Council on behalf of Mime Action Group published for consultation in *Magazine*, No. 1, Autumn 1984. Joseph Seelig was using the terms 'mime' and 'visual theatre' at this time and championed the term 'visual theatre' a decade later at MIP, suggesting that the time has come to drop both 'mime' and 'physical theatre' (Keefe, 1995: 27; Chamberlain, 1997: 86).

2   The Centre for Performance Research (CPR) hosted both of these events.

3   Ensembles of creative actors can work with a director, but there is a difference of distance between Barba and Odin and, say, McBurney and Complicité. Barba stays in the role of director, whereas McBurney shifts between the roles of 'actor' and 'director'.

4   See also Murray, 'Tout Bouge', in Chamberlain and Yarrow (eds, 2002).

5   Franko B, Granary Theatre, Cork, October 2005.

6   www.stelarc.va.com.au/obsolete/obsolete.html, accessed 13 April 2006.

7   www.symbiotica.uwa.edu.au/info/info.html

References and further reading

Berghaus, Günter (2005) *Avant-Garde Performance: Live Events and Electronic Technologies*, Basingstoke: Palgrave Macmillan.

Boal, Augusto (2002) *Games for Actors and Non-Actors*, London: Routledge, 2nd edition.

Callery, Dymphna (2001) *Through the Body: A Practical Guide to Physical Theatre*, London: Nick Hern Books.

Chamberlain, Franc (1992) 'Fragments of a Dixi Training' *TDR* (T134): 118–25.

Chamberlain, Franc (1995) 'Digging Beneath the Surface', *Total Theatre* 7 (4).

Chamberlain, Franc (1997) 'Moving into Performance', *Contemporary Theatre Review* 6 (1): 85–96.

Chamberlain, Franc (2000) 'Theatre Anthropology: Definitions and Doubts', in Anthony Frost (ed., 2000) *Theatre Theories from Plato to Virtual Reality,* Norwich: Pen & Inc.

Chamberlain, Franc (2005) 'Body States: The Pilot Project', *Total Theatre* 17 (4).

Chamberlain, Franc (2006) 'Ways of Working: Ten Fragments from Sixteen Years of Interaction', in *A Performance Cosmology*, Abingdon: Routledge, pp. 36–41.

Chamberlain, Franc and Ralph Yarrow (eds, 2002) *Jacques Lecoq and the British Theatre*, London: Routledge/Harwood.

Craig, Edward Gordon (1981) *On the Art of the Theatre*, London: Heinemann Educational Books.

Giannachi, Gabriella (2004) *Virtual Theatres: An Introduction*, London: Routledge.

Keefe, John (1995) *Moving into Performance: Report*, London: Mime Action Group.

Lehmann, Hans-Thies (2006) *Postdramatic Theatre*, Abingdon: Routledge.

Sánchez-Colberg, Ana (1996) 'Altered States and Subliminal Spaces: Charting the Road towards a Physical Theatre' *Performance Research* 1 (2): 40–56.

Smart, Roger (2004) 'In Depth with Franc Chamberlain', *Acting Now* 4 www.actingnow.com/four.html#

CHAPTER 21

Steven Berkoff

Introduction and *East*, scene 4

Producer's note

THE FOLLOWING PLAYS WERE performed by the London Theatre Group, a collection of actors welded together by a common purpose. To express drama in the most vital way imaginable; to perform at the height of one's power with all available means. That is, through the spoken word, gesture, mime and music. Sometimes the emphasis on one, sometimes on the other.

At first, in searching for material for these plays, I found the finished play too finite a form, simply a mass of dialogue, with no resonances of inner life, where the actors hurled situational chat at each other. Far more inspiration came from the short story form, or classic text, which gave the whole situation, the inner and outer life and subjective thought of the characters. Here the environment constantly shifts in the same way that the processes of the imagination can take you outside the boundaries of time and space. In fact, we worked closer to music and the scenario of the film. Instead of a dead setting on the stage fixing us firmly in the conscious world of the now the actor became the setting and the environment. His body, his voice and his text were made into a language malleable to swift changes of situation.

We always attempted an analysis of the play rather than a realistic rendering. Realism can eventually have a deadening effect since it only mirrors a conscious world and is more suited to TV drama. What we attempted in the following plays was a grotesque, surreal, paranoiac view of life such as is conjured up in dreams . . . the schizoid personality of man as he undoubtedly is . . . and the staging took on this manner in its exaggerated and enlarged forms. Naturalism, both in the writing and performing of plays, often leaves me with pangs of embarrassment, especially when witnessing actors playing this game of pretence. What we sought for was a critical analysis where we performed what was unreal and not perceivable in everyday life, and expressed drama less through impersonation than through revelation, hoping that a greater degree of reality would be shown by these methods.

Steven Berkoff 1977

East, Scene 4

> MIKE and LES *commence* 'If you were the only Girl in the World' *which covers the bringing on of the only props — a table and chairs. On the table are toast, a teapot with steaming tea, a tureen of baked beans, a packet of margarine — in fact the normal tea time scene. They sit around the table and eat. During* DAD's *long speech he eventually destroys everything on the table in nostalgic fury. The table and contents become a metaphor for the battle of Cable Street — his rage becomes monstrous and gargantuan.*

Ma and Pa

DAD. Mum?

MUM. What?

DAD. What time does Hawaii 5–0 come on?

MUM. What time does it come on?

DAD. Yeah!

MUM. I don't know dear. . . .

DAD. She doesn't know, she watches it every night, and doesn't know.

MUM. *(Reading)* . . . What's a proletariat?

DAD. A geyser who lassoes goats on the Siberian mountains.

MUM. In one word I mean. Six letters.

DAD. Panorama's on first . . . yeah that's worth an eyeful . . . Then we can watch Ironside, turn over for the Saint and cop the last act of Schoenberg's Moses and Aaron.

MUM. Charlton Heston was in that.

DAD. Machinery has taken all the joy out of work . . . the worker asks for more and more money until he breaks down the economy hand in hand with the Unions who are Communist dominated and make the country ripe for a takeover by the red hordes.

MUM. You haven't paid the Licence.

DAD. She's a consumer on the market, that's all, not even a human being but a consumer who's analysed for what she buys and likes by a geyser offering her a questionnaire at the supermarket — makes her feel important . . . I try to educate it but 'tis like pouring wine into the proverbial leaking barrel.

MUM. Suppose they come round.

DAD. Nobody visits us any more.

MUM. They might then you'd go to Court and it would be all over the Hackney Gazette.

DAD. You don't want to believe all that rubbish about detector vans. That's just to scare you . . . make you think that they're on your tail . . .

anyway if anyone knocks on the door we can whip the telly out sharpish like and hide it in the lavatory until they're gone . . . simple . . . say . . . 'There's been a mistake . . . your radar must have been a few degrees out and picked out the hair dryer performing on her curlers.'

MUM. But anyone can knock on the door . . . you'll have to start running every time someone knocks.

DAD. When was the last time we had a visitor – especially since the lift's nearly always broken by those little black bastards who've been moving in, and who's going to climb 24 floors to see us except the geyser for the Christmas money – so if anyone knocks on the door it can only be one of two things – the law enquiring after Mike since they think he's just mugged some old lady for her purse, or the T.V. licence man – in either case I can shove it in the loo!

MUM. Mike doesn't do things like that – I won't have you uttering such dreadful libels – my son takes after me – you won't find him taking after you – he is kind to old ladies – helps them across the road on windy days.

DAD. That was only a subtle jest you hag, thou lump of foul deformity – untimely ripped from thy mother's womb – can't you take a flaming dash of humour that I so flagrantly waste on you – eh? What then . . . what bleeding then – thank God he's not a pooftah at least already so soon – Eh . . . where would you put your face then – if he took after me the country would rise to its feet – give itself an almighty shake and rid itself of all the fleas that are sucking it dry . . . *(Wistful)* He could have . . . Ozzie* had the right ideas – put them into uniforms – into the brown shirts – gave people an identity. Those meetings were a sight. All them flags. Then, they knew what to do – take the law into your own hands when you know it makes sense. That beautiful Summer in '38 was it? – When we marched six abreast to Whitechapel – beautiful it were – healthy young British men and women – a few wooden clubs just in case they got stroppy down there, just the thoughts of the people letting the Nation know it weren't stomaching any more of it – the drums banging out a rhythm in the front and Ozzie marching at our head. We get to Aldgate – if you didn't know it was Aldgate you could smell it – and there were us few loyal English telling the world that England is for us – and those long-nosed gits, those evil smelling greasy kikes had barricades up – you couldn't even march through England's green and pleasant, the land where Jesus set his foot – they had requisitioned Aldgate and Commercial Road but our lads, what did they do, not turn back – not be a snively turn-coat but let them have it. They soon scuttered back into the tailors shops stinking of fried fish and dead foreskins – and with a bare fist, a few bits of wood, we broke a skull or two that day – but Hebrew gold had corrupted our fair law and we were outnumbered – what could we do – the oppressed still living there under the Semite claw sweating their balls out in those stinking sweat shops – could only shout 'come on lads' – they had no stomach for it, no strength. It were for them that we had to get through. But we were outnumbered – the Christian Soldiers could not get through this time – not then, and what happened – I'll tell you what happened – by not getting down Commercial Street . . . by not getting down Whitechapel – Alie Street, Commercial Road and Cable Street, Leman Street we opened the floodgates for the rest – the Pandora's bleeding box opened and the rest of the horrors poured in. That's what happened mate. *(Suddenly)* What's the time?!

MUM. Eight o'clock.
DAD. We've missed *Cross-Roads*!!?!

(Blackout)

* Oswald Mosley

CHAPTER 22

Samuel Beckett to music by John Beckett

Act without words

A mime for one player

Desert. Dazzling light.

The man is flung backwards on stage from right wing. He falls, gets up immediately, dusts himself, turns aside, reflects. Whistle from right wing.

He reflects, goes out right.

Immediately flung back on stage he falls, gets up immediately, dusts himself, turns aside, reflects.

Whistle from left wing.

He reflects, goes out left.

Immediately flung back on stage he falls, gets up immediately, dusts himself, turns aside, reflects.

Whistle from left wing.

He reflects, goes towards left wing, hesitates, thinks better of it, halts, turns aside, reflects.

A little tree descends from flies, lands. It has a single bough some three yards from ground and at its summit a meagre tuft of palms casting at its foot a circle of shadow.

He continues to reflect.

Whistle from above.

He turns, sees tree, reflects, goes to it, sits down in its shadow, looks at his hands.

A pair of tailor's scissors descends from flies, comes to rest before tree, a yard from ground.

He continues to look at his hands.

Whistle from above.

He looks up, sees scissors, takes them and starts to trim his nails.

The palms close like a parasol, the shadow disappears.

He drops scissors, reflects.

A tiny carafe, to which is attached a huge label inscribed WATER, descends from flies, comes to rest some three yards from ground.

He continues to reflect.

Whistle from above.

He looks up, sees carafe, reflects, gets up, goes and stands under it, tries in vain to reach it, renounces, turns aside, reflects.

A big cube descends from flies, lands.

He continues to reflect.

Whistle from above.

He turns, sees cube, looks at it, at carafe, reflects, goes to cube, takes it up, carries it over and sets it down under carafe, tests its stability, gets up on it, tries in vain to reach carafe, renounces, gets down, carries cube back to its place, turns aside, reflects.

A second smaller cube descends from flies, lands.

He continues to reflect.

Whistle from above.

He turns, sees second cube, looks at it, at carafe, goes to second cube, takes it up, carries it over and sets it down under carafe, tests its stability, gets up on it, tries in vain to reach carafe, renounces, gets down, takes up second cube to carry it back to its place, hesitates, thinks better of it, sets it down, goes to big cube, takes it up, carries it over and puts it on small one, tests their stability, gets up on them, the cubes collapse, he falls, gets up immediately, brushes himself, reflects.

He takes up small cube, puts it on big one, tests their stability, gets up on them and is about to reach carafe when it is pulled up a little way and comes to rest beyond his reach.

He gets down, reflects, carries cubes back to their place, one by one, turns aside, reflects.

A third still smaller cube descends from flies, lands.

He continues to reflect.

Whistle from above.

He turns, sees third cube, looks at it, reflects, turns aside, reflects.

The third cube is pulled up and disappears in flies.

Beside carafe a rope descends from flies, with knots to facilitate ascent.

He continues to reflect.

Whistle from above.

He turns, sees rope, reflects, goes to it, climbs up it and is about to reach carafe when rope is let out and deposits him back on ground.

He reflects, looks round for scissors, sees them, goes and picks them up, returns to rope and starts to cut it with scissors.

The rope is pulled up, lifts him off ground, he hangs on, succeeds in cutting rope, falls back on ground, drops scissors, falls, gets up again immediately, brushes himself, reflects.

The rope is pulled up quickly and disappears in flies.

With length of rope in his possession he makes a lasso with which he tries to lasso the carafe.

The carafe is pulled up quickly and disappears in flies.

He turns aside, reflects.

He goes with lasso in his hand to tree, looks at bough, turns and looks at cubes, looks again at bough, drops lasso, goes to cubes, takes up small one, carries it over and sets it down under bough, goes back for big one, takes it up and carries it over under bough, makes to put it on small one, hesitates, thinks better of it, sets it down, takes up small one and puts it on big one, tests their stability, turns aside and stoops to pick up lasso.

The bough folds down against trunk.

He straightens up with lasso in his hand, turns and sees what has happened.

He drops lasso, turns aside, reflects.

He carries back cubes to their place, one by one, goes back for lasso, carries it over to the cubes and lays it in a neat coil on small one.

He turns aside, reflects.

Whistle from right wing.

He reflects, goes out right.

Immediately flung back on stage he falls, gets up immediately, brushes himself, turns aside, reflects.

Whistle from left wing.

He does not move.

He looks at his hands, looks round for scissors, sees them, goes and picks them up, starts to trim his nails, stops, reflects, runs his finger along blade of scissors, goes and lays them on small cube, turns aside, opens his collar, frees his neck and fingers it.

The small cube is pulled up and disappears in flies, carrying away rope and scissors.

He turns to take scissors, sees what has happened.

He turns aside, reflects.

He goes and sits down on big cube.

The big cube is pulled from under him. He falls. The big cube is pulled up and disappears in flies.

He remains lying on his side, his face towards auditorium, staring before him.

The carafe descends from flies and comes to rest a few feet from his body.

He does not move.

Whistle from above.

He does not move.

The carafe descends further, dangles and plays about his face.

He does not move.

The carafe is pulled up and disappears in flies.

The bough returns to horizontal, the palms open, the shadow returns.

Whistle from above.

He does not move.

The tree is pulled up and disappears in flies.

He looks at his hands.

CURTAIN

CHAPTER 23

Emilyn Claid

Re-dressing the girls

WENDY HOUSTOUN, FORMER DV8 DIVA, now makes her own work as performer-choreographer, crossing the boundaries between theatre and dance. I watch Wendy perform *Haunted, Daunted and Flaunted* (1997). The stage is empty except for an upstage microphone and a jacket hanging over a chair. Over the speakers, a voice makes an announcement about an assault on a young woman. The disembodied male voice informs me that this performance will be a re-construction.

Wendy appears, simultaneously speaking and dancing. She describes the events leading up to the attack, the journey the woman took and how she was watched. Wendy's text interweaves the description of the event with comments on her own movements. 'She carried on, on the diagonal, everything seemed to have returned to normal. As she reached behind her, she suddenly had a feeling she was invisible. As she rolled away it could be awhile before she went out again' (Houstoun 1997).

In the next scene, Wendy sits in the chair talking into the microphone. She now takes the role of the woman herself post-assault: 'Sometimes I try saying hello. Sometimes I just make weird faces. Sometimes I cross the road at a shallow diagonal' (Houstoun 1997). The text is rhythmical, giving it a dream-like quality. She puts on the jacket. 'Sometimes I just change my name. Sometimes I try to be invisible' (Houstoun 1997). She picks up the gun. Wendy's poetic, hypnotic, inwardly focused text abruptly changes. She faces the audience. She walks, zigzagging sideways towards the audience, then stands looking out. 'My name's Veronica.' She begins to panic. 'What are you looking at, what are you looking at, sod off you fucking creep, just piss off' (Houstoun 1997). A loud crashing sound interrupts – rock music begins. Wendy dances. Her legs, thrown from the hips, sharply kick, stab and circle. Her leg movements dominate the language; they are her weapons, warding people away. She holds the gun in her right hand. She rolls on the ground, tosses her body, performs tiny steps on the spot and hesitates in stillness. She lifts her right leg; the gun is aimed along the line of her leg. Her leg and arm open and circle round behind her. Wherever her foot points so does the gun. 'She is a spanner in the works . . . Twisting and lunging back and forth, she randomly fires off the gun, until suddenly she finds it poised by her head. The image is unsettling' (Dodds 1998: 13).

The mood changes: Wendy steps into the role of storyteller. She becomes lyrical; her arms and back become liquid. The mood changes again as Wendy, now smoking, drinking and joking, talks about herself. She goes back over her past memories, provoking images from different years. She says, 'I remember in 1989 I did this a lot' (Houstoun 1997), flinging her right arm from her chest outward to the side. She traces back to being a baby. The text and movement work together in present time to describe the past. This is comic entertainment. She switches to minimal action and a more sinister mood. Towards the end, the words and actions drift into abstraction, hypnotic once more. 'I stole away, I hid, I hid away, I hid away from hurt, I dragged, I dragged up, I dragged up the dirt' (Houstoun 1997). Wendy holds the gun close to her body, points it towards herself, twisting and writhing on the floor.

Embodying different perspectives of the story, blowing the narrative apart, Wendy brings the audience into an active play for meaning: who, she asks, is watching whom and from what perspective? Wendy shifts her personae between the objective and subjective, from observing the scene to being the tragic victim, playing many figures of herself in the narrative. Dangerous and exciting, Wendy is haunted by her own life.

Wendy embodied both movement and text, physical and spoken languages. Each was rich in content, articulate and complex in its humanity. The movement and text were not creating a unity. The text ironically commented on the action and vice versa. Sometimes the words gave identity to the gestures but when gestures were repeated with different words, the meaning was displaced. Often, quite arbitrary movements were juxtaposed with text, displacing the emotional drama of the words, words and movement working out of rhythm with each other. There were different styles of text: argumentative, autobiographical, documentary and fictional. Painful personal memories were displaced by poetic verse, different tenses, first person, third person and sometimes by addressing the audience as 'you'. Wendy's presence was sometimes in front and sometimes behind the text, alternating between playing directly to the audience and focusing inward, letting the words dominate. Movement and text merged with one other as harmonized poetry in motion only towards the end. Sometimes the movement slipped off Wendy's body with ease, sometimes with tension and contradiction. Nothing was comfortable. The movement languages shifted between balletic articulations, fluid-released gesture, and parodies of jazz and English stage-school dance styles. With her articulate technique, Wendy performed a love/hate relationship with her dance history, always human, often dismissive. Teetering on the edge of the suicidal and the self-reflective, acting as victim and aggressor, she inhabited and commented on the text and the movement. Wendy parodied the tragedy with her ironic use of text and movement, without pretension, without hierarchy – with wit and a small black gun. She hovered at the place where irony becomes self-destructive. Wendy's presence slipped into the gaps between her performed identities. She was a comic, angry, abstract, theatrical and pedestrian figure. She was tragic and mocking. She was all and none of these things, an intriguing figure between fully lived and performed surfaces.

References

Dodds, S. (1998) 'A spanner in the works', *Dance Theatre Journal*, 14(1): 12–14.
Houstoun, W. (1997) *Haunted, Daunted and Flaunted* performance text, London.

CHAPTER 24

Norbert Servos

Bluebeard

WITH *BLUEBEARD* THE CREATIVE innovations that were outlined in *Rite of Spring* and in the Brecht/Weill evening became the stylistic principle, are here the intrinsic choreographic elements. Theater of movement drawn from mixed genres, the combination of elements from dance, opera, spoken theater and mime, becomes established as an uncompromising dance theater art form.

For the first time, the program notes make no references to such terms as 'dance opera' (as in the Gluck choreographies) or 'ballet' (as in *Rite of Spring*), but speak simply of 'scenes'. Like the revue format of the Brecht/Weill evening, this expresses the sense of the fragmentary, the rejection of a continuous choreographic structure. Opera is not translated or interpreted into dance terms, as in *Iphigenia on Tauris* or *Orpheus and Eurydice*. In contrast to the frequently supplementary function of music as a tonal embellishment in classical ballet, in *Bluebeard* the music has the status of an independent, indispensable element of content of equal rank with the other scenic elements. The complete title of the work becomes *Bluebeard – While Listening to a Tape Recording of Bela Bartok's Opera 'Duke Bluebeard's Castle'*. The main property, appropriately, is a tape recorder mounted on a wheeled table, the flex run over an overhead reel.

With the total integration of the music into the theatrical performance, the tape recorder assumes a significance beyond that of a piece of technical equipment. It achieves the status of a performer, is incorporated into the action, wheeled about, and used choreographically to divide the performing space. The musical level of the dance theater evening, determined by the tonal and dramatic complexity of Bartok's opera, parallels the level of portraiture . . .

The action is led by the music. As the performance begins, Bluebeard is seated at the tape recorder, listening to the introductory bars of the opera. He stops the tape, rewinds it, starts again from the beginning, stops it again, and, repeating the procedure several times, allows himself to be captivated by his memories and associations. Like the isolated Krapp in Beckett's *Krapp's Last Tape*, who discovers the futility of his existence through a dialogue with recordings of his own voice, Bluebeard searches in violent desperation for the tenderness, the affection, the love he once knew. While the tape repeats the same excerpt from the score, he races to Judith who is lying motionless on the floor with arms angled to receive him, the woman absolute. Bluebeard throws himself on top of her, rapes her, and then with great effort drags her across the floor. The man does as he pleases. The woman offers no resistance . . .

Sex is reduced to its animal function in a mounting crescendo of violence. With the removal of the veil of harmony and union, the struggle for power is revealed. Bodies collide as opponents tear, push, shove and torment one another. Exhaustion climaxes in the renewed search for physical contact . . .

Moments of quiet and contact are interspersed among the moments of violent extremity, although even these shift to reveal latent aggression and resignation. As Bluebeard sits at his tape recorder, the women crowd around him and monotonously pipe the 'Thank you' from Judith's aria, as they stroke his face and shoulders in an attempt to possess him. The partners inflict wounds of equal depth upon one another . . .

The important rank of *Bluebeard* in the Bausch repertory is due not so much to its theme, which is central, in one form or another, to all the works, but rather to the continuity it provides for the sustained development of dance theater as a form of theatrical representation.

With greater consequence than in the previous Brecht/Weill revue, Bausch expands the boundaries of the traditional theatrical apparatus through implementation of the tools of the various genres – dance, spoken theater, opera and mime. She combines these ingredients, however, without fusing them into the unified 'total work of art' as defined by *Ausdruckstanz*. The various theatrical elements do not combine into a harmonious whole, but instead retain their independence. These dissonances are acknowledged and incorporated into the concept of the work.

The movement canon is drawn directly from everyday existence. The dancers do not dance as they did in the earlier works. Here they walk, run, jump, fall, crawl, slide and so on. The repetition of the same movement as often as ten times or more physicalizes the fatality inherent in the state of being bound up in the course of events. The intolerable nature of the immediate situation is directly expressed through the choreography . . .

Bluebeard is a further variation on the subject of role antagonist. Bluebeard and Judith are forms of Everyman and Everywoman. Bausch presents behavioral schemata, longings, and clichéd roles as existential conditions. The analysis is concentrated on the mechanisms of oppression, not on their causes . . .

With the dissolution of role differentiation, the audience is no longer offered the convenience of conventional character identification. The dramaturgy of the plot no longer supplies a base for moral judgement on the various events. The cooperation of the audience is required. The individual audience member is rationally and emotionally included in the stage proceedings and must make his own decisions. The fact that *Bluebeard* is one hundred and ten minutes in length and performed without an intermission, a radical break with standard theater procedure, compels the audience to do so.

In her subsequent works, Bausch reinforces these foundations of the dance theater aesthetic and further develops the scenic theater of movement demonstrated in *Bluebeard*.

CHAPTER 25

Forced Entertainment;
Text by Tim Etchells

Club of no regrets

'On the edge of a dark wood the scenes of strange play are enacted at gunpoint . . .'

CLUB OF NO REGRETS WAS Forced Entertainment's 10th project for theatre spaces. In it a central figure, Helen X, who claims to be lost in the woods, orders the enactment of a series of fragmentary scenes by a pair of performers inside a tiny box-set, centre-stage. The box-set is a crude plywood room with sawn-out windows, the walls of it painted black and scrawled with writing and drawings in chalk. Behind this crude house is a large plywood wall also painted black and covered in chalk drawings which depict an overgrown cityscape, the whole picture blurred and distorted with smudged chalk.

To facilitate or perhaps hinder the enactments ordered by Helen, a second pair of performers function as stagehands or captors who, having tied the other two to chairs and threatened them with guns, proceed to bring them the texts and props they might need for the performance. The enacted scenes are replayed many times as though Helen is unsure as to their true order or correct arrangement. The scenes themselves, reproduced below, are fragmentary and to some extent incomplete, unconnected sections of made-for-TV dialogue, thriller nonsense, love story, psychic detection. Each scene is titled, the titles drawing attention to their found, clichéd and more or less iconic status. The scenes are framed by a further text from Helen, a confused narration of her fairy story/history which she calls *Club of No Regrets*.

Collected together here are the key texts spoken during the performance: those from the central figure Helen X and those enacted repeatedly as 'scenes' by the performers inside the tiny box-set. The texts are presented in order as they appear in the performance, excluding the considerable repetitions and without annotation. (Not reprinted here.) Immediately following the text is a short section which maps the structure of the performance and makes some account of the action-track surrounding the text.

Like *Emanuelle* before it, *Club of No Regrets* creates a fiction in which theatrical material is being ordered, enacted and explored by the protagonists. Its movement is from a chaotic enactment of its scenes to a transformation of the same material via repetition, interruption and gradual mutation.

Club of No Regrets lasted one hour and 25 minutes. It was conceived and devised by Forced Entertainment under the direction of Tim Etchells. It was performed by Robin Arthur, Richard Lowdon, Claire Marshall, Cathy Naden and Terry O'Connor. The assistant director was Ju Row Farr, design was by Richard Lowdon, lighting by Nigel Edwards and soundtrack by John Avery.

Structure of the performance

What follows is an attempt to map or diagram the structure of *Club of No Regrets*. The position of the various texts in the piece is indicated alongside notes and annotations concerning the action track and tone of the performance. Throughout the piece Helen calls for the scenes to be enacted again and again, repeating them, switching their order. Helen is erratic, jumpy and volatile, declaring that the scenes are 'completely wrong' or 'too sad' or simply 'too black and white'. Her struggle is to get them in the right order, or, more certainly, to forge some more poetic sense from their unpromising substance.

As Helen calls for the scenes to be enacted, Richard and Cathy function as brutal stage-hands who bring texts and props to enable the performance. Their action is often disruptive – drawing one's attention away from the scenes themselves, obliterating dialogue with noise and distraction. The annotations for the piece give only a crude and partial account of the action and of Helen's more-or-less impromptu responses to it.

Helen text one

Helen wandering, reading and talking to herself in the darkness of the stage.

Robin and Claire enter as somewhat reluctant performers, with Richard and Cathy as stage-hands. Robin and Claire are gagged and bound to chairs using parcel-tape. Helen is above the set, looking down into the room, consulting her papers and drinking from various bottles throughout the piece.

Scene Order	Staging Notes/Terry's reactions
BLOCK ONE	Robin and Claire are bound and gagged throughout.
A Procedures Scene	Text largely inaudible, glasses brought for Robin and Claire.
A Questions Scene	Text obscured by Cathy banging behind set. Helen: Is that it?
A Questions Scene	

Telegram One (Claire)	Claire still gagged, text inaudible. Helen leaves her place overlooking the room to come down stage left.
Helen Text Two	Helen returns to her vantage point.
BLOCK TWO A Procedures Scene	Robin and Claire are bound and gagged throughout. Interrupted by constant changing of props in the room.
A Just As They're About To Kiss The Telephone Rings Scene*	Robin and Claire hop towards each other, bound to their chairs. The telephone arrives late, the scene an absurd failure.
Telegram One (Robin)	Helen: Completely fucking wrong. We'd better do another.
Telegram Two (Claire)	Claire is still gagged text inaudible. Helen has her head in her hands.
A Look How I'm Crying Scene	Helen: Too short we'll have to do it again.
A Look How I'm Crying Scene	Robin's mouth has finally been untaped.
A Troubled Scene	Robin cut out of chair by Cathy using knife, Richard pushes the standard lamp into the room through the window.
A Questions Scene	Claire's mouth untaped, a gun placed in Robin's hand. Helen leaves her place above the room to come down stage left.
Helen Text Three	Helen returns to her vantage point.
BLOCK THREE A Look How I'm Crying Scene	Water from bottles thrown onto Robin and Claire's faces as tears.
A Questions Scene	Text inaudible again due to Cathy banging behind the set.
A Look How I'm Crying Scene	Glasses doused with water for tears.
A Questions Scene	Helen reads aloud from a book as the scene proceeds.
Helen Text Four	As Helen reads Richard and Cathy bring a coloured shirt for Robin and a dressing gown for Claire, gesturing at gun-point that they should put them on.
Telegram Four (Robin) A Shoot Out Scene	A trickle of fake blood sprayed on Robin, a single squirt of talcum powder sprayed in the air as smoke. Richard with a gun through a window of the room.
A Troubled Scene	Richard and Cathy pelt the windows of the room with 'rain' from bottles.

	Helen: It needs more colour.
A Troubled Scene	Cathy puts a blue shirt on the table, more water thrown in the windows.
	Helen: Too black and white.
Helen Text Five	Helen pacing behind the set, then returning to her place.
A Troubled Scene	More water thrown in the windows, Helen ghosting Claire's words.
	Helen: I've completely lost the thread of it . . .
A Kiss/Telephone Scene	The phone arrives just in time to disrupt the kiss.
A Kiss/Telephone Scene	The phone arrives just in time to disrupt the kiss.
A Kiss/Telephone Scene	The phone arrives just in time to disrupt the kiss.
A Kiss/Telephone Scene	Helen given microphone.
A Kiss/Telephone Scene	The phone arrives just in time to disrupt the kiss.
A Drug Trip Scene	CHAOS: Richard flashing the practical lamp on and off, drawing circles of light in the air, Cathy throwing talcum powder into the room.
	Helen: More cops! We need more cops, we'll have to do it again.
A Drug Trip Scene	Helen waving a tin-foil star, whoops and yells, circles of chalk, Claire crying into the telephone.
Telegram Four (Robin)	
Telegram Four (Claire)	
A Kiss/Telephone Scene	The phone arrives just in time to disrupt the kiss. Robin and Claire have been parcel-taped to the walls of the set by Richard and Cathy – since they cannot move the scene is a dismal failure.
	Helen: Shit.
Helen Questions	Helen enters the room and poses questions to Robin and Claire.
Helen Text Six	Helen returns to her place above the room.
BLOCK FOUR	Richard and Cathy no longer pass text to Robin and Claire, except for telegrams.
A Procedures Scene	Robin and Claire still taped up.
A Questions Scene	
A Troubled Scene	Richard and Cathy deluge the room with water, talcum powder and leaves.
A Look How I'm Crying Scene	
A Kiss/Telephone Scene	
Telegram Six (Claire)	
A Drug Trip Scene	More manic than ever.
A Shoot Out Scene	Claire's face and neck sprayed with blood.
	Helen: Oh, she's dying, she's dying, oh God, she's dying . . .

A Questions Scene	Robin shouting against the music.
A Shoot Out Scene	Robin's face and neck sprayed with blood, leaves and talcum powder thrown into the room.
	Helen: Oh, he's dying, he's dying, oh God, he's going to die . . .
A Look How I'm Crying Scene	Helen: It's too sad, we'll have to do it again.
A Look How I'm Crying Scene	Helen leaves her place above the room.
Helen Text Seven	Helen returns to her place above the room.

BLOCK FIVE

Helen calls the scenes faster and faster. Richard and Cathy are running themselves into the ground. They pile on the leaves, talcum powder water and fake blood. Robin and Claire are soaked, their voices at their limits from shouting.

A Questions Scene
A Troubled Scene
A Just As They're About To Kiss The Telephone Rings Scene
A Just As They're About To Kiss The Telephone Rings Scene
A Just As They're About To Kiss The Telephone Rings Scene
A Look How I'm Crying Scene
A Drug Trip Scene
A Troubled Scene
A Questions Scene
A Look How I'm Crying Scene
A Procedures Scene
A Troubled Scene

Robin and Claire give up enacting the scenes. They stand in the centre of the room as Richard and Cathy deluge it with water, leaves, smoke and sprayed blood, the 'stage-hands' continuing to do the special effects and props-continuity long after the actors have stopped. Frenzy. Helen continues to call scenes in random order, doing the dialogue herself, mis-remembered, jumbled, confused. In the end the music lulls.

Helen text eight

Helen calms and continues to speak, leaving her position above the room and moving to the front of the stage. Richard and Cathy gently arrange objects in the room as she speaks: delicate arrangements of books, guns, leaves, bloodstains.

After a time they stop arranging objects in and around the room, and assume Helen's previous position looking down into it at Robin and Claire who are still embraced. When they've looked for a while they get down and start to clear the crude room set and all the things in it, leaving Robin and Claire embraced alone in the centre of the cleared space, visible against the backdrop wall of chalked buildings. Robin and Claire drop their embrace and join Richard and Cathy at the back.

Terry calls for the music for the 'big escape routine'.

CODA:
CHAIRS DANCE/ESCAPE ROUTINE
R&B music plays.

Richard and Cathy are bound to chairs with parcel tape and gagged. A frightening dance follows; somewhere between brutal ballet and the climax of some well-dodgy thriller. They struggle to escape, madly slipping and falling over as Robin and Claire dance. Often the chairs break.

Meanwhile Helen chalks a circle on the floor at the front on each side of the stage. Using the knife and a hammer, running from side to side of the stage she dances, a thrashing with the knife that suggests her cutting her way out of the woods. Richard and Cathy escape from the chairs and immediately tape-up Robin and Claire. The R&B music ends. Richard, Cathy and Helen/Terry are all breathing hard. Piano music comes on and the escape routine repeated in another key by Robin and Claire. Helen stays at the front, her 'getting out of the woods' dance going more and more slowly. Robin and Claire escape. The piano music ends. There is silence.

Terry pours water on the chalk circles on the floor at the front, erasing them with her foot. She walks to the right hand side of the stage, takes off her wig and picks up the microphone. The others watch as she speaks.

Helen final text

* There are two scenes that Helen calls for which involve no written dialogue. The first is entitled *A Just As They're About To Kiss the Telephone Rings Scene* and in it Robin and Claire make their way toward each other in the tiny room, get closer and closer as if they are about to kiss and then break off at the last moment, usually prompted by the noisy arrival of the disconnected prop telephone. Richard and Cathy change the meaning of this scene (and others) by placing props into the hands of Robin and/or Claire as it is enacted. A Robin advancing on Claire to kiss her is transformed by Cathy arming him with a large rusty saw for example, or by the addition of an old bottle-thick pair of glasses.

The second scene which does not feature written text is entitled *A Drug Trip Scene*. The action for this develops and changes throughout its various repetitions but it basically consists of Robin and Claire feigning hysterical and/or manic hallucinations while Richard and Cathy draw circles on the walls of the room in chalk, make the hands of the prop clock go round and round very fast and use a practical lamp to crudely create the effect of shifting, swimming and flashing lights, and place objects and bursts of smoke (talcum powder) in the room to disorientate Robin and Claire.

CHAPTER 26

Mike Pearson and Cliff McLucas, John Keefe, Simon Murray

'On Brith Gof', a montage of material about and concerning the work of Brith Gof, a Welsh Theatre Company

My Balls/Your Chin,* Mike Pearson

I want to tell you about Antonin Artaud and me.

I want to tell you about the work of RAT Theatre with whom I performed in 1972 and 1973. Of whom the programme for the Festival Mondial du Théâtre in Nancy said, 'few could, like them, legitimately, lay claim to Artaud, at least with regard to the manifesto on cruelty', and of whom Dutch newspaper *Het Parool* said, 'It is "Poor Theatre" and "Theatre of Cruelty" taken to their furthest extremes' . . .

I want to tell you about *The Lesson of Anatomy*, a performance in four sections based on Artaud's various writings about the body – the body physical, the body social, the body spiritual, the body transcendental – presented by Cardiff Laboratory Theatre at Oval House in London early in 1974. I performed the first section, which was called *Flesh*. First time I ever shaved my head, as an artistic statement then of course, not the last hope of a balding, middle-aged man! Sitting on a marble slab, exposing bits of my anatomy as if for dissection – patient, specimen, case-study. Of the text, all I recall is 'All writing is pig-shit!', read from the label on my jacket pocket.

* 'My Balls/Your Chin' is a piece by Last Exit from *Best of Live*, Enemy Records EMCD 110 1990

I want to . . . but I can barely remember. It's all so long ago and there's so little to help me. For this work – marginal, ephemeral, disposable – was never recorded, documented, analysed, held up for scrutiny. All that survives – the traces which devised performance leaves behind – is a few scars, the odd photograph, an occasional anecdote . . .[1]

Y Llyfyr Glas

McLucas
The things that were important, or that I felt were important, about those pieces of work were no longer present, they weren't around. Then you start thinking that if we use some of that stuff from the time, and augment it with stuff from now, you get two orders of material, one trying to be a kind of supratext for the other one. So the idea emerges of just treating it all as memory . . .

Pearson
Well, devised performance has no record to authenticate it or to legitimize it. It doesn't produce play scripts, and so any effort to document work, to talk about our work, is a kind of political project. It may be that we appear very inarticulate, illiterate almost, in relation to those forms of theatre that do produce texts. Therefore I think we have a constant need to find different ways of talking about our work. The one important thing about devised work is that it is bound up in an oral culture, it's a set of practices that are passed on from performer to performer, from mouth to mouth actually, so it is perhaps more valuable to apply techniques of oral history to this kind of work . . .[2]

I want to tell you about my friend Dave Levett.

Dave is a physical performer and computer musician: he controls his keyboard with his nose. When he was born, Dave was not breathing. This caused damage to his brain, affecting his motor functioning. Dave is neither mentally disabled, nor, as he is fed up of telling strangers who rush to his assistance in the street, is he deaf! Ten years ago he would have been called a spastic. Today he is regarded as 'having' – or 'suffering from' – cerebral palsy. In contemporary parlance he is 'disabled', not 'handicapped'.

Dave cannot stand unaided. Nevertheless, he generates tremendous pull and grip with his arms, and push with his legs. He refuses to use an electrically powered wheelchair, which he feels defines his 'status of dependency', and instead uses a standard manual chair, which he operates by pushing himself backwards with one foot. He cannot turn the wheels with his hands. Yet he achieves a precision of turn, spin, reverse, effectively with one toe. He communicates by laboriously pointing to a given vocabulary on a board on his lap or to individual letters to spell out more complex words. He also speaks, in gurgling tones. His voice, with its broken rhythms and swooping articulations – on the breath, against the breath – demands our attention, demands that we listen and interpret. And that we relax, that we accept that there is meaning here. His is a language that one has to learn. As his lungs don't inflate or deflate greatly, the nuances are subtle and there is extreme brevity and clarity in his words. Which is why he likes verbal puns so much.

Five years ago we began to make physical theatre together. The rehearsal process meant the daily breaking of taboos. How do I touch a disabled man? How do I hold him? Will I damage him? Three moments I remember clearly from our early work:

– I was on my hands and knees. Dave was kneeling beside me. His action was to throw his body over mine. I remember his hand on my back and the enormous force of will as he imagined his goal and ordered his physical effort, and time, in a supreme effort of catching the moment. The feeling of organizing the body, directly experienced by those of us who hold and touch him in performance.

– I once dropped him. And he fell like a stone. Fortunately his body is tough. But he has no defence, no protective mechanism. To work with Dave is to know total responsibility.

– After the first performance, the audience was clearly moved. But not by Dave's disability. He despises pity and self-pity. By the fact that they realized that they knew what he meant. Yet he was not making anything close to a conventional gesture, rather a hovering net of gestural hint and suggestion. But with him isolated on the bare stage, with no redundancy of action on his part and no wavering of attention on our part, with a deep and extraordinary concentration, a will to communicate, to be understood, we experience him 'as signing', signalling through the flames perhaps. Exotic, fascinating, irresistible. We are attracted by his humanity, by his heat.

Dave's body is in a kind of rebellion with itself, suddenly jerking into spastic movement or channelling creative impulse into stereotyped gesture. His body is decided. Yet he works with the actions his body wants to make. So 'pull' can become embrace, hold, grip, fight, tear. And 'push' becomes caress, reject, threaten. Or he can hitch a ride on the randomness and fury of physical abandon – shaking, jerking, spasm-ing. He once told me that the one thing he can never do on stage is die, some part of his body is always in motion. His fingers always want to trace the most intricate and delicate of patterns. Yet just occasionally he can give a deep sigh and achieve the most awesome and terrible of silences. This is a dance of impulses: intended, random and spasmodic.

In our duet in *Black and White*, Dave worked both in and out of his chair. In *D.O.A.*, the chair was nowhere to be seen: Dave worked on a bed, on the floor, supported and carried by his two colleagues.

For me, Dave's work begins to pose fundamental questions about the nature of physical performance. What is the distinction between ability and disability, for his body can adopt positions, engage in actions which mine never can? What is the purpose and nature of training for the disabled body which will never achieve athleticism? What does a notion such as choreography mean to the disabled performer? Or timing and dynamic, when action is the result of chance and will? Can the work of the disabled performer be confined by stylistic labels such as melodrama? Is 'what it is' as significant as 'what it portrays'?

Dave's work is impossible to notate; it resists the document. We will never come close to understanding his strategies. Only he will ever know what it feels like. We can never train to be like him. And video is not sophisticated enough to see the delicacy of hand gestures or the micro-movements of face and eye which communicate his precision of emotion and dramatic intent . . .[1]

Brith Gof, *Arturius Rex*, Cardiff, November 1994

Bussed from Chapter Arts Centre to a cold, barren industrial shed. Inside a long, narrow performing space filled with beds; to be transformed by the performers and audience.

Arturius Rex shows the scummy, demeaning, dirty death of a hero, of the Celts, of every society at the hands of another. Power given to anyone with *carte blanche* to use it turns neighbours into torturer, rapist, killer. Becomes ethnic cleansing, the release of evil.

All this is **shown**, through a physical theatre of tenderness, violence, ideas; that embraces and distances. The physical and emotional proximity makes us voyeurs, victims, torturers.

Images:

> chalk drawn outlines of bodies are scrubbed out in physical and cultural genocide.
> a text of raw poetry, rhythm & repetition, and thrash music.
> hospital beds become torture frames, rape & death cage.
> the audience gets out of the way or is pushed aside.
> water over floor, over us.
> a fractured singing of *Mae Hen Wiad Fy Nhadau/Land of my Fathers* makes patriotism ironic and broken.
> Dave Levett thrown onto the bare bed springs, his own physical 'disability' standing for all the broken bodies of torture, war, genocide making his own 'physical theatre'.

This was a performance total in the commitment of performers and audience. It was raw and moving, making insipid most of what passes for physical theatre. A theatre of body, mind, emotion that made an image both simple and complex.

It was a very special experience.

John Keefe[3]

I begin to feel uneasy.

I feel uneasy that the demand for the document is part of a process of legitimization that is turning our practice into an orthodoxy and our life-wishes into a profession. As more and more university drama departments turn their attention to performance studies we begin to seek academic approbation and authentification. At best, this might cause us to be reasonable, rational, logical about work that is naturally none of these things. At worst, it may begin to represent a proprietorial struggle as to who is authorized to speak about, and for, the work and in what terms. And how ironic that more and more academic attention begins to focus upon less and less work.[1]

Chasing shadows: stories of stories of stories . . . impressions from two documenters

Mind the Gaps – a conference organized by CPR and Lancaster University – attempted to explore and rethink the relationship between performers and documenters. Out of suspicion, the quest for a positive embrace. Many words, much cleverness and shifting positions. At one extreme: 'Interpretation is the revenge of the intellect upon art', at another: 'All theatre is ephemeral, so documentation is the only way to re-present our work to history'. A rough and unstable consensus that documentation is a means of starting and maintaining a dialogue between different groups: what matters is the nature of the relationship.

Some agreement, too, that there can be no objective record – too many truths and lies. How to document the peripheral, the accidental, the surprises and that lack of clarity which are part of the process of making theatre.

Below is a personal documentation of Panel Presentation 2 – a panel of academics/professionals from non-theatre disciplines each talking about how they deal with recording and documentation.

Memories of an undisciplined documenter

- I remember the anxieties of the pathologist and the lawyer.
- I remember the bodies and the infinite number of ways there are to sit on a chair.
- I remember the fallibility of technology.
- I remember 3 pairs of sandals and 3 pairs of dark socks.
- I remember 6 men on chairs and no women.
- I remember the shuffling of papers and transparencies.
- I remember the fishbowl reflection of the auditorium in the glasses of the women sitting in front of me.
- I remember the black and silver of the trunk and wishing I could have one.
- I remember the desire, which kept returning for 7 or 8 minutes.
- I remember the Sociologist twice tripping, nearly falling, saving himself.

Simon Murray

In all languages – A five day workshop with Mike Pearson of Brith Gof.

- 'In All Languages' – a two-part record by Ornette Colman. The first part created in 1964 and the second 25 years later in 1989.
- 'In all languages': Brith Gof's exploration of 10 sets of 10 movements or gestures, done in solos, pairs, groups in different articulations. A vocabulary of 100 'words' to form the basis of a text of articulate physicality, combined in performance with texts of words, sounds and images.
- A group of practitioners, teachers, under and post graduates going across levels of practice and skills creating within a day a high degree of physical and mental trust.
- An intense, stimulating, exhilarating workshop.
- The clash between processes of/in the group and university documentation: the students are required to observe, take notes, write essays. But First Injunction: Let the mind and body remember and then record later. Authenticity confronts the idea of 'accurate' records; with illusions of true documentation. Documentation is *mimetic*.
- Second Injunction: Do not treat this work as another ingredient in the cocktail of training – do not consume the 'words' and just reproduce them – explore, develop, then learn and use them as a model for one's own vocabulary and process.

- Little formal discussion, but a sharing of reactions, ideas and feelings that grows out of the work. Contrast the discussion sessions with members of other two workshop groups which prove that work (unlike ideas) cannot be known by talking, only a degree of understanding.
- Group decision not to make plenary session: just Mike making statements in Welsh – the workshop cannot be reduced to simplistic statements perpetuating delusions of knowing – the unrolling of two wonderful paper murals by a participant that sense and distil the work as impressions, fragments of energy, movement and articulations.

John Keefe[4]

For me, it's always been a political project. When I started with RAT Theatre in 1972, our work was a critique of the torpid youth culture – shrouded in a dope haze, 'flapping in flares' – of which we were part. We were fuelled by a set of attitudes to the body physical and the body politic; our gobs were full of situationist slogans. If we had been able to play guitars, we would have formed a band.

Instead, we made physical theatre – aggressive, violent, disturbing, ugly stuff – form and content locked in one semi-coherent outburst of energy. Theatre was our only option, but at least it was ours. No training, no teachers, no peers. Arrogance, bad attitude, maximum exposure and effect. I feel uneasy turning performance into an object of study. I can teach technique but not attitude. We need more passion and less pedagogy. More dumb insolence in the face of those twin pillars of theatre – tradition and prudence – which refuse to tumble. The means will always follow the motive . . .[1]

Pearson
There are only three modes of performance – dramaturgy, by that I mean the way in which some narratives are unfolding, choreography and art. There is an unfortunate perception that if you are not staging dramatic literature then you must be 'Performance Art', and these definitions have slipped and slopped around. If you read national criticism of work you can very quickly see where all of the major critics stand. If the work is non-verbal, or running several narratives in juxtaposition, then they have extreme difficulty and it's always defined as 'Performance Art'. I have difficulty with that because I think most of our work is constituted as dramaturgy, but it may exist in gaps between all of them. I suppose in the end one defines it by Company; if you want to see Brith Gof, if you like Brith Gof then you go for the Brith Gof experience . . .

But I began to realise that if in our work performers were working in three dimensions and that they may be in many different physical relationships with each other, and with an audience, and that if we were putting pressure on all three of those sets of relationships, performer to performer, performer to spectator and spectator to spectator, then we might be able to begin to work with the other elements, and the under-considered elements I think, of physical communication. Almost every theatre practice uses gesture, kinesics, physical movements, but I also began to think that perhaps we could begin to generate material which was entirely based on proxemics, the distances between people. Whether that be the distance between performer and performer, or indeed between performer and spectator – because that is something, you know, when you're sitting in your seat in the theatre you never expect to be close to a performer, to feel a performer breathe, to feel a performer sweating – and one can generate exciting material by that. Equally to begin to work with haptics, which is touch of self and others, and we touch each other in all sorts of ways, and I thought we could go to work with that, once again in all those sets of relationships varying degrees of touch might be possible . . . because we make physical performance, I think there's a way in which that's often characterised as some kind of athletics, not least because the traditions of physical theatre which have grown up in the 80's are the ones of choreography. I think we do work with dramaturgy, I come from an older tradition, and so I think very often . . . You know that our performers singularly are not athletes in many ways, what they are is extremely committed so that to deal with on one level the active environment and at the same time to be making meaningful, communicative gestures, kinesic but also proxemics and haptics, is what is demanded of our performers . . .[2]

I feel uneasy.

I fear that theatre is already an anachronism: speedier media have already got 'replication' and 'representation' sewn up. And performed behaviours, social simulations and staged events may already be happening in sophisticated ways elsewhere, not least in everyday life. In an era of surveillance, we are all constantly 'on stage'.

I feel uneasy.

I can no longer sit passively in the dark watching a hole in the wall, pretending that the auditorium is a neutral vessel of representation. It is a spatial machine that distances us from the spectacle and that allies subsidy, theatre orthodoxy and political conservatism, under the disguise of nobility of purpose, in a way that literally 'keeps us in our place'. I can no longer dutifully turn up to see the latest 'brilliant' product of such-and-such in this arts centre, where I saw the latest 'brilliant' product of others only yesterday, a field ploughed to exhaustion. I can no longer allow the programming policies and the black boxes of a circuit of venues to define the form and nature of performance . . .[1]

McLucas

What happens in Wales is that you get two kinds of worlds slipping against each other. One is built around the whole tradition of the Eisteddfod which receives massive and passionate support from, in inverted commas, 'the Welsh speaking community'. People will work endless hours for nothing and produce astonishing amounts of work. Sitting on top of that you've got this thing called 'Art', which is, well, an incredibly bald statement to make, but is almost all an import, in terms of its forms and techniques . . .

Pearson

I think Cliff's right. It may be that we are already working in a deeply anachronistic medium. It may be that the theatrical impulse, the impulse to represent society, the function of theatre in certain ways, has already gone elsewhere . . .

McLucas
On all those edges where hybridization is taking place and where clever thinking is being imported from one field into another such as archaeologists or architects . . .[2]

Brith Gof, *Tri Bywyd (Three Lives)*, Lampeter, October 1995

Once more taking the road to Wales, now further into the mid-West. Once again by coach to the performance site but now deep in the forests. This shared journey becomes a semi-ritualistic travel into the site, the place of magic and transformation. And the site is magic, is magnificent. Stages growing out of the ruined walls, out of the trees – yet the trees grow out of and through the stages. We sit literally in/by the trees looking at the array of platforms and ladders. It evokes the mediaeval theatre; not the stations of the cross but the stations of a contemporary secular morality play.

5 performers tell the intertwining stories of victims and rooms; clambering through poles & trees, criss-crossing the stages as we are shown the life of a house, the death of a prostitute, the dying of a fasting girl with the parallels of places, events, violences. We are confronted by the sordid realities of undignified lives and deaths. A soundscape reverberates around the trees as lights swing from one figure to another. We are surrounded by nature but here nature does not carry salvation; it is ironic, the mute setting only for the events of a broken society.

The piece does not have the incessant pounding power and physical impact of *Arturius Rex* nor the mythic level that links us with the events across time. There is not the physical connection between performers and audience, leaving us only as observers. Rather it is the totality, the vision of the space that resonates this time; the sheer presence of the stages, trees, stone walls, roots, darkness and lighting, sound, figures all intertwined and growing from each other as the space itself overarches the action.

John Keefe[5]

I feel uneasy.

I have an urgent need to readdress my practice, to challenge and dismantle my own notions. Jerzy Grotowski's early work was dedicated to finding an authentic communication between one performer and one spectator – spatially, physically, emotionally. I imagine that he got up one morning and realized that the single thing which prevented such communication was theatre. And that's when he left. It will require that clarity of vision.

So what do I want?

I want to get rid of the theatre 'object', the play, the 'well-made show', the *raison d'être* of the critic. I want to constitute performance as a strip of anti-social behaviour and incoherent activity, as a 'special world' where extra-daily occurrences and experiences and changes in status are possible.

I want to constitute performance as a 'field' of activity that will tend to escape definition, description and representation, there being no singular or external vantage point from which to view it. I want to create 'radically unfinished work', awkward, uneasy stuff which defies commodification as the latest product to buy, sell, hype in Europe.

I want to dislocate and confound the preconceptions, expectations and critical faculties of the audience. I want to problematize and renegotiate all three basic performance relationships: performer to performer, performer to spectator (and vice versa), and spectator to spectator. Standing, moving, running with, running away . . . So that we may have to ask, 'Who is who?', 'Whom do I watch?', 'What's going on here?'

I want to find different arenas for performance – places of work, play and worship – where the laws and bye-laws, the decorum and learned contracts of theatre can be suspended.

I want to make performances that fold together place, performance and public.

I want to make 'hybrids' – of music, action, text and site – that defy conventional labels.

I want to make slippery, sliding performances that are not a mirror of some social issue or a simplification but a complication, which defies instant scrutiny.

And I want to reduce the critic to bystander.

I want to constitute performance as a discontinuous and interrupted practice of different modes of expression, of varying types and intensities, in which different orders of narrative can run simultaneously, in which dramatic concept may spring from site, not story, and which may include rapid changes in mode and material . . .

So that we find a 'way of telling' about it which has personal and communal currency. So that we can endlessly replay it, thrill again to it, enshrine it in our mythology.

So that perhaps, in the end, the best we can ever do is to ask, 'How was it for you?' Which probably tells you quite a lot about Antonin Artaud and me.

(Versions of this provocation were presented at the Centre for Performance Research/ Lancaster University Summer School of Theatre symposium 'Mind The Gaps'/ Performance: Process and Documentation, Lancaster, England, July 1994, and at the Centre for Performance Research symposium 'Past Masters: Antonin Artaud', Aberystwyth, Wales, November 1996.)[1]

Key to sources

1   *My Balls/Your Chin*
2   *Y Llyfyr Glas 1988–1995*
3   *Arturius Rex*
4   *Chasing Shadows*
5   *Tri Bywyd*

CHAPTER 27

Franc Chamberlain

MAG – the next five years 1997–2002

Vision and definition

PHYSICAL-BASED PERFORMANCE; I guess that the word 'body' isn't used
here because 'object animation' is included. I have a problem which, for me, refuses
to go away and which the current definition makes worse. What would it mean for a
piece of theatre to be non-physically based? As soon as it's theatre it's physical (if we
take this far enough even a piece of radio drama has the bodies of the actors producing
sound which is recorded/transmitted). Theatre *is* physical-based in the broad sense. If
we want to oppose physical-based theatre to text-based, or image-based, theatre then
I think there's still a need for a clearer definition than we've got.

In *On the Art of the Theatre*, Edward Gordon Craig wrote against the idea that literature
was at the root of theatre and argued instead that: 'the Art of the Theatre has sprung
from action – movement – dance' (1980: 139). We can take this idea backwards into
history and prove, if we wish, that Craig wasn't the first person to have suggested this.
Fine, but the point is that this statement, which was originally published in a 1905 essay,
signifies that the attempt to define theatre in terms of what made it a distinctive art form
was underway and that one strand of this definition is that theatre is not a branch of
literature. From that point on, it seems to me, all of the key developments in actor-
training have involved a physical-based approach. Stanislavski's work at the First Studio
and his later 'method' of physical actions; Meyerhold's interest in the commedia dell'arte
and then his development of biomechanics; Copeau's interest in the commedia and in
the work of the Fratellini Brothers; Michel St Denis' insistence on the importance of
gesture and movement and so on. I could add to the list Michael Chekhov, Grotowski,
Boal, Bing, Pagneux, Decroux, Pardo, Castrillo, Lecoq, Schechner, Barba, Beck, Suzuki
and Brecht. If I look to non-Western forms, e.g. kathakali, Beijing Opera, No, kabuki,

once again we can look at the training and see the importance of starting from the body; the early-morning kathakali eye-exercises for example. Indeed, if we think of it historically in terms of what we know about the importance of gesture in actor-training from previous centuries it becomes difficult to see where our non-physical based theatre lies, at least in terms of the actor's training. It seems obvious to me that even training someone to act 'naturalistically' is to train them in the use of the body in an 'unnatural' situation. And where does dance fit in?

But, of course, we all know that there's something which we recognise as 'physical theatre', or at least there used to be. But wasn't it a code word, for Lecoq or Decroux-based theatre where the performer needed 'quelque chose à dire' and the starting point was their own body and experience? Or was it something else? Something which was marked out in opposition to mainstream theatre where the task of the actor was to interpret the text under the eye of an (often) literature-trained director? Or both of these things?

To return to Craig again, for a moment. He was reacting against a theatre which was text-based and this involved the re-valuing of the actor's physicality. With this re-valuing came a possibility which Craig didn't follow through, much to Copeau's annoyance. What everyone 'knows' about Craig is that he wanted to get rid of the actors and replace them with puppets and yet, in the very same essay which is quoted as the source of this idea, 'The Actor and the Ubermarionette' (1908), Craig offers what has proved to be a far more significant solution to the problem:

> I see a loop-hole by which in time the actors can escape from the bondage they are in. They must create for themselves a new form of acting, consisting for the main part of symbolical gesture. Today they *impersonate* and interpret; tomorrow they must *represent* and interpret; and the third day they must create. (1980: 61)

This idea of the actor creating may, of course, be interpreted in many different ways but I think that it is another key idea which Craig is identifying (again, it's not important to my argument whether or not he 'originated' it). There is a constant struggle in twentieth-century theatre between the actor as the puppet of the director and actors as creative artists in their own right (and this tension is in Craig's work), but when we put the idea of creativity together with the idea of movement as the basis of theatre then I think that we can begin to recognise something of what we used to mean, at least, by 'physical theatre'; Moving Picture Mime Show, David Glass, Trestle Theatre, Mummer&dada, Théâtre de Complicité, etc. I think this is still there in the work of Talking Pictures, Commotion, Bouge-de-là, Brouhaha.

Perhaps the word 'create' or 'creativity' here should be re-written as 'devise' or 'devising' because that's what I think I mean.

These two things together would connect to Tom Leabhart's idea, presented at the European Mime Foundation meeting in 1994, of the 'liberated actor'. Leabhart called this liberated actor a 'mime', which, if we accepted it, would bring us right back where we started: Mime Action Group. In Leabhart's formulation, however, I didn't get a sense of the importance of 'movement', but perhaps that should be taken as implicit given his background.

I have a strong interest in non-European forms of performance and have had for a long time, yet I would have to exclude many of them from my definition here because most of them are not 'creative' in the terms I've identified. In kathakali and No, for example, performers learn pre-existent texts which they perform in, more or less, pre-determined patterns. The instant Kalamandalam Vijayakumar works together with a group of other kathakali performers to devise a version of 'Snow White' (*The Oppression of the Innocent* (1995)), however, then the work may be said to be a piece of 'physical theatre'. The same would be true of No, Kabuki, Beijing Opera, etc.

The physical training of kathakali actors pre-sets the way in which any topic can be approached. That, however, would be true, again to a greater or lesser extent, of all forms of actor-training, which doesn't get us very far.

Insofar as dancers are creating work they would also have to come under the definition. Dancers' training is clearly physical-based but they are not always trained to be creative artists in Craig's sense, but interpreters. DV8, who call their work 'physical theatre' anyway, would fit into the definition neatly enough but Ballet Rambert or the Royal Ballet wouldn't. What I'm unsure of here is how the term 'physical-based' performance would exclude the Royal Ballet – if it doesn't exclude them then it seems to me that we fall back into some naive position which argues that dance is 'physical-based' whereas drama is 'text-based' and thus all 'physically based' theatre becomes dance.

I still want to hold on to the idea that physical theatre, as a term, however flawed it might have been, actually said something which physical-based performance can't (although physical performance might). [. . .]

[Out would go] Théâtre de Complicité's *The Visit* and any number of other pieces we might want to save as examples of physical theatre. So, a pre-existent text can be there but there must be an approach towards it; there must be a devised response to the text which takes the body as the starting point. But this doesn't seem as simple to me as it sounds. As a member of the audience, how would I tell if the 'body' had been taken as the starting point? Unless there is an identifiable set of practices, I don't see how I can. Actually this question opens up onto another problem; if I'm watching a show created without a pre-existent (theatrical) text, how will I know whether movement/gesture has been the starting point? [. . .] The traditional page-to-stage approach, where the text is used as a blueprint which the actor manifests on stage, is what is meant by text-based [. . .] whatever the starting point in the rehearsal process as the 'devised' or 'creative' dimension is excluded.

So, one week a company presents a piece of physical theatre, the next week they present a piece of text-based theatre. That's OK. Do we need them to be fixed? However, when I read a review of Complicité's *Foe* in *Total Theatre* I have to ask why I didn't see a review of *The Machine Wreckers* which was at the National (and which had Paul Allain as movement director). Presumably because Complicité are defined as a physical theatre company irrespective of what they do or who's in the company. This seems to me to reduce the term physical theatre to a marketing label which, in the end, says nothing about style, approach, or training.

[. . .]

I'd now like to turn to the inclusion of 'object-animation' in the definition. Once again this is work which interests me, but I'm not sure about its inclusion as such. Where the 'object-animation' is a page-to-stage approach (e.g. staging literally a pre-existent text written for 'puppets') then it would not be a piece of physical performance as I'm defining it. I'm also uncertain as to why we would want to include 'object-animation' at all in a definition of physical-based theatre, except insofar as a piece of physical theatre might include 'object-animation' (as in Nada Theatre's *Ubu* or Bouge-de-là's *The Man Who Ate His Shoes*). What about Punch and Judy? Do we even need a live human performer for a piece to be physical-based if we remove the idea that physical = centered on the movement of the human body? A few weeks ago I was at a degree show and conference at Dartington and there were some very interesting 'performances'. One involved several blocks of ice hanging above a white-painted trolley on which there was a monogrammed handkerchief, an old black-and-white photograph and a collection of file-card size transparencies with pieces of text. From underneath the trolley came some faint music. Inside each of the blocks of ice was a handkerchief and the ice was dripping on to the table. When the ice melted sufficiently the handkerchief would fall to the table; for those who were impatient there was a hammer. It was a very beautiful and moving piece. What stops this from being a piece of physical-based performance?

I have other questions and other problems and, as you can see, I haven't thought all of these through in great philosophical detail. To sum up my definition of physical theatre I'd restate that (i) both process and performance are based on the principle that the movement and gesture of the live human body is the essential component of theatre and (ii) that performances are devised by the performers whether in response to a pre-existent text or from their other material and (iii) that without either of the above two components we lose what made the idea of physical theatre distinctive. [. . .]

I think that if we don't want to stick to some manageable definition of physical theatre and we do want to expand the terms of MAG in order to take into account all of the members' performance interests then perhaps we should change our name. I think that we all exist with multiple identities and that MAG gives space to one (or two) of mine; I don't think it would be MAG if it tried to take account of all of the diversity in the world of performance. But if we're going that way, why continue to call ourselves 'Mime Action Group' because we're abandoning the idea of mime except in an all-embracing sense which ultimately says nothing? Perhaps we should be called Total Theatre Group (TTG), not such a sweet acronym of course, and say that we're interested in all things to do with theatre (Pantheatre?).

In the end then, I don't find the new definition helpful except insofar as it demands that we think our definition more rigorously. Let's get more debate going!

Afterword (July 2006)

In this response I was still trying to keep alive the idea that there was something which we could define as 'physical theatre', although I thought I might be going against the tide. I didn't (and don't) think it made sense to say that physical theatre was somehow 'indefinable' and I attempted a simple definition in this report. I felt that the proposed alternative, 'physical-based performance', wasn't particularly helpful and there were other members of MAG with similar concerns. Mark Evans, for example, recognised the need for a 'more flexible term than mime', if the changes in practice since the mid-1980s were to be reflected. He was, however, sceptical about the term 'physical-based performance', feeling that it lacked definition, and was also concerned that:

> MAG should not be a forum that simply validates anything that 'moves' – though dialogues with associated forms is important – neither should it stand as judge and juror – it should however assert the value of the 'physical performance' with passion and authority. If we are not careful our 'difference' will disappear as we widen to encompass too much. (Evans, 1996)[1]

I suggested the name Total Theatre Group as a way of indicating that the organisation might be going too far away from the core of mime/physical theatre, but it wasn't something I was comfortable with. There's perhaps an irony that MAG mutated into Total Theatre Network after this, but my belief is that the decision had nothing to do with my response.

Notes

1   Evans' response to the MAG vision statement is an unpublished document and I'm grateful for his permission to quote from it. In my report on the Moving into Performance Symposium, which was in press from 1994 but didn't appear until 1997, I wrote: 'Rigid definitions and boundaries of the different genre of performance are undesirable and could result in mime being redefined in terms of the silent whiteface. On the other hand boundaries which are too ambiguous could leave mime/physical theatre practitioners without any sense of identity or community. Perhaps all we can realistically hope for is a provisional grouping around Wittgensteinian notions of "family resemblance"' (Chamberlain, 1997, p. 89).

References

Chamberlain, Franc (1997) 'Moving into Performance', *Contemporary Theatre Review* 6(1): 85–96, Amsterdam: Harwood Academic Publishers.
Craig, Edward Gordon (1980) *On the Art of the Theatre*, New York: Heinemann.

SECTION 4

Preparation and Training

Essay 4

Reframing the journey

■ Lorna Marshall

THE FIELD OF PHYSICAL PERFORMANCE and its training processes is wonderfully rich and diverse, but it can be very confusing for both students and teachers. Ironically, most problems and arguments within this field do not originate in the actual work of the body. They originate in the mind. We do not always think with sufficient clarity about our practice.

First, there is a term 'physical performance' which implies there is such a thing as 'non-physical performance'. This is a false distinction; all performance is 'physical'. No performer can sing an aria, dance in *Swan Lake*, swing on a trapeze, act in *Hamlet*, kill her husband in a television soap opera, or do stand-up comedy without a body. No one can even perform on radio without the voice passing through the physical matrix. What the audience sees and hears is a body (which includes the voice) manifesting thought, action, reaction, and feeling, within concrete time and space, and within a particular style. The style may vary from virtually abstract movement patterns (in the case of classical ballet), through clear, but non-demonstrated physical choices (in the case of 'naturalistic' acting in film and television), to bodies that are not visibly present (in the case of radio). Sometimes the body advertises its expertise and sometimes the skill is concealed, but the body itself is always present. And since the key site of performance is the human body, it is clear that training for all performers, irrespective of style, should be focused here.

There is nothing new in this idea; for decades practitioners have acknowledged the primacy of the body in performance, and the need for training to reflect this reality. In addition, there is currently great interest on the part of the students, and clear desire on the part of the providers of training. There is also no lack of intelligent and creative analysis (as is clear in the excellent selections in this section). Teachers continue to devise inspired exercises, students search for classes that enable them to work in this area, and training administrators attempt to find space for the latest 'Physical Technique'. But somehow all of this expertise and enthusiasm is failing to produce concrete results; this should be a golden age for performers in all styles, and yet, somehow, the physical potential is not being realised.

So where does the problem lie, and how can it be addressed? The core issue is insufficient clarity about the training journey, and a lack of understanding about the factors that influence its effectiveness.

We can create a framework for training consisting of three elements; outcome, process, and applications. *Outcome* refers to what we desire training to achieve. *Process* refers to the exercises or technical systems that the student experiences in order to achieve some aspect of the desired outcome. *Applications* refers to the factors that promote or impede the work. Simply expressed, *applications* affect *process* in the achievement of *outcome*. Since there are many excellent *processes* available and plenty of discussion on methodology, I will focus my attention on the other two areas: *outcome* and *application*.

When designing a training journey (for yourself or your students) it is important to start your thinking with *outcome* (what you want to achieve) not *process* (which technique you use to get there). Unfortunately, the opposite tends to occur; teachers and students too often focus solely on *process*. In addition, people can become emotionally attached to certain systems or techniques, believing that the chosen approach is innately superior, or a universal panacea. When this occurs, debate on training becomes a competition between strongly defended *processes*; people argue about which exercises or systems of training are superior. In fact most *processes* are in themselves useful and effective, so this debate is counter-productive.

The real question is, does *process* X offer the best means of achieving *outcome* Y? If your desired *outcome* (on the level of physical skill) is slow, relaxed flow of movement, then Tai Chi is a good *process*. If your desired *outcome* (also on the level of physical skill) is sharp reactions and rapid changes in rhythm, then Tai Chi is no longer the most effective alternative, and you would need to look elsewhere. Defining your *outcome* clearly and precisely at every level of the training journey enables *process* exercises and techniques to find their appropriate context and role.

So the first requirement when thinking about training is to create a clear and detailed definition of *outcome*. Most people, either formally or informally, have desired outcomes built into their training, but quite often these are unspoken and unshared. It is useful for outcomes to be overt, tightly defined, and multi-levelled. And shared. Otherwise what the teacher thinks they are teaching and what the student thinks they are learning may be quite different.

We need at least three time-based levels of outcome; *broad outcomes* (that reflect long term goals, e.g. the definition of what kind of performer is being trained), *mid-level outcomes* that reflect stage by stage goals (what you wish to achieve year by year and term by term), and *task-specific outcomes*, which focus on short term detail (what is encountered in that particular day's journey). There is another axis of outcomes which reflect the specific focus or subject; is the outcome a *technical skill* (e.g. the ability to manipulate the body according to the stylistic demands of classical ballet), or a *deep process* (e.g. practising the skill of independent creation without supervision), or a *professional/personal skill* (e.g. the ability to assess the usefulness of criticism and use or ignore it accordingly)? These two types of outcome (time-based and focus-based) need to be integrated with each other. They also need to be flexible and responsive to the abilities and needs of the particular student cohort.

As mentioned above, it is also important for both students and teachers to check whether the student's own desired *outcome* matches that of the teacher. Students, either consciously or unconsciously, are always pursuing their own goals in a learning context. And when this goal is different from the teacher's desired *outcome*, confusion arises. If the student is pursuing 'wild, free release' and the teacher wants 'precision and attention to detail', there is a need for discussion, and negotiation. In addition, some students subconsciously pursue non-relevant *outcomes* (such as 'being popular'). Again this requires discussion and clarity on both sides.

Once *outcome* has been defined, *process* is selected. Choices are made about which techniques, exercises and encounters will be most effective in achieving the desired *outcome*.

The third key element in considering the training journey is *applications*. We need to examine what factors could promote or impede learning, once *outcome* has been defined and *process* selected. These might be *structural* factors such as timing and duration (repeated classes versus a single extended workshop), *interpersonal* (various aspects of the teacher–student dynamic) or *sociological* (cultural factors). Obviously, there are many application factors, which cannot be discussed in the space of this essay. Instead I will select one element of *applications* (cultural philosophy of the body) and examine how it impacts on a single area of training (the warm-up).

As a teacher, my desired *broad outcome* for training is 'a performer who fully owns his or her body and can use it easily and confidently, to communicate accurately to the audience, within a wide variety of contexts and styles'. This goal is fairly universal; other people might use different words, but essentially most teachers and students have a similar aim. This *outcome* in turn requires an essentially positive and active engagement with the body on the part of the performer, in order to create confident use and ease of action and exploration. Yet in the West, our culturally embedded attitudes to the body are essentially negative. Despite the rhetoric of fitness, health and beauty, there is a strong current of distaste for the body within the broader society. We may dutifully change our physicality (through exercise, training, diet, or surgery) to fit some particular ideal, but there is very little delight in or curiosity about the body's subtle workings. Nor is there a real understanding of its prime role in our encounters with the world. This essentially negative viewpoint is the precise opposite to the body attitude that most performers need. This cultural element impedes the *application* of *process*, and it does so in a detailed and precise fashion.

There are two main cultural models of the body in Western cultures, and both of these involve dualistic thinking about the body (in the context of this essay I am discussing Western models of training and encounter, with a primarily Eurocentric focus). The first is derived from Early Christianity (although it had its roots in the ideas of Plato). In this model, the body and the soul/mind were seen as distinctly separate, and actively opposed. The 'higher functions' of thought, imagination and conscience resided in the soul/mind, while the body was seen as inherently sinful, inferior and brutish, and operated as an active impediment to the soul/mind's development. It required discipline, punishment and strict control in order to prevent it returning to a state of lazy bestiality, and so damaging the soul's capacity for union with God. This concept was re-invented by Descartes during the Enlightenment; he re-formed the religious dimension of the soul/mind, but kept the idea of the body's innate inferiority, and its problematic nature. And this sense of the fundamental inferiority and untrustworthiness of the body still permeates our society, manifesting in many different ways.

For performers, this attitude affects *how* we work with the body. Irrespective of style, many training practices emphasise discipline, rigour and transcendence of discomfort, and elevate these concepts to ideals. What is won through difficult endeavour is seen as worthwhile, while what comes easily is devalued. This was clearly evident in the 'no pain, no gain' ideology which came to the fore in the 1980s, alongside the boom in the fitness industry, but it has more subtle manifestations in the fundamental belief that the only way to 'train' a body is via focus and control, and relentless effort. Hard work is good, while discomfort is often welcomed as a sign of positive change. Pleasure in body use is seen as a form of self-indulgence – you might have the occasional fun 'game' in class – but it is seen as separate to the serious work of training. Yet how can a performer be playful and creative with a body that is seen as requiring harsh control? There is a contradiction here between the actual requirements of a performer, and the unspoken cultural belief that influences the process of training.

The second key cultural attitude to the body reflects nineteenth-century engineering principles. With the advance of scientific thinking after the Renaissance, involving the rediscovery of classical principles of methodical enquiry, there was a more accurate understanding of how the body actually functioned; how the blood flowed, how the muscles operated, and so on. In the nineteenth century this became allied to the ideology of advancement via industrialisation. From this 'engineering' viewpoint, the body was seen as a series of mechanical functions, of levers, pulleys and pumps, which could be rendered more efficient via the intelligent control of the mind. Again the mind (which had usurped the position of the soul as the seat of self/intelligence) was seen as fundamentally separate and superior; this time as the driver in the control box, supervising the smooth running of the machinery.

In terms of training, this philosophy helps ensure that bodywork techniques respect the actual anatomical structures and functioning of the body, which is valuable and essential. But it also contains the unspoken idea that the body itself is an inert structure, requiring external manipulation and control.

This perspective also led to another unhelpful concept for performer training – the unexamined use of the word 'movement' to define all aspects of physical engagement. This linguistic description frames the body as a passive object moved by the mind in accordance with consciously chosen patterns. This philosophy of conscious control and patterned manipulation of the anatomy has shaped dance training, and is of clear use in this context, but it is not directly relevant to other performing styles. The aim of a dancer is to *move well* within the patterns of the given dance style, but other performers do not have this as a prime objective. Singers and actors may occasionally need to *move well* (be able to dance or use stylised gesture) but fundamentally their broad aim is *connected physical life*, whereby the body is capable of revealing thought, feeling and reactions, plus the ability to transform according to the demand of character. Which is not the same as *moving well*.

In addition, the use of the term 'movement' reinforces the cultural attitude of separation between the body and the other aspects of the performer (mind, emotions and voice). In terms of actor training (compared to dancers) this creates a problem, which is further reinforced by the separation of movement from voice and acting in most drama school syllabuses. While there are some very good reasons for discrete classes (such as the provision of sessions of technical detail), there is a risk of actively impeding the development of *connected physical life*, which is the desirable *outcome* for actors.

Which brings us to the core of the problem with this aspect of *application*; neither of these two cultural models is based on an accurate understanding of how the human organism actually functions.

The common use of the two words 'mind' and 'body' in everyday speech and training vocabulary reflects a false perception; in reality the organism is already a single physical/ electrical/chemical unit. What we call 'mind' (thoughts, feelings, reactions, memories) can be witnessed scientifically as a dizzyingly rapid and complex series of connections within the brain, which is itself a physical organ. When a strong thought or emotion or reaction arises in the brain it will then trigger electrical or chemical signals, which pass via the blood and/or nervous systems to organs and muscles, which in turn provoke muscular shifts leading to movement, or stimulus to organs leading to chemical alterations, including release of hormones and brain neurotransmitters. These in turn feed back to the brain, producing different signals in different parts of the organ itself, which in turn triggers new thought/feeling/response. And so on; an endless electrical-chemical feedback loop. In fact the mind and body are like the palm and back of the hand; opening or closing the palm of the hand inevitably affects the back of the hand, and vice versa. This fused cycle exists in our daily lives. We are nervous; our pulse rate speeds up, our palms get sweaty, we need to go to the toilet, we fidget, and our thoughts run around like mice in a cage.

This is a simplistic explanation, and the detailed research into how the physical matrix functions in practice is still in its infancy, but the basic position is clear. The organism is a single inseparable unit, and our physical being (including the brain) is the actual site of emotions, thought, reactions, and other aspects of the inner landscape. What this understanding means is that the body is not a brutish inferior requiring control, discipline and occasional punishment. Or a machine to be kept running at maximum efficiency. Rather it is our 'self'.

This lack of understanding of how the human organism actually functions, combined with cultural beliefs that foster separation and debasement of the body, affect *application* of training at every level. The warm-up is a good example.

Although most performing styles promote warm-ups as a valuable part of performer preparation, the precise operation is rarely examined. To begin with, embedded cultural attitudes shape ideas about the desired *outcome* of a warm-up. Typically, people cite safety issues as the prime objective. But this focus is a consequence of the engineering view of the body; the machinery must be made ready to function efficiently. While safe physical use is obviously a very important factor, it is not the whole picture. The true *outcome* of a warm-up is not smooth engagement of the machine but transformation. Performers need to shift from a daily sense of self and physical use to the place of 'full ownership and easy and confident engagement' within the given context of that particular day's work. And the latter point is important; a warm-up for a comedy should be different from that for a tragedy, since the desired outcome in terms of performance is different.

Cultural models also affect the *process* used in a warm-up. Many warm-ups consist of fixed exercises that are repeated each time; people tend to create a mechanical programme of warm-up exercises that they do as a matter of habit. As noted above, this prevents the warm-up responding to the specific needs of the performing situation. It can also actively promote disconnection. When warm-ups follow this pattern, the performer processes the body like a machine through the routine while the mind wanders elsewhere.

Then there is the emotional dimension. It is very easy for a warm-up to become boring and dutiful, or even something unpleasant that has to be endured. And these reactions in turn connect to the Christian/Cartesian idea of the body as the site for discipline and subjugation. In this way, a mechanical warm-up can confirm and reinforce both of the negative cultural attitudes to the body. Which creates a paradox; since performers need to actively engage with their bodies in order to communicate effectively to the audience, a warm-up that promotes disengagement and duty is counterproductive. Ideally, warm-up exercises need to help the entire organism come alive and alert, and engender a sense of pleasure and ownership.

In addition, a good warm-up truly understands and utilises the interconnection of the mind and body. The transformation offered by a warm-up is for the entire entity, not just the physical structure. Many years ago I was working in Australia with Gregorii Ditiatkovski, a director from the Maly Theatre (St Petersburg) on a production of *A Doll's House*. Each morning he would tell me exactly which creative impulse he wanted the actors to use in that day's rehearsal, and I would lead the warm-up in such a way as to encourage that precise outcome. Once it was emotional availability, the next day it was clarity of perception, while on a third day it was attention to moment-by-moment unfolding of the situation. As a director, he understood the connection between body experience and inner response, and he also knew how to use the power of a warm-up to transform the actors in precise mental and emotional ways.

A warm-up is a central part of a performer's preparation, yet lack of clarity on *outcome*, together with unexamined cultural assumptions about the body which shape *application*, can prevent the *process* (often involving very useful exercises) from achieving the goal of supporting dynamic performance.

Unfortunately, this lack of clear thinking about what we do permeates the wider field of training, and sadly prevents the many excellent training approaches having their full impact. Too often we focus on *process* alone, rather than initially defining *outcome*, and then selecting *process* accordingly; a case of cart before horse. In addition, the third element – *applications* – is rarely considered, yet its impact is enormous. One key area within the field of *applications* that must be addressed is our assumptions about what we are working with; what is the human entity? There is ignorance about how the organism actually functions, and instead of a genuinely useful understanding, we too often have unspoken beliefs (based on outmoded cultural models) which derail the journey. As both teachers and students, if we do not understand the process involved in creating a useful learning journey, or understand what we are actually working with, the wonderful ideas, excellent techniques and approaches, and enthusiastic commitment are rendered ineffective.

Useful reading

Damasio, Antonio (2000) *The Feeling of What Happens*, London: Heinemann.
Damasio, Antonio (2004) *Looking for Spinoza*, London: Vintage.
Gibbs, Raymond W. (2006) *Embodiment and Cognitive Science*, Cambridge: Cambridge University Press.
Marshall, Lorna (2001) *The Body Speaks*, London: Methuen.
Marshall, Lorna (2008) *Getting It Right*, London: Methuen.

CHAPTER 28

Étienne Decroux

Photo essay: *Sports*

Photographs by Étienne Bertrand Weill

THESE UNDATED PHOTOGRAPHS show the 'essence' of Decroux's approach to the body. Wearing the minimum of clothing to 'free' the body and his version of the 'neutral mask' to remove the expressive face, they present 'poses' which reveal the angles and dynamics of the articulate body; it's musculature and lines. The title *Sports* perhaps indicates the purpose: to show the body as something that has weight and grace, that works and must be worked.

Figure 28.2. Photograph by Étienne Bertrand Weill.

Figure 28.1. Photograph by Étienne Bertrand Weill.

Figure 28.4. Photograph by Étienne Bertrand Weill.

Figure 28.3. Photograph by Étienne Bertrand Weill.

Figure 28.6. Photograph by Étienne Bertrand Weill.

Figure 28.5. Photograph by Étienne Bertrand Weill.

CHAPTER 29

Michael Chekhov

To the actor; Appendix: a practical guide to the application of the Michael Chekhov psychological gesture (PG) technique.

Translation and commentary by
Andrei Malaev-Babel

> To George Shdanoff
> who shared with me the strenuous work, excitement and joys of the Chekhov
> Theater. His directorial ability and pedagogic experiments with the principles
> of the method I introduce in this book were stimulating influences.
>
> This new publication of *To the Actor* is dedicated to the memory of Beatrice
> Straight (1918–2001). With admiration and thanks for her all-important role
> in the original creation of this book.

THE CONCEPT OF PSYCHOLOGICAL GESTURE remains one of the most
popular aspects of Michael Chekhov's creative heritage. The goal of this appendix
is to provide every actor and reader with a detailed guide to the practical application of
the Psychological Gesture (PG) Technique . . .

Fantastic PG

Michael Chekhov is widely known not only as a great theatrical master-teacher and
theoretician, but also as one of Russia's greatest twentieth-century actors. As an actor,
Chekhov followed a unique trend in theatrical art, one described by the Russian director
Evgeny Vakhtangov as 'fantastic realism'. All of the characters created by Chekhov at the
Moscow Art Theater . . . had a tendency to appear larger than life, or even exaggerated.
At the same time, they never became flat or psychologically shallow, and never turned

into caricatures. In other words, the actor always realistically justified his characters, both emotionally and psychologically. His characters remained complex human beings, but perhaps the kind of human beings one might see in a dream or imagine in their fantasies.

> You can make your PG resemble more or less everyday naturalistic gestures. You can also create a *fantastic* PG. Through it you will be able to convey the most intimate, the most original artistic concepts.

These Chekhov words as well as the very term of the Fantastic PG provide us with an invaluable insight into the hidden goal of the Chekhov Method . . .

> (1) For the role as a whole.
>   You can use the PG to master the character as a whole.

For example, while working upon the part of The Mayor from Gogol's *The Inspector General*, you might discover that his will has a tendency to strive forward (gesture) in a cowardly manner (quality). You create a simple PG, corresponding with your first impression. Let us assume that this gesture will be the following one (see drawing 1). Having fulfilled and concretely

Figure 29.1 Drawing 1

experienced it, you will now feel an urge for its further development. Your intuition might prompt you: *down to the earth* (gesture), *heavily and slowly* (quality) (see drawing 2). The new experience of the PG will lead you to new movements. Now it might become, perhaps, like this: the gesture receives an inclination to the side (canniness), hands clench into fists (intense will), shoulders lift up, the entire body slightly bows towards the earth, knees bend (cowardliness), feet are slightly turned inside (secretiveness) (see drawing 3) . . .

(3) For separate scenes.

With the help of the PG you can also penetrate, regardless of the role you perform, into the essence of each *separate scene*.

The essence of the scene is determined by characters' actions, their relationships, characterizations, atmosphere and the style of the scene, as well as its place within the composition of the entire play. While gradually creating the PG for the scene, always appeal to your creative intuition. The scene will appear before you as an *entirety*, despite all the variety and complexity of its elements. With the help of the PG, you will be able to see the predominant will and emotion of the scene clearly.

Figure 29.2 Drawing 2

Figure 29.3 Drawing 3

Let us take an example from *The Marriage* by Gogol (Act I, scene 19) . . .

With the arrival of the last groom, following the moment of awkward silence, the gesture of the scene looms before you. The waves of hope and fear ascend and descend heavily and awkwardly within the space that seems huge and empty. From the very beginning the characters in the scene are surrounded by an atmosphere of tension. While seeking a gesture for a scene, you might experience a desire to embrace as much space around you as possible. Your arms sway slightly, as if they were holding a large sphere, filled with air (see drawing 4). Your arms, shoulders and chest contract slightly. The quality of hope and fear permeates your gesture. The destiny of all the participants in the scene should be decided within the period of five to ten minutes. Emptiness and uncertainty become unbearable. The grooms initiate a conversation on the subject of the weather. The tension grows, and the space contracts further:

Figure 29.4 Drawing 4

your hands press the sphere and grow steadier. The increasing tension is now fraught with explosive energy. The grooms, as if throwing themselves into the fire, approach the awkward subject closely. The space around you, that used to be huge and empty, becomes extremely contracted and tense: your arms lower and press the space surrounding you with the utmost force (see drawing 5). The bride, being unable to tolerate this tension and shame, runs away – the atmosphere explodes! (see drawing 6) . . .

Figure 29.5 Drawing 5

Another important component of the PG Technique that clearly appears in both Chekhov's example and Remisoff's illustrations is the category of the imaginary space. Chekhov first describes the space as a large sphere, huge and empty. (This sphere is almost visible in drawing 5.) What follows is the transformation of the space under the influence of the gesture. The sphere is first being gradually contracted, its quality changing from emptiness to tension, and finally the sphere explodes.

> (4) For the score of atmospheres.
>   You can use the PG in order to master the score of atmospheres.
>
> As I already mentioned, the atmosphere has its predominant will (dynamics) and feeling and, according to these elements, the atmosphere can be easily

Figure 29.6 Drawing 6

realized by means of their inherent gesture and quality. Let's take another example. The final scene from Gorky's play *The Lower Depths* gives us a characteristic example of a strong atmosphere that appears unexpectedly. The tenants of a shelter are preparing for their nightly debauchery . . .

With the arrival of the Baron the atmosphere changes abruptly. It starts with a shock, and its tension in the beginning is at a maximum. Its strength gradually weakens by the end. Its predominant initial quality can be experienced as sharp pain and amazement. It changes into melancholic despondency by the end. You are making your first attempt to discover the PG. It might be, for example, like this (see drawing 7): your hands are thrown up (amazement) quickly (power, force), your fists are clenched (pain and force). Perhaps you will discover that the quality of pain from the first shock can be more strongly realized through a different gesture; having thrown up your arms, you cross them above your head (see drawing 8). After a pause, you will slowly lower your arms with an increasing quality of melancholy, and hold them close to

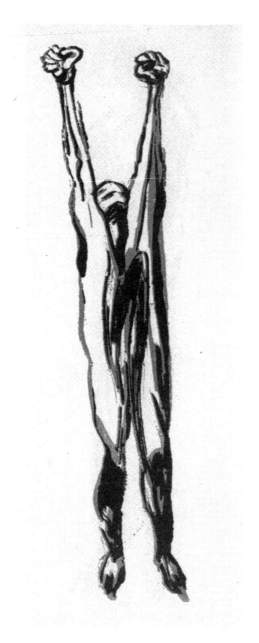

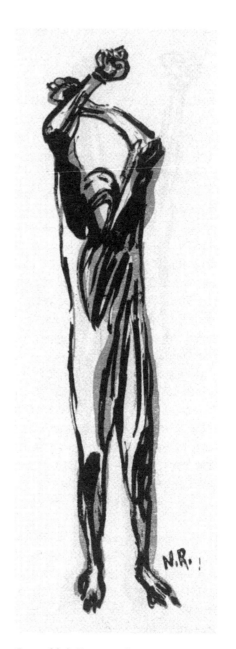

Figure 29.7 Drawing 7

Figure 29.8 Drawing 8

your body (depression). The ending phase of the atmosphere is associated with helplessness – you will gradually unclench your fists, lower your shoulders, stretch your neck and straighten your legs while pressing them tightly against each other (see drawing 9).

Having executed these kinds of PG's, you and your partners will get the feeling of the scene's atmosphere. It will radiate into the audience through any blocking suggested to you by the director and any lines given to you by the author. It will unite you with both your partners and the audience; it will inspire your acting and free you from clichés and bad stage habits . . .

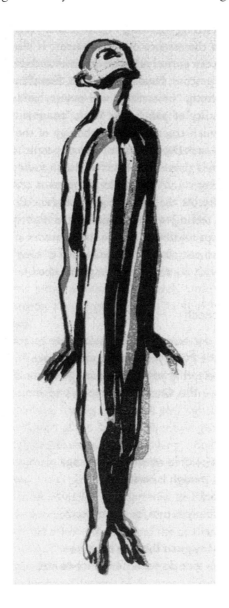

Figure 29.9 Drawing 9

(5) For the speech.

I will attempt, by example, to demonstrate to you the practical application of the PG in your work upon the role.

Let us suppose, that you are preparing Horatio's monologue in the scene where the Ghost first appears to him (Shakespeare's *Hamlet*) . . .

As before, you are appealing to your imagination. While listening carefully to Horatio's speech and looking closely at his movements, you make the first attempt to create a PG for his speech. It appears to you as an ardent, violent *thrust forward*, as a desire to detain the Ghost and *penetrate* its mystery. Suppose the first 'draft' of your PG was like this: a strong thrust forward with your entire body, your right arm also striving forward and upward (see drawing 10). You rehearse the gesture many times and then try to say the lines of the monologue (this time without a gesture), until you can hear the general character of your gesture with its qualities affecting the lines that you say.

Figure 29.10 Drawing 10

Now step-by-step you start searching for the details of the monologue. Perhaps the first moment, prompted by your creative intuition, will be the contrast distinguishing the beginning of the monologue from its ending. Horatio starts addressing the Ghost firmly, and yet with a feeling of awe. A plea can be heard in his words. Yet the Ghost starts to leave without giving an answer. Horatio's efforts are useless. He's growing impatient. His confidence is now turning into bewilderment, his awe is replaced with offensive insistence, his plea becomes an order, and instead of solemnity it is harsh irritability that can now be heard in his words. You already have two gestures: one mirrors the will and the quality of the beginning, the other – the will and the quality of the end (see drawings 10 and 11). They are based upon the principle of polarity . . .

Now let's take a look at the first part of the monologue: imagine the vague expectation accumulating in Horatio's heart as he is waiting for the meeting

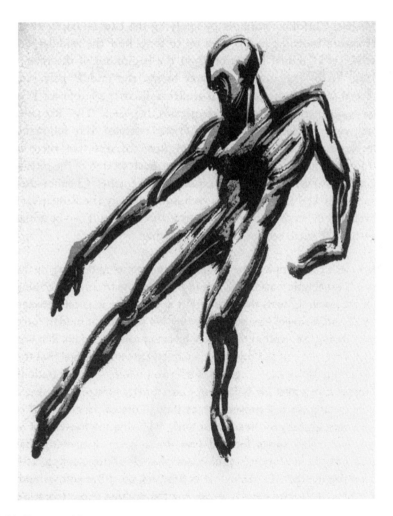

Figure 29.11 Drawing 11

with the mysterious Ghost. The tension between belief and disbelief has been agitating his soul! What hidden force has already lived within him before he ever pronounced his first line in the presence of the mysterious Ghost! Do you now feel that the beginning of the monologue has its own prelude – a preparation? Express it in a gesture: before your arm thrusts forward, it makes a wide, strong yet soft movement, as though drawing a circle within the space above your head. Your body, following the movement of your arm, also sways forward (see drawing 12). Everything that accumulated in Horatio's soul in anticipation of the meeting, as if *preceding* the speech, comes out in this prelude . . .

You also might encounter a case where what's taking place on the stage happens to be one of the important moments of the play, where not only every movement but every sound and quality of your voice plays a crucial part in the development of the action. At the same time, the lines provided by the author are insignificant, inexpressive and even weak in their content. In this case, all the responsibility lies upon you as an actor. You should fill the insignificant lines with the power and depth of the moment. Here the PG might do you an invaluable service. You will create it based on the psychological content of the given situation, and you will use it as a foundation for both

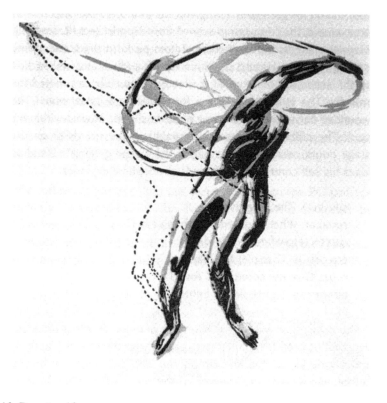

Figure 29.12 Drawing 12

your acting and the author's text. Let's take as an example the 'mousetrap scene' from *Hamlet*. Hamlet presents a play at court. Actors perform the scene of poisoning the King. Hamlet observes King Claudius, and his reaction to the scene will tell Hamlet if Claudius has truly committed the murder. The tense atmosphere foreshadows a catastrophe. The wounded conscience of the king arouses chaotic powers within his soul. The crucial moment is approaching; the murderer on the stage pours poison into the ear of the sleeping 'king'. Claudius loses his self-control. The pregnant atmosphere explodes . . .

You are searching for a PG. Despite the complexity of the moment, your gesture should always remain clear and simple. Perhaps your creative intuition prompts you to *a wide gesture of falling backward, flat on your back*, into the realm of unconsciousness and uncertainty, into the darkness. Your hands and arms are powerfully thrust upward and thrown back along with the entire body and head. Your palms and fingers open in self-defense, *in pain, fear and coldness* (the gesture's qualities).

Having thrust backwards up to the bodily limits, you continue to fall deeper and deeper in your imagination (drawing 13). Rehearse the gesture, perfecting and developing it, and when all its forces and qualities start resonating in your lines, they will fill your phrase with the previously lacking significance of the moment . . .

An imaginary space and time.

Exercise. Start with simple gestures: lift up your arm in a moderate tempo, while imagining that *a long period of time* is passing. Do the same gesture, accompanying it in your imagination by the notion of *a very short period of time*.

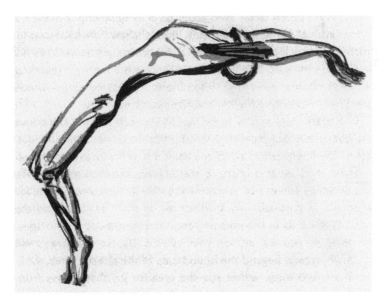

Figure 29.13 Drawing 13

Continue with such simple exercises until you feel that your imagination has gained a certain convincing power.

Do the gesture of opening in a moderate tempo (see drawing 14). Continue it in your imagination for an indefinite period of time, spreading it upon an endless distance. Imagine the same gesture produced instantly within a confined space, while actually doing it in the same moderate tempo.

Do the same with the gesture of closing.

Start with an opened gesture and then close it, contracting a formerly endless space to the size of a tiny dot (see drawing 15). Do this gesture first in a long period of time, then, in a short period of time. The same gesture

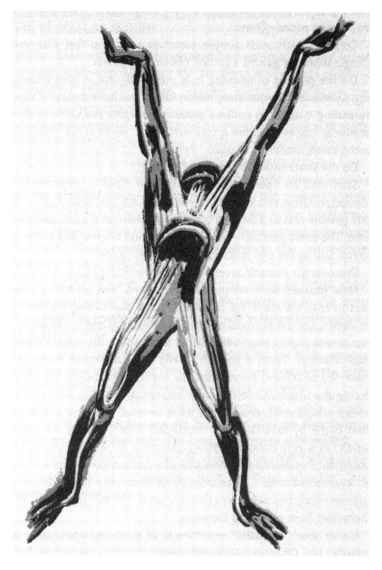

Figure 29.14 Drawing 14

– first in a long period of time, in a confined space, and by the end quickly, in an endless space.

Discover for yourself several variations with the PG . . .

Michael Chekhov calls on the contemporary actor to master concepts of imaginary time and space. For an actor, just becoming aware of these categories, it can bring new depth and complexity to their work on stage. However, it is the trained ability to transform time and space on stage with the power of the actor's imagination which helps actors to convey the inner life of their characters and gives them true power over their audience. The technique of creating imaginary time and space can be applied directly in rehearsal and performance. It can also be used in the actor's work upon the Psychological Gesture . . .

The concept of the PG would not be complete without these two categories. The deep inner connection that exists in between imaginary time, imaginary space and Psychological Gesture should be explored and exercised by every actor interested in mastering the principles of the Michael Chekhov Technique.

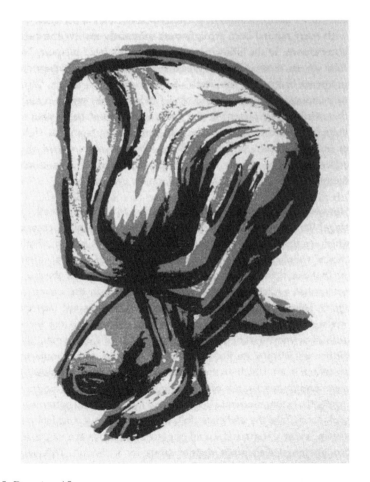

Figure 29.15 Drawing 15

CHAPTER 30

Anne Dennis

The articulate body

The physical training of the actor

In memory of Étienne Decroux

The actor's physical language: important concepts in preparing the articulate body

THE NEUTRAL BODY, IMMOBILE, breathing, is ready to act; the elements of motion – rhythm, intensity, and design – are at its disposal. The theatre space is ready to come alive.

The neutral – a beginning

'I am', 'I have presence', 'I have weight', 'I exist in space', 'I am ready to act (move)' – this physical state we will call the 'zero'. We are describing the physical and emotional neutral. It is from this point that the actor will be free to build and discover. The neutral is the takeoff point and landing place for the actor.

It is exactly that – a neutral body. The actor is immobile, breathing gently, weight somewhat forward, secretly relaxed . . .

Immobility – 'a living immobility' (Decroux)

In neutral, the actor is immobile. An actor without skill finds stillness very difficult. He squirms, unable to sustain and express that which he has identified inside . . . However, it is in stillness that the actor begins to create. He senses the inner rhythm through his breath. Through the breath the actor becomes and remains vibrant, alive, ready. It is when these moments cannot be sustained that the actor finds his body dying in the space. Character and motivation become lost. The actor becomes an empty shell, waiting for a piece of business or words that will offer him a lifeline into shallow, but safe, waters . . .

Stillness commands great power and authority in the theatre space. An actor must learn how to use it. Stillness gives clarity to relationships. It brings focus to a moment or rest to the end of a thought (much as a full stop does in diction). It gives the audience space in which to take in the process leading up to and causing an action; stillness permits the transitional moments to be seen . . .

Breath – communicator of feeling

Neutral, immobile, the actor breathes . . . Breath expresses emotion. The slightest movement of the chest can betray all that is happening inside. One image that Decroux used that I find very useful, but which is often misunderstood, is the idea of the 'nipples as eyes'. One has just to look at an actor whose face is covered to discover the enormous clarity with which feelings are expressed through the chest. It is through the chest that all the subtleties of the interior become visible.

Three elements of movement – the basis of the actor's grammar

Decroux noted and defined three elements at the actor's disposal when using movement as his means of dramatic expression. As physical actors, we have the design, the intensity, and the rhythm of a movement or movements with which to work, in bringing our ideas to their visual theatrical form. It is important to understand how these elements may serve the actor and how they affect that which the audience sees and understands:

> *design*: the line created in space, the aesthetic use of space
> *intensity*: the amount of intensity given a moment or a movement
> *rhythm*: accents and lengths through which movements' relationships are
>   expressed

1 *Design* refers to the image created by the actor(s) in the space, and what the audience sees and understands by these images. The positioning of a body or bodies creates what I call a 'stage picture', and it is through these theatrical images we communicate our specific ideas to the audience . . .

The design created by movement has both a narrative and aesthetic value. It can be however limiting and two-dimensional. It is through the intensity and rhythm with which the movement is executed that meaning and dramatic value are achieved. All movement can be analysed as a rotation, inclination, or translation, or some combination thereof. This is to say that all movement can be categorized as being an example of one of these possibilities. The movement can be composed of isolated movement (a combination of any of the isolated parts of the body) or the movement can be created by the total movement of the body, as in a block . . .

2 *Intensity* refers to the level of tension a movement uses in conveying a theatrical moment. It is the primary means we have to focus the audience on what we deem important . . .

Much like the close-up in film, intensity forces the audience to look at the specific. For example, if there is one relaxed hand and one tense hand, the tense hand will dramatically dominate, and that is where the audience will be focused.

> Intensity replaces time.
> Effort is shown through intensity.
> Quickness and intensity results in the compression of time.
> Repeated, intense rhythm can give feeling of mass heartbeat, the feeling of
>   the mob, for example.
> Intensity is the means by which the actor directs the audience's attention.

3 *Rhythm* is the speed at which a movement is executed. Rhythm controls the level at which the audience will take in an action. An audience's understanding and clarity will differ depending on whether it has been offered a fleeting glimpse or a long, focused stare. It will help dictate what the audience sees and in what detail.

Highly stylized theatre will usually use non-natural rhythm as a means to get to the essence of a movement.

For the actor, rhythm is dictated by dramatic need, not a specific beat or music. Through rhythm the actor controls how the audience looks upon a specific dramatic event . . .

The body in space – using the theatrical space to make clear dramatic statements

When speaking of creating the stage picture we mean simply the actor's use of his physicality as a means to create a theatre image . . . Lines in space communicate specific ideas and specific relationships and are based on shared, learned understandings. The slightest change in image can easily change the audience's perception of a given moment . . .

Many things can happen to an image given the slightest change in the use of what I call the 'lines of space'. For example, an audience's understanding of an action will be determined by whether the action is carried out in a direct line, facing the audience or on an oblique line, using the diagonal. Proximity (how close the characters are to one another) and attention (where they are looking) will influence how the audience interprets a relationship . . .

The actor will need to find a way technically to sustain, night after night, in new spaces of differing dimensions, differing shapes, and differing proximity to audience all that he has found through the process of rehearsal and previous performance. The same ideas must be conveyed through the same rhythms, tensions, designs. The actor depends on his physical awareness to make this possible.

CHAPTER 31

Jacques Lecoq

Movement technique

Physical and vocal preparation

Giving meaning to movement

THE STUDY OF HUMAN ANATOMY enabled me to develop an analytic method of physical preparation, directed towards expressivity and bringing into play each part of the body: feet, legs, hips, chest, shoulders, neck, head, arms, hands, getting a feel for the dramatic potential of each in turn. I have discovered, for instance, that when I move my head in ways dictated purely by geometry (side, forward, back) the result is: 'I listen', 'I look', 'I'm frightened'. In the theatre making a movement is never a mechanical act but must always be a gesture that is *justified*. Its justification may consist in an indication or an action, or even an inward state. I raise my arm, to indicate a place or point something out, to take an object off a shelf, or just because an inner emotion makes me feel like raising it. *Indications, actions, states*, these are the three ways of justifying a movement. They correspond to the three major dramatic modes: indications are related to *pantomime; actions take us towards commedia dell'arte, and states bring us back to drama . . .

Physical preparation does not aim to emulate a particular physical model, nor to impose established dramatic forms. It should assist everyone towards the fullest realisation of accurate movement. There should be no sense of the body 'getting in the way', nor of it feeding parasitically off what it should be conveying. Its foundation is *dramatic gymnastics*, in which every gesture, every attitude or movement is justified. I use elementary exercises, such as swinging the arms, forward or sideways bends of the trunk, swinging the legs, etc. These are all exercises generally used in physical warm-ups, to which we give meaning.

Arms raised and extended, a forward fall from the trunk flexes the body which bounces back up to the starting position.

When accomplished in a precise sequence, this movement exemplifies how we proceed in all our dramatic gymnastics. We begin by carrying it out mechanically, very simply, in order to see how it goes. Next, we try to enlarge the movement to test its limits, filling the largest possible space. The third stage is to concentrate especially on two essential phases in the movement, trying to understand their dramatic dynamics. They are the starting point, with arms extended, just before the trunk collapses, and the end of the movement, with the trunk upright again and the arms in the vertical, when the body is once again extended and the movement is about to fade, imperceptibly, into immobility.

These two moments, which precede and follow the extension of the body, carry a strong dramatic charge. The state of suspension just before the beginning is part of the dynamics of risk (risk of falling) and includes a sense of anguish which emerges clearly. Conversely, the concluding suspension is one of landing, returning to a state of calm, coming gradually closer to immobility and serenity.

Next, breathing comes into play. The same movement is done on a single exhalation, covering both the fall and the rebound, inhalation coming only after the return to the immobile, extended position. Once this breath control has been mastered, I begin to suggest parallel images, which introduce a dramatic dimension into the movement. Still using the same movement, the students imagine they are looking out to sea, following the rhythm of the waves. That can lead on to imagining a ball being thrown up into the air and falling back, with the fascination exerted by the beginning and the end of the movement: what is this instant of immobility between flying up and falling back? Does the ball remain for an instant suspended in mid-air? How? In this kind of movement drama makes its appearance at the very moment of suspension. Beforehand we are simply dealing with sports. Everyone who saw Nijinsky dance says that he remained suspended in mid-air. But how?

Dramatic gymnastics also have a vocal dimension, for it would be absurd to claim that voice can be separated from body. Each gesture possesses its own sonority, or voice, which I try to help the students discover. The utterance of a voice in space shares the same nature as the execution of a gesture: just as I can throw a discus in a stadium, I can throw my voice in space; just as I can aim for a mark, I can address someone who is some distance away from me. In the waves of the sea or in the bounce of a ball, just as in any other movement, gesture, breathing and voice join to form a single movement. In this one movement, it is possible to throw out a sound, a word, a poetic sentence or a dramatic line . . .

My conception of physical preparation is in disagreement with one aspect of the movement methods recommended to many actors. Frequently, these are gymnastic methods which I call 'comforting', since their principal aim is a feeling of wellbeing for those who practise them. The various relaxation methods which are invading drama training may possibly serve to calm certain fears, or to help an individual recover their sense of personal harmony, but they never deal with the relationship to acting. For an actor, the only internal harmony that matters is that of *play.

I reject the impulse which makes a teacher want to get his students to like him at any cost. This is pure demagogy . . .

Purely athletic exercises are equally insufficient for actor training. I have known actors who were extremely stiff in the gym, who nevertheless moved with wonderful suppleness on stage, and others who were very supple in training, but who were incapable of creating an illusion. Some had acting talent, others lacked it.

Another distortion can be caused by premature apprenticeship in the formal gestures belonging to styles or codes of classical dance or of fixed dramatic forms like those of oriental theatre. Such formal gestures, often insufficiently practised, set up physical circuits in the actor's body, which then become very difficult to justify, especially when the actor is young . . .

Finally, exercises in group dynamics – e.g. holding hands before beginning a performance – are very nice and helpful for the group. But not for a company of professional actors . . . In Italy they go on stage and play. That's my idea, too . . .

Movement analysis

Movement analysis applied to the human body and to nature, charting the economy of physical actions, is the foundation of the school's physical work. The things I had practised as an athlete naturally carried over into action mime. When I started, I used Georges Hébert's 'natural method', which analyses movement under eleven categories: *pulling, pushing, climbing, walking, running, jumping, lifting, carrying, attacking, defending, swimming.* These actions lay down circuits in the human body, through which emotions flow. Feelings, states and passions are expressed through gestures, attitudes and movements similar to those of physical actions. Young actors have to be aware of how the body can 'pull' or 'push' so that, when the need arises, they can express the different ways in which a character can 'pull' or 'push'. The analysis of a physical action does not mean expressing an opinion, but acquiring physical awareness which will form an indispensable basis for acting.

The foundation: natural everyday movements

I begin by analysing the movements of the human body based on three natural movements which occur in everyday life: *undulation, inverse undulation* and *eclosion.*

I discovered *undulation* as the principle of all physical effort in the sports stadium. It was on the stage of the theatre at Grenoble that I discovered *eclosion*. And it was at the rue du Bac, the first home of the school, that I perfected *inverse undulation*, discovering the meaning of conflict and character. This is how I identified the three principles of bodily movement, and with them the three main pathways of my teaching method.

Beyond their simple basis in physical movement, these three principles also provide analogous pathways to those of masked performance. *Eclosion* corresponds to the *neutral mask; undulation* to the *expressive mask in its first image; and *inverse undulation* brings us back to the *counter-mask . . .

Undulation is the human body's first movement, the one underlying all locomotion. Fishes in water undulate to achieve forward motion. Snakes in the grass also undulate. A child on all fours undulates as well, and humans in the upright position continue to undulate . . . Any undulating movement progresses from a point of leverage to a point of application. Undulation takes its leverage from the ground and effort is gradually transmitted to all the parts of the body until it reaches the point of application . . .

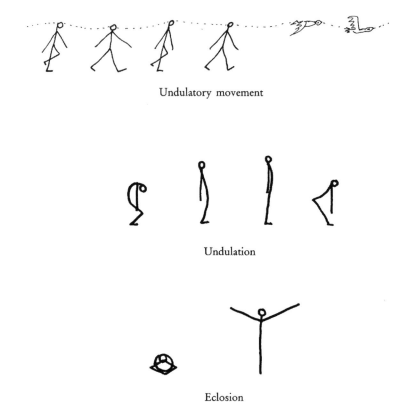

Undulatory movement

Undulation

Eclosion

Figure 31.1 Lecoq diagram of 'undulatory movement', 'undulation', 'eclosion'

Inverse undulation is the same movement, but inverted. Instead of starting from the leverage of the feet on the ground, it starts from the head, which initiates the movement by taking its lead from something outside me that sets me in motion . . . In a movement like this, which starts from the head, the whole body is mobilised. The mode employed is one of *dramatic indication*. Whereas undulation is a voluntary action, initiating movement from one point to another, inverse undulation always expresses dramatic reaction. In reality, all drama *inverts* the techniques of movement . . .

Balanced between the two preceding movements, *eclosion* opens up from the centre. It starts from a crouched position down on the ground, the body occupying the smallest possible space, and opens up to finish on the 'high cross' position, upright, legs together and arms extended above the horizontal. Eclosion consists in moving from one position to the other without a break and with each segment of the body following the same rhythm. Arms and legs arrive simultaneously at the extended position, no one part of the body preceding another. The difficulty is to find exactly the right balance and an unobstructed dynamic. Too often the upper part of the body reaches the end before the arms, simply because more attention is being given to it. Eclosion is a global sensation which can be performed in both directions: expanding or contracting.

Glossary

The following is a brief outline of technical terms or terms given special technical meanings by Jacques Lecoq in this book.

character mask See *expressive mask.*

counter-mask A mask which is played for the opposite of what it appears to represent.

dramatic gymnastics Exercises originating in the discipline of gymnastics which are put to use in developing acting students' physical and vocal abilities.

eclosion One of the movements drawn from nature that are explained in the section entitled 'Movement analysis'.

expressive mask A mask representing a particular character. Also named 'character mask'.

inverse undulation See undulation.

neutrality, neutral state The state prior to action or character creation, when the actor is in a state of perfect balance, presenting nothing but a neutral generic being. 'A character experiences conflict, has a history, a past, a context, passions. On the contrary, a neutral mask puts the actor in a state of perfect balance and economy of movement. Its moves have a truthfulness, its gestures and actions are economical. Movement work based on neutrality provides a series of fulcrum points which will be essential for acting, which comes later.'

neutral mask '. . . a perfectly balanced mask which produces a physical sensation of calm. This object, when placed on the face, should enable one to experience the *state of neutrality* prior to action, a state of receptiveness to everything around us, with no inner conflict. This mask is a reference point, a basic mask, a fulcrum mask for all the other masks.'

pantomime Type of performance in which gestures replace words because the actor accepts the constraint of not being able to use spoken language. White pantomime conveys the style of silent performance common in the eighteenth and nineteenth centuries, when Pierrot became the central character and which was immortalised in the film *Les Enfants du Paradis.*

play Lecoq's conception of acting is founded on an approach that could be called playful or improvisatory. He exploits to the full the overlap of meanings contained in the words 'play' and 'player' between child's play and drama, games and performances. His own definition of play is as follows: 'when, aware of the theatrical dimension, the actor can shape an improvisation for spectators, using rhythm, tempo, space, form.'

replay In order to stress the importance of *play*, the term 'replay' is used to indicate a first stage in building up improvisation work: 'We approach improvisation through psychological replay, which is silent. Replay involves reviving lived experience in the simplest possible way [. . .] with no thought for spectators . . .'.

states Term used to indicate the main orientation of a character and to avoid the actor relying on imitation of pre-existing models.

undulation and inverse undulation Two of the three natural movements observed in nature (the third is *eclosion*).

Tout bouge.
Tout évolue, progresse.
Tout se ricochette et se réverbère.
D'un point à un autre, pas de ligne droite.
D'un port à un port, un voyage.
Tout bouge, moi aussi!
Le bonheur et le malheur, mais le heurt aussi.
Un point indécis, flou, confus, se dessine,
Point de convergences,
Tentation d'un point fixe,
Dans un calme de toutes les passions.
Point d'appui et point d'arrivée,
Dans ce qui n'a ni commencement ni fin.
Le nommer,
Le rendre vivant,
Lui dormer autoritée
Pour mieux comprendre ce qui bouge,
Pour mieux comprendre le Mouvement.

Everything moves.
Everything develops and progresses.
Everything rebounds and resonates.
From one point to another, the line is never straight.
From harbour to harbour, a journey.
Everything moves . . . as do I!
Joy and sorrow, confrontation too.
A vague point appears, hazy and confused,
A point of convergence,
The temptation of a fixed point,
In the calm of all the passions.
Point of departure and point of destination,
In what has neither beginning nor end.
Naming it, endowing it with life, giving it authority
For a better understanding of what moves
A better understanding of what Movement is.
             (Jacques Lecoq, Belle Île en Mer,
                        August 1997)

CHAPTER 32

Myra Felner

Circus and the actor

An interview with Hovey Burgess

QUESTION: Since you are teaching in theatre departments, there must be a specific value in circus techniques for an actor. Can you describe the nature of the link between these disciplines?

BURGESS: The union is at a basic level. There is a great benefit to the actor because he can learn about his own body movement, about himself – his courage, fears, physical potential, how he can change it, where he can go. Circus enables an actor to trust his physical instincts. It is not important for an actor to juggle before an audience, but he must be able to do so if the play requires it. Talented actors have a theatrical feeling for circus. Historically actors have had access to these techniques. Sophocles was a juggler and an acrobat. It is not a new thing.

QUESTION: What is the dividing line between the actor and the circus performer?

BURGESS: Circus is useful to the actor up to a point. An actor lives through an emotion to create a specific impression. The circus performer is called on to physicalize certain things. He may try to create an emotion, but not through emotion. He works alone, while the actor works with a director. In contemporary theatre, where there are no strong character roles, the actor becomes much more like a circus performer . . .

QUESTION: The goals of the actor are different from those of the circus performer. How does your method of instruction deal with the actor's specific needs?

BURGESS: A circus performer must have a gimmick in order to make an act work. He must be either very good, or very original. Therefore, when I am dealing with circus performers, I go after the original well done trick. I try to find out what they could do better than anyone else in the world and develop that skill to a very high degree. It's a very different thing when working with actors. It's a little ironic, but I'm actually interested in what they don't do well. I try to give them a progressive circus approach toward self improvement. If they are not flexible, I go for that . . .

QUESTION: How does your work differ from Lecoq's?

BURGESS: Lecoq has said that he is interested in the range of expression between mime and theatre. I am concerned with circus as it relates to theatre. Lecoq is in touch with basic principles of movement that are also circus. He tries to capture movement in a time-exposure way, attempting to get people from uninspired to inspired physical states. Breathing is an important part of movement. It is vital for the actor's voice production. It can also affect gesture. The same gesture on an inhalation means something different on an exhalation. This categorization of gesture is Lecoq's work, and I admire it, but it is not my emphasis . . .

QUESTION: Could you expand on the skills you teach, explaining why and how they are taught, and the benefit to the actor?

BURGESS: One of the first things I teach actors is how to balance an object – a broom, or a cue stick. The technique requires keeping the top from moving. I start with that because it is simple, and most people have done it. Balance is the basic necessity for all exercises. The actor needs gesture for expression. This skill can break through limitations in movement by indicating a way to re-educate all the muscles of the body . . .

Through the warm-up and other exercises I try to develop balance and flexibility of the human body. Later on, I get to the manipulation of objects with the body. Tumbling and juggling come later because some of the people I teach are so stiff, so unacquainted with movement that they require something very simple in order to attain a degree of success, to be interested in going on . . .

There is concentration on the objective of trying to keep the balls going while remaining as relaxed as possible. Actors, therefore, improve their movement without becoming self-conscious about it. They gain an awareness of how they can change their patterns. It isn't the juggling that is important, but what the actor learns in the process . . .

Ted Hoffman, a professor of drama at New York University, once said that when someone is ready to fly through the air and do somersaults they are ready to start acting. There is great truth in that. Circus skills enable the actor to understand the vitality, intensity and freedom that must exist under the spoken lines if the audience is not to be bored. If only the people who could leap through the air were actors, the theatre might be more exciting. Meyerhold understood this . . .

QUESTION: Has the work of Grotowski influenced you?

BURGESS: His early writings influenced me a good deal, but more in terms of directing than in terms of training techniques. His teaching of physical and acrobatic exercises is not done progressively; he asks actors to do things that I consider dangerous. Knowing how the human body works, I do not put such demands on my students. He accomplished a great deal in doing this, because he is quite right that the mind and body are one; that through confronting people with things they are capable of doing but cannot do and making them do it they can learn a lot about themselves. But he is notorious for putting people in the hospital, and that is not my intention. When you don't know how to do an exercise you get hurt. I work my way into a difficult activity. I have been greatly influenced in my teaching by Joe Price, and he deals with slow progressions. Grotowski, when he watched my class, seemed upset with the progressiveness. He felt that the actor should be pushed further for the work to be relevant to his idea of theatre . . .

QUESTION: Do you foresee the 'new' theatre as moving toward circus?

BURGESS: Yes, that is fair to say. But it comes from a new emphasis on the physical in the world today. Grotowski revitalized it in the theatre. I hope that the actor, capable of performing circus techniques, stimulates this feeling of physical re-awakening in the public.

CHAPTER 33

Yoshi Oida and Lorna Marshall

Moving

Directions of movement

IN EVERYDAY LIFE, WE TEND TO keep our attention focused inside our skin. We move the body around, pick up objects, avoid bumping into chairs, and negotiate our way along crowded streets. And during all this activity, we rarely think about where our body is actually situated in the space around us.

However, the actor's body exists within the unique space of the theatre, and it needs to 'expand' in order to fill it. As well as being aware of your skin and bones, you must be able to sense all of the directions that surround your body. Just stand somewhere in the performing space and ask yourself the following questions. Where is the front, the back, the side, up, and down? And in relation to the audience, are you facing directly towards them, or are you standing on a slight-diagonal?

This sense of space can be codified into eight directions. In relation to the audience these are: directly front, directly back, to the sides on the right and left, and the four diagonals in between. This creates a kind of eight-pointed star, which forms a clear pattern in space: a basic template for action, although other geometric patterns, such as the circle, can be used. As well as helping the actor gain a sense of the body in space, it also creates a very clean stage picture from the audience's point of view.

There is an exercise that helps you experience the eight-direction 'star'. Stand facing the front (the audience), with the feet placed in parallel position, about hip width apart. The right foot steps directly forwards into a lunge, and the whole body goes with it. As you step, the arms also swing forward till they reach shoulder height. When you arrive, your right leg will be bent, while the left leg will be nearly straight. The weight will be mainly on the front leg, while the spine remains straight and upright.

Then the whole body swivels 180 degrees to face the back, without changing the position of the feet. You just pivot on the spot turning your whole body, without lifting either foot. You end up facing the back wall, away from the audience with the left foot in 'front'. As you pivot, you let the weight swing forward on to the left leg, ending in a lunge position with the left knee bent. During the turn the arms swing back and then forward again to this new 'front'.

Then the whole process starts again from this position: the right foot steps out again, this time directly to the side on your right. It moves from 'behind' the left leg, directly to the new position, becoming the new 'front' leg, facing stage right. Then you follow with another 180 degree swivel to the opposite side ending up facing stage left. You have now traced the front, back, right side, and left side arms of the star.

The pattern then continues to the four diagonals. Step the right foot 'forward' to the right-hand diagonal facing away from the audience (in theatre parlance: upstage right). Pivot 180 degrees, so that you are facing the audience on the downstage left diagonal. Now, step the right foot forward to the downstage right diagonal, facing the audience and then pivot so that you are facing away from the audience, on the upstage diagonal. You are now ready to start the whole 'star' again, by stepping directly towards the audience again with your right foot. The sequence is always 'step right foot forward, pivot, step right foot forward, pivot'.

Each time you change direction, the whole body turns to the new 'front', not just the feet. This helps you gain a real sense of the stage space in relation to the audience.

In a stylised performance, this star-shaped floor pattern is very clearly indicated, but it isn't necessary to be quite so obvious when you are working realistically. You can stay aware of the eight directions, and base your performance on them, without becoming mechanical. Your actions will still look very natural, while at the same time retaining a quality of clarity and spaciousness. In addition, movements involving the spatial planes work the body on a more fundamental level. They help you to sense your basic human connection to the world around you.

In terms of our relation to the earth, we know that prostrating the body on the ground has a profound effect. It can bring you into a state of deep calm and inner balance. I don't know how it happens, but it is very powerful. Which is probably why so many religions use it.

Even in daily life, it is useful to think about how and where you place your body. According to Japanese tradition, when people's bodies are being prepared for burial, they are always placed with their heads to the north. Statues of the reclining Buddha always have the body lying on the right side while the head points to the north. There is also a belief in Japan that you cannot sleep well if your head points to the west. The logic of this is based on the direction of the earth's spin. If you sleep with your head travelling in the same direction as the spin (i.e. to the east), the sensation is different from that where your head is oriented to the west, in which case you are travelling feet first. So if you have to sleep with your bed parallel to the equator, place your head to the east. However, the most-recommended position for sleeping is with your head facing towards the nearer pole, in other words to the north, if you live in the northern hemisphere. I suppose if you are living in the southern hemisphere, you should sleep with your head to the south.

I don't really know if all these traditional beliefs are true or useful, but it is clear that lying in different positions produces different inner sensations. We all know that lying on our right side feels quite different from lying on our left, and that we each have definite preferences about our sleeping positions.

In a sense, we exist in a web of time and space. Our bodies are situated at the centre of north, south, east, west, up, down, right, left, past, future, birth, and death.

SECTION 5

Physicality and the Word

A tiny gesture

Like these women's friendship, the play happens almost entirely in the silences between the 121 words of text. It is like dropping a pebble into a well and hearing a distant splash that reverberates for eternity. At the end, the women clasp hands, a tiny gesture of solidarity and exquisite tenderness. It is such a fruitless defence against a merciless world that it makes you want to weep.

Lyn Gardner reviewing 'Come and Go' (Beckett),

The Guardian, 4 April 2006

Essay 5

Physical theatre and text

■ Phelim McDermott

Imagine a sign with 'physical theatre' written on it. It's in the middle of the stage. It's pointing offstage left. There are some performers underneath the sign talking about it . . .

How I inadvertently became involved in physical theatre

THE FIRST SHOW THAT I directed professionally was an adaptation of a Ted Hughes poem, *Gaudete*. I created it with Julia Bardsley for our company 'dereck dereck Productions' in 1986. It was the story of a vicar kidnapped by the spirits and replaced by a changeling magically hewn from an oak log. The unleashed spirit wreaks sexual havoc and turmoil within a quiet English village. For about ten weeks, self-funded, we worked away at this piece of incredibly muscular narrative verse and, provoked by the potent text, we created a piece of visual theatre. It was highly stylised: the characters narrated themselves and their own stories; there were very few moments of spoken dialogue and the whole was overseen by a chorus of Grannies from a Giles cartoon who moved in a demonic fashion as they spoke the poetry. We used a lot of dramatic Bernard Hermann music from Hitchcock films and the set was an incredible amount of old furniture and second-hand clothes from junk shops.

It subsequently won a *Time Out* award and was hailed as an example of the new 'physical theatre' of the time. This was all news to us! In making *Gaudete* we had not set out to create any particular kind of theatre except what we yearned to see. We felt we were doing what the text was demanding of us; to make it live onstage. However we got known as a company who 'did physical theatre', as they used to say to me when I went for auditions.

Physical theatre in the mid-eighties

At the same time as this, other companies such as 'Théâtre de Complicité' and 'Lumière and Son' were gaining a reputation for using physical performers rather than actors who concentrated on the voice. The idea that there was a physical theatre movement happening was probably constellated around the fact that a lot of young performers were choosing to go to Paris to train with Jacques Lecoq and/or also attending Philippe Gaulier's 'Clown' and 'Bouffons' courses in London and Edinburgh.

Physical theatre enters the mainstream

The point at which this work broke through into the mainstream on my own particular journey was when Richard Jones employed me and a number of other performers from the fringe in his production of *Too Clever by Half* at the Old Vic. Through subterfuge and bloody-mindedness he managed to combine the stylistic elements of so-called 'physical theatre' with a bold visual language into a major show.

There was no physical theatre movement

The reason I mention these shows is that there seemed to be a point during this time at which people were talking about 'physical theatre' as if it were an organised or co-ordinated movement. As if a group of people had got together and said 'let's do physical theatre'. Actually I just wanted to make good theatre and if, as a performer, that involved bringing my body along as well as my mind and voice then so be it! From the outside I guess it was a convenient way for the press to group together these young companies and say we might be doing something different. It was a good topic for theatre articles. Movements are very often identified by people who aren't in them! Perhaps it was a good way to name work that couldn't quite be categorised. This could also explain how radically different the shows were, yet grouped under this same banner. For the artists themselves maybe it was a way to argue a case for support and innovation from funding bodies.

I don't like physical theatre

To be honest I never really liked the term 'physical theatre'. Like all potential jargon it has its values and its drawbacks. In emphasising one mode of communication there is an implicit statement that we stop using our brains. In fact we just brought them in at a later stage of the creative process. If the term 'physical theatre' comes up in conversation I often find myself asking these questions: what do we really mean by 'physical theatre'? Why did or do we need to talk about it as such? Is this still a useful term and might there be some better ones?

What I feel was more important about this work was its emphasis on the performers being artists, the creators of their own work and the potential authors of their own theatre, rather than any idea of exploring physicality. However, behind these different shows and companies there were common elements. One of them was an excitement about devising, adapting and starting the work from an improvisational approach rather than an intellectual one. Using the imagination as an 'embodied activity' rather than only a mental one.

> Imagine a signpost. On it are written the words 'physical theatre'. It was put up in the eighties and is still there. Another group of people are standing under the sign. They talk about the sign . . .

What is the mainstream perception of physical theatre?

Now that the term has been around for a while it seems it can often be used in a derogatory way suggesting an emphasis on form over content. I remember reading a Michael Billington review of a show in which he implored the performers: 'Don't just do something . . . Stand there!' On a spectrum it seems that physical theatre can be a means to fire the imagination or to make the flesh crawl! So what is good about the idea of 'physical theatre'? More importantly, has it really helped us create better theatre?

What was good about physical theatre?

A few weeks back there was a review of *The Royal Hunt of the Sun* at the NT (London 2006). The reviewer noted that

> . . . it was as if the productions of Complicité and Robert Le Page had never happened.
> (Paul Taylor in *The Independent*, 14 April 2006)

It intrigued me to ask what was it that this production hadn't learnt from these practitioners who had a different outlook on theatre? The review talked about its approach to physicality in the show. Was it a certain attitude to devising and physical presentation that was missing? In some way the production hadn't quite got what physical theatre could be. This is not just an inclusion of movement but an engagement with the 'embodied imagination'. Ironically, on its first performance the play was noted for its radical stage direction 'They cross the Andes'.

The reason for physical theatre to be used is that it can create imaginative worlds; it can stretch the imagination. Don't pretend you can't afford a set when you can. Don't try to create 'physical theatre' if that's not authentically true to where you're coming from.

If we look at the emphasis on 'physical theatre' during the 1980s and 1990s in context, we can see that it was a reaction to a perceived over-intellectualised approach to performing and the historical emphasis on text as the primary source of creating theatre. This trend could be seen as a plea to create a theatre that was more alive and immediate. The championing of a way of working which began by getting up in the space and showing before discussing. As Spolin used to side-coach, 'Out of your head and into the space!'

There is however a danger that it could be misconstrued as an emphasis on the physical alone rather than a plea to not forget our bodies or to 'remember' that we have one. The body is a place where images and the emotions are felt and arise for the performer as well as the head and as such should be an equal partner in the making of our shows.

The dream is not just of a physical theatre but of an embodied theatre that combines the body, the imagination, the emotions and the voice. This performance also has a relationship beyond its own body in-the-space and is in energetic dialogue with other performers, the design environment and light, and the audience. This whole energy field is a system in constant flux as it relates to itself and organises the system of emotions, impulses, intellect and storytelling. Surely the term 'physical theatre' is inadequate to describe what it actually points us towards if we think this ends at the body itself.

> Imagine a sign on the stage. It has two pointers: one points offstage left; it says 'Physical Theatre'. The other points offstage right; it says 'Text'. Beneath it a group of people are discussing the sign . . .

Wrestling with text

As I mentioned earlier, my first explorations with making shows often involved working with texts that weren't plays or adaptations. I remember being given advice by Roger Rees at the National Student Drama Festival that the best way to bring a text to life when adapting something was to respect it. This didn't mean being careful but standing up to it and getting into a relationship with it. Start by tearing it up, ripping pages out and trusting that it could stand up for itself. I believe it's true not only for adaptations but also for how to approach making any text work in performance. In order to make text sing you have to wrestle with it and play with it with your whole self.

(My mother, an English teacher, once surprised me by telling me she had to squat down in front of a Blake poem before she could fully understand it.)

Improvisation is more interesting than plays

In was not long after I left college that I did a workshop with Keith Johnstone. Here I lost my attachment to perfection. It was through his work with improvisation that I started on a journey attempting to bring the same spontaneity to text as to 'improv'. Although Keith's work is primarily about improvisation, his work could equally be termed 'physical theatre'. So many of his techniques are about getting performers to be easy in their bodies and to recreate the relaxed 'kinetic dance' that happens between people in life. Keith calls bad theatre 'the theatre of taxidermy'; we do not so much forget the body as become painfully aware of it and its rigidity.

After getting excited by the immediacy of improvisation, returning to work with text was a challenge. It seemed so often to be less alive than the work which was being created in the moment. I realised that I began to enjoy what happened in workshops and rehearsals more than finished shows. I enjoyed mistakes in performance more than skill. The things that grabbed me seemed to be less about doing it well and more about keeping the body, the voice, and the mind open as channels so that performance seemed to happen through them. The stimuli could come from other performers but it could also come from the space, the environment or the atmosphere and energy of the audience. As I worked on text it seemed to me the biggest challenge was not how to get the performers to say the text well but how to make a written script as dynamic as one that was being improvised there and then.

A scripted play must be made up every night

As I worked on scripted plays I noticed that when performers are awakened by the meaning they discover in the text for the first time they were more present. I decided that it is our job as performers to work at the creation of words that live. The sustaining of an illusion that the actor does not know his lines well but is forming them in the moment as he would in the midst of a passionate conversation. The text arises from his whole being. In fact, if this process isn't happening then the text could actually be dulled by his very understanding of it. What would it be like to not conquer the text with our understanding of it but with our curiosity to help the text reveal itself each time we explore it as if it were a cave we have never been into? The text must surprise the performer every night or at least she must keep digging for new meaning and be open to let new understandings reveal themselves each time the text is spoken and acted.

Of course this is an artifice. We know the actors know what they will say next but the nature of the collusion is that we are asked to create a situation where although we know the performers are speaking in iambic pentameter, they are still making it up then and there. What is it that makes this possible? If the work is good can we forget the artifice enough to enter a dream-world? The essential need for this is made clear when we know the outcome of the play but on some level must believe the performer might still be considering the other story possibilities. Maybe tonight the story of Hamlet won't end the way we know it! The performer must be constantly daring the other possibilities to happen. That tonight Hamlet may do what he hasn't done before. By its nature this means it cannot energetically alone exist within the head. It must include the body.

I also noticed that when performers had actually been present and brilliant they didn't always know it and had to be told afterwards. It was not only unfamiliar to them, it also felt uncomfortable. I got less interested in the skills of one particular performer and more interested in the energies that happened in the invisible space between performers.

Dead collaborators are easier to work with

I began to explore Spolin's use of space as a concentration point. This was a theatre training method which emphasised the actor's whole instrument. An obvious contender for the term 'physical theatre' with its side-coaching imperative 'to get out of the head and into the space!' The concentration of the work is not on physicality so much as on an aim for the performer to be present and awake in the moment to the changing nature of the theatre space. The constant attention to 'the invisible made visible'.

I sought out practitioners whose writing was about presence and the moment rather than skill. I was on a journey of rediscovering their experiments for myself and not worrying about whether I was doing a technique correctly. So I invented my own way to do their practices. Do it in the space and then notice if it worked.

Michael Chekhov was a great help in his writings and teachings. His 'Future Theatre' was a physical one including the possibility of the grotesque but his exercises were 'psycho-physical', always stressing that the work was not gymnastics but acting. The exploration of the 'Psychological Gesture' was an exploration of the body that must always go beyond and radiate into the space around the physicality. This work was not just about the body, it was the body and the spirit. One of the dangers of physicality is that it can take us on a journey but it can also alienate us. It can make us feel as an audience 'I'd never be able to do that'. But this is not theatre; it is circus. Skills that are developed to impress are not the same as skills which expand the imagination of the audience.

Whelan recording technique – the missing link

A major breakthrough for me in dealing with the challenge of text and physicality was to start using the late Jeremy Whelan's recording technique. This is the most integrated way I have come across to tackle the issue of how to get performers improvising and truly exploring varied meaning in a text. What excites me about it is that the performers immediately engage with the script in the space and they are straightaway forced to dig deeper to the sub-text in a non-intellectual way. Without scripts in their hands the performers are liberated to fully explore the physical aspects and emotional impulses within a text. The actors are forbidden to learn their lines in isolation at home so no pre-decided meaning can be imposed. All interpretation must be forged from the crucible of ensemble interaction. As I started playing with this technique I became very excited as it seemed to be a link between the freedom of improvisation and devised work without undermining any technique which aims to honour a text.

The physical message in the ritual of the curtain call

In thinking about 'physical theatre' I keep thinking about a theatre ritual which is present in most shows: the curtain call. I've often wondered why I got so angry at shows where I wasn't allowed to applaud. There is an extraordinary dynamic present when an audience is refused the opportunity to clap and they are sent out into the night without being able to applaud. When this has happened to me as an audience member I have been surprised by how unsatisfying I found this. In fact I felt insulted.

How often, after watching a boring piece of theatre, I notice how suddenly the performers come alive in the curtain call. Where have they been all evening? I have been intrigued by the curtain call as the manifestation of the body-in-theatre. It is my theory that even in text-bound productions the curtain call is an embodied version of the contract between performers and audience.

What is happening during a curtain call? The standard interpretation is that it is our opportunity as an audience to give congratulations or, at worst, a sycophantic moment between audience and performer. We are allowed to show our adulation of the wonderful performers and the vain actors lap this up. Of course sometimes this is exactly what is happening. However perhaps there are some deeper meanings in this ritual.

On another level the curtain call seemed to be a recognition that I was part of creating the performance that had happened that night. I noticed that in the process of clapping I was brought back into my own body and 'grounded' in some way. In my imagination, part of me had been onstage and now was returning to my own body. Also, the performers were bowing to me and in so doing were giving me status. Perhaps I had allowed them to be more than human for a while and they had been privileged enough to take advantage of my dreaming in this respect. I had left my body and lived a story through theirs for a while. I now needed a ritual process to bring me back into my own body.

I had trusted them to show me aspects of themselves and myself which are normally marginalised. I wouldn't let them do that in ordinary life so easily. At the same time in this process they were returning to being ordinary human beings again and separating themselves from what had happened during our allotted time in the dark together.

'Yes we were great performers tonight but actually we are all just like you.' A necessary ritual for the banishment of a spell I had partaken in. The performers were acknowledging it would not have been possible without me. Their bow to me seemed to say to me that I was an important part in what had happened tonight.

All this communicated through the body and its movement and the sounds it can make.

> Imagine a sign centre stage. It points offstage left. The sign says, 'Physical Theatre'.
> It has another sign underneath which says 'Text'; it is pointing the same way.
> A third sign says 'Dream'.
> There is no one underneath the sign . . .

Provocative statements for adventures in physical theatre

There is actually no such thing as physical theatre.

The term physical theatre is useful if it is seen as a signpost but not the destination.

The dream is one of not just the body but the whole being an 'embodied theatre' or a 'radiant performer'.

When was the last time you went onstage without your body?

Physical theatre has the ability to say one thing and to be doing another. To tell stories and to engage the imagination of an audience in a way that film and television do not.

What is it that physical theatre can give us which simple text work can't? Remember it as a means to a freedom of the imagination. Use the physical in the creation of worlds of the imagination and mythological realms.

What is interesting is not that a production might be physical but that our imaginations are stretched beyond the mere representation of what is present. The ability to create parallel worlds is the chief virtue theatre has in the face of the onslaught of film, TV, game consoles, and the Internet. Theatre has the ability to create these worlds simultaneously: what is happening on the stage and what is happening in the eye of the imagination. Don't forget.

It is not just gymnastics! Work the body to reveal the soul.

CHAPTER 34

Bertolt Brecht

On everyday theatre

(Poems of the Crisis Years 1929–1933)

You artists who perform plays
In great houses under electric suns
Before the hushed crowd, pay a visit some time
To that theatre whose setting is the street.
The everyday, thousandfold, fameless
But vivid, earthy theatre fed by the daily human contact
Which takes place in the street.
Here the woman from next door imitates the landlord:
Demonstrating his flood of talk she makes it clear
How he tried to turn the conversation
From the burst water pipe. In the parks at night
Young fellows show giggling girls
The way they resist, and in resisting
Slyly flaunt their breasts. A drunk
Gives us the preacher at his sermon, referring the poor
To the rich pastures of paradise. How useful
Such theatre is though, serious and funny
And how dignified! They do not, like parrot or ape
Imitate just for the sake of imitation, unconcerned
What they imitate, just to show that they
Can imitate; no, they
Have a point to put across. You
Great artists, masterly imitators, in this regard
Do not fall short of them! Do not become too remote
However much you perfect your art

From that theatre of daily life
Whose setting is the street.
Take that man on the corner: he is showing how
An accident took place. This very moment
He is delivering the driver to the verdict of the crowd. The
  way he
Sat behind the steering wheel, and now
He imitates the man who was run over, apparently
An old man. Of both he gives
Only so much as to make the accident intelligible, and yet
Enough to make you see them. But he shows neither
As if the accident had been unavoidable. The accident
Becomes in this way intelligible, yet not intelligible, for both
  of them
Could have moved quite otherwise; now he is showing what
They might have done so that no accident
Would have occurred. There is no superstition
About this eyewitness, he
Shows mortals as victims not of the stars, but
Only of their errors.

Note also
His earnestness and the accuracy of his imitation. He
Knows that much depends on his exactness: whether the
  innocent man
Escapes ruin, whether the injured man
Is compensated. Watch him
Repeat now what he did just before. Hesitantly
Calling on his memory for help, uncertain
Whether his demonstration is good, interrupting himself
And asking someone else to
Correct him on a detail. This
Observe with reverence!
And with surprise
Observe, if you will, one thing: that this imitator
Never loses himself in his imitation. He never entirely
Transforms himself into the man he is imitating. He always
Remains the demonstrator, the one not involved. The man
Did not open his heart to him, he
Does not share his feelings
Or his opinions. He knows hardly anything
About him. In his imitation
No third thing rises out of him and the other
Somehow consisting of both, in which supposedly
One heart beats and
One brain thinks. Himself all there

The demonstrator stands and gives us
The stranger next door.

The mysterious transformation
That allegedly goes on in your theatres
Between dressing room and stage – an actor
Leaves the dressing room, a king
Appears on the stage: that magic
Which I have often seen reduce the stagehands, beerbottles in
   hand
To laughter –
Does not occur here.
Our demonstrator at the street corner
Is no sleepwalker who must not be addressed. He is
No high priest holding divine service. At any moment
You can interrupt him; he will answer you
Quite calmly and when you have spoken with him
Go on with his performance.

But you, do not say: that man
Is not an artist. By setting up such a barrier
Between yourselves and the world, you simply
Expel yourselves from the world. If you thought him
No artist he might think you
Not human, and that
Would be a worse reproach. Say rather:
He is an artist because he is human. We
May do what he does more perfectly and
Be honoured for it, but what we do
Is something universal, human, something hourly
Practised in the busy street, almost
As much a part of life as eating and breathing.
Thus your playacting
Harks back to practical matters. Our masks, you should say
Are nothing special insofar as they are only masks:
There the scarf peddler
Puts on a derby like a masher's
Hooks a cane over his arm, even pastes a moustache
Under his nose and struts a step or two
Behind his stand, thus
Pointing out what wonders
Men can work with scarves, moustaches and hats. And our
   verses, you should say
In themselves are not extraordinary – the newsboys
Shout the headlines in cadences, thereby
Intensifying the effect and making their frequent repetition

Easier. We
Speak other men's lines, but lovers
And salesmen also learn other men's lines, and how often
All of you quote sayings! In short
Mask, verse and quotation are common, but uncommon
The grandly conceived mask, the beautifully spoken verse
And apt quotation.
But to make matters clear: even if you improved upon
What the man at the corner did, you would be doing less
Than him if you
Made your theatre less meaningful – with lesser provocation
Less intense in its effect on the audience – and
Less useful.

Note

On everyday theatre (Über alltägliches Theater). GW 766, Ged. 4, 171. Included in the Messingkauf poems.

Brecht's typescript is dated 1930 by the Bertolt Brecht Archive, though this seems uncertain. It is in a folder of about 1938 marked 'On the theatre' and anticipates the essay 'The street scene' of June 1938 (*Brecht on Theatre*, 1978, p. 121), which was to be taken up, in some form, in the Third Night of the *Messingkauf Dialogues*.

CHAPTER 35

Jonathan Kalb

Rockaby and the art of inadvertent interpretation, and Considerations of acting in the early plays

Rockaby and the art of inadvertent interpretation

IN *ROCKABY* A WOMAN, DRESSED in black and 'prematurely old', sits in a rocking chair alone on a dark stage. Though her feet do not touch the floor, the chair rocks on its own to the soothing regular rhythm of tape-recorded lines spoken in the woman's voice. As the play opens she says 'More', and the rocking begins, seemingly in response to her word. During the next fifteen minutes, the play's approximate length, the rocking slows to a stop four times and the woman reacts each time but the last by saying 'More', after which the rocking immediately starts again; the final time her head slowly sinks as the taped voice echoes more and more faintly. The recorded text, separated by the 'Mores' into four sections, is repetitive, like a litany, and tells of a woman who goes 'to and fro', looking 'for another/another like herself', until 'in the end/the day came . . . when she said/to herself/whom else/time she stopped'; on some repetitions of 'time she stopped' the woman speaks along with the tape. The voice goes on to describe her going 'back in' (presumably she was outside) to sit at her window 'facing other windows/other only windows' looking for 'another like herself/a little like/another living soul', but finding 'all blinds down/never one up'. In the final section we hear that she 'went down . . . down the steep stair . . . into the old rocker/mother rocker/where mother rocked/all the years/all in black . . . off her head they said . . . and rocked'. Thus 'in the end', as she rocked 'off' seemingly toward death, she 'was her own other/own other living soul' – 'other' asserting itself in the theater as a rhyme for 'mother'.

The action is richly ambiguous. We hear a moving, almost sentimental tale but are not sure what the action onstage has to do with it; we are given insufficient evidence to determine either who the stage character is or if she has really died. We hear near the end that she ultimately came to function as 'her own other', so we naturally reconsider the preceding story in that light and suspect that its third person point of view is a result of her having become that 'other' at some point; like the narrator in *Company*, she 'speaks of (her) self as of another'. This possible split in the character is suggested to us in very conventional terms, similar to the age-old practice of suddenly unveiling new information about a character's background near the end of a drama, but it is more unsettling than that because it raises the possibility that the voice is lying – in the sense that many Beckett narrators lie (in *The Unnamable*, *Company*, *Cascando*, and many other works), by making up tales that seem somehow connected to their survival while also functioning as pastimes.

The mention of 'mother' rocking permits several different responses: we may conflate mother and daughter, viewing the woman as a composite character who incarnates certain tendencies passed down through all generations; we may continue to view her as a singular character whose self-objectification has taken the form of identifying with her mother; or we may even speculate that the voice belongs to a true other, perhaps a daughter telling a story to 'rock her (mother) off', or some other alter ego (perhaps the mysterious force that rocks the chair) who happens to have a voice similar to the woman's. As in *Waiting for Godot*, *Play*, *Act Without Words 2* and many other Beckett works, the action seems to be a section of an endlessly repeated cycle – i.e. a process the daughter's daughter will also go through, etc. – but no confirmation is given that such repetitions ever occurred or will occur, and the story heard about the past may or may not be a narration of events leading up to the action seen onstage.

Lyons feels that this unverifiability is the essence of Beckett's originality as a dramatist.

> Many of the moments that we witness in the theater encompass two kinds of significance: they enact a unique moment in time and, simultaneously, they function as representations of typical moments in the complete lives of the characters. In other terms, they operate both as complete or self-sufficient representations of a temporal unit and as metonyms of a larger temporal unit (an illusory wholeness that cannot be represented). I make this point to suggest that Beckett's use of partial or fragmented temporal units builds upon a fundamental convention of dramatic structure: the use of isolated or discrete moments in time as the expression of the quality of a large us as spectators.
>
> (Lyons 1982/83: 306)

She (Billie Whitelaw) begins her roles by listening to Beckett read his texts. Her metronome-like hand movements seen in the documentary are an old habit from her meetings with the author prior to each opening, at which they conduct one another like musicians. She says,

> When I work with Sam we don't analyze the plays at all. My first task is to find the music of it. At first you don't know if it goes fast or slow, or where to put the Metronome . . . What on earth people do trying to tackle Beckett without having Beckett at their side I don't know. I've always had the man close to me. I've never done any of his plays without him.
>
> (Edelstein 1984: 81)

Whitelaw's approach to Beckett might be summarized as follows. She listens to the music of the text in Beckett's reading and uses it as a guide to meter, tempo and phrasing.

Then, as she herself reads the words over and over in rehearsal, they affect her internally, first as music but later also as language. She allows those words to evoke visual images, sometimes from her own life, and in the end arrives at ideas about the play's meaning despite her aversion to analysis and her continuing emphasis on melody in her delivery. Thus her performances benefit from ideas through the avenue of music. One might well ask whether someone who works so much with subjective response can be called a Beckett 'interpreter' at all, but in a way the semantic ambiguity of that appellation illuminates her approach.

When we say that an actor or musician *interprets* a text, we use the word neutrally to describe a more or less physical process of learning, and then speaking or playing, words or notes. But when we say that a critic *interprets*, we refer to a huge and problematic tradition of assigning meanings, in which most actors prefer not to participate. The truth is that although actors such as Whitelaw may not set out to, or wish to, interpret in the latter sense, and neither may audiences, interpretation happens anyway because some type of understanding is an inevitable part of anyone's significant entry into an imaginative work. As Richard Gilman once said to me about Susan Sontag's *Against Interpretation*, to ask for an erotics of art is itself an interpretation; we should question not the spectator's ability to feel but the denigration of mind implicit in drawing simplistic thought/feeling polarities. Thus, let us for the sake of argument call Whitelaw an inadvertent Beckett interpreter, and use that to facilitate a parallel with Beckett's spectators.

Considerations of acting in the early plays

As in all Beckett's productions, the stage movement is extremely calculated and non-naturalistic. Walter Asmus, Beckett's Assistant Director for *Godot* and many other productions, describes a typical piece of direction in his rehearsal diary:

> Beckett walks on the stage, his eyes fixed on the ground, and shows the movement as he speaks Estragon's lines; 'You had something to say to me? . . . You're angry? . . . Forgive me . . . Come, Didi. Give me your hand . . .' With each sentence Beckett makes a step towards the imaginary partner. Always a step then the line. Beckett calls this step-by-step approach a physical theme; it comes up five, six or seven times, and has got to be done very exactly. This is the element of ballet.
>
> (Asmus 1988: 143)

Almost any section of the production could be used as an example of these graceful, highly polished gestures, which usually become part of some visual symmetry, and which are usually executed in silence because of Beckett's rule about separation of speech and movement. Didi and Gogo make their stage crossings in long, arched paths and frequently stop to pose for tableaux – e.g. the heights of Bollmann, Wigger and tree in identical proportion (apparently one of Beckett's favorites). At one point they walk arm in arm across the vast stage, which takes at least fifteen seconds, keeping in perfect step the whole time, only to turn around when they reach the other side and return. And at another point Bollmann travels toward Wigger by means of a standing broad jump, after which they clasp hands and broad jump together in another direction.

In description this type of activity sounds contrived, but in the theater it actually turns out to be strikingly natural. Like the 1961 Schneider production, this world defines its own sense of the natural, only without a full commitment to illusionism. Wigger/Didi and Bollmann/Gogo's world *is* a staged performance, and they express their emotions, so to speak, geometrically: it seems completely reasonable to us that Bollmann might do something like a standing broad jump just to entertain himself, and find Wigger joining him a moment later; the more surprising the invention the better because surprise breaks monotony. Since those geometric expressions are in no way arbitrary – Beckett's *Regiebucher* for all his productions contain hundreds of detailed notes for systematic activities intended as 'subliminal stage imagery' – Didi and Gogo's movement is like a shared code that serves to entertain, primarily them but also others. And that code creates an atmosphere on stage in which different degrees of realism make no sense. In most *Godot* productions, as in Brecht, some lines are directed outward, or addressed to the audience, in the context of all others being directed inward in a quasi-normal fashion, but no such distinction exists here. Any action, any line, any gesture, can be interpreted two different ways: as a performance, or as a 'real' event in the characters' fictional lives . . .

What Beckett's production shows clearly, then, is that the two realms of meaning, presentational and representational, can be blended into a consistent atmosphere of ambiguity without the actors having to make constant shifts back and forth between them. Because it commits to an internal logic of clowning, his *Godot* is light-spirited, physical, and sensible. And because it is choreographed with such a firm hand, it transcends that simple clown-sense without forcing its clowns to act as authorial mouthpieces. From a stance of simplicity and humility it succeeds where countless slick and intellectually ambitious productions have failed, eventually leading the spectator's mind toward questions of presentational action without destroying the integrity of its representational action. One's thoughts quickly finish with local questions – Who is Godot and why doesn't he arrive? Why do Didi and Gogo stay together and keep returning? – moving presently, almost automatically, on to more comprehensive ones: for whom is any performance given and with what expectations? Why am I in the theater, and what am I waiting for?

References

Asmus, Walter (1988) 'A Rehearsal Diary', in Dougald McMillan and Martha Fehsenfeld, *Beckett in the Theatre: The Author as Practical Playwright and Director*, London: John Calder.

Beckett, Samuel (1984) 'Rockaby', *The Collected Shorter Plays*, NY: Grove Press.

Edelstein, David (1984) 'Rockaby Billie', *Village Voice*, 20 March, p. 81.

Lyons, Charles R. (1982/83) 'Perceiving Rockaby – As a Text, As a Text by Samuel Beckett, As a Text for Performance', *Comparative Drama* 16, Winter.

CHAPTER 36

Mike Alfreds

A shared experience

The actor as story-teller

This interview with Mike Alfreds was held in June 1979 in London. The interviewer was Peter Hulton.

PH. The question of story and of narration, of narrative, of narrator, of the relationship between actor and narration, of the relationship between audience and the given narration, the presence of story within the theatrical event seems to have been quite an insistence in the work which you have done up to this point in time, leaving aside *Cymbeline* or the work that might come after. And this insistence is somewhat remarkable in that much contemporary theatre activity for a while (though it is returning now) would deny the story the right or the place that Brecht, let's say, gave it, and attempts to see the theatrical event as more experiential or dramatic in other kinds of ways than those that hinged upon the manipulation of narrative. I think that as we talk about story the presence and importance of the actor will become evident.

MA. It was never my intention to be a story-telling company. The story-telling was a step towards something else; the fact that we stayed with it so long was because it opened up richer avenues than we had expected.

Before I formed Shared Experience, I had become very disenchanted with theatre, had begun to doubt its validity as a medium; what vitality could it have for a contemporary audience? Compared to film, say, it seemed slow and clumsy; the component parts of most productions were inconsistent, the various participatory skills far too variable a standard to command the sort of absorption achieved by a film. Other media seemed to deal much better with whatever theatre had to offer: TV was more up-to-the-minute and more available; a fiction could explore ideas and character in considerably more breadth and depth; film could tell stories more rapidly and was visually way ahead of anything theatre could do; literature was better read; dancers created more exciting movement than actors . . .

The fact of the 'live' presence of actors and audience threw up another area of theatre practice for reconsideration. The actor, too, from his side, is aware of the audience. His endeavours should affect them; their response could affect him. This exchange was totally impossible within the fixed forms of the technical media. So, since human beings were the vital element of theatre – and the actors, the generating force of a performance – it seemed logical not to attempt the 'fixed' perfection of film, but to take advantage of the 'rough' quality implicit in the unknown inter-action between actors and audience from night to night and in the fact that the actor was a human being who, even if he wanted to, could not be exactly the same at each performance; in short, to treat theatre as a living process rather than a pro-duct pre-packaged for passive consumption . . .

Theatre is a communal event; this is evident in the fact that, while most of us can quite happily watch TV on our own or enjoy a film in an empty cinema, we (and the actors) feel uncomfortable and unfulfilled with a small audience. Theatre is the occasion on which we confirm our shared humanity. The actor, by transforming himself and therefore transcending himself, confirms that untapped potential within us all to understand and express ourselves beyond our apparent abilities. In a way, he is saying 'Look! I am a human being – like you. I have, like you, the capacity to go beyond my seeming limitations. I am ordinary – like you. I am also extraordinary – like you. Our only difference is that I have developed the skills to release this potential, to give form and meaning to our common experience, to prove for you that we all contain part of each other within us, to confirm the vast possiblities within us all. This is what you have come here for and this is what I shall try to give you.' Performance can create life-giving energy; the actor can transfer his vitality to the audience. In an idealised sense, the actor becomes a sacrificial victim who undergoes the enactment of pain and joy to celebrate our common humanity. He helps us through our own pains and releases our own joys by expressing them before us in an intensified form. If theatre has a 'purpose', this, surely, is it . . .

PH. Could we just stay on this decision to use story for a little longer? You used the word dehumanised, and said that story does not do that. Would you agree that back of the story, as at the end of a word, even if the story is about animals, let us say, there is somewhere a human being?

MA. Absolutely. There must be a recognisable human experience. Stories are about people. Theatre is about people. And people are the essential material from which theatre is created. What sort of experience – ideas, themes, attitudes – is secondary in importance to the fact of the experience itself. In itself, no one theme is necessarily better than another. The important thing is that the experiences portrayed should be recognisable, identifiable – an unfashionable word, but if the audience can't identify, how can they relate? . . .

PH. Could you talk a little about the techniques of narration?

MA. The techniques of narration. Before we started work on *The Arabian Nights*, we had an extensive workshop period where we took different types of stories and tried to tell them theatrically. Out of this we discovered three basic modes of narration:

one – with the narrator outside the action; two – with the narrator from within the action, narrating in the first person; three – (and this was another of our 'great discoveries') with each actor being *both* his own narrator *and* character, and the narration being given in the third person.

Number One is, of course, the most obvious and most frequently employed. You have the fairly classic example of the narrator standing down right while the main event gets played centre stage, which seems a fairly sterile convention. The narrator is usually little more than a link-man, there to fill in bits of exposition the writer (frequently the adapter of novels to the stage) is too lazy to incorporate into the action . . .

But he can, of course, be extremely interesting. First, his detachment from the action allows him to view it from any number of vantage points – sympathetic, satirical, angry, didactic; then, where he is placed in relationship to both audience and action of the story has a great effect on his attitude and function. We experimented a lot, having him seated downstage in front of the action; behind the audience, urging their focus on the action; behind the action; moving amongst the action; even touching or manipulating the characters of the story . . .

The second mode – the first person narrator – took us to the other end of the story-telling spectrum. Here, the narrator emerged from the action and had both to participate in it and comment on it. So there was an interesting acting problem of the narrator/character straddling two time sequences. There were also difficult decisions as to his or her emotional attitude. In his narration he could either relive the emotional state of his past experience or experience the emotional response of observing past events and his former behaviour from the distance of time . . .

The third mode provided each character/actor with the opportunity to contact the audience. It gave all the characters an even weight and the actor had the best of both worlds – talking to the audience as the narrator of his character's actions – describing his character in the third person – and then acting out that character, actually becoming that character in varying degrees and ways – from a naturalistic creation to a rapid crayon sketch. This opened up a huge range of acting choices for the actor. He could narrate as himself and then make a sharp transition into character; he could give his narration totally in character . . .

PH. What special things are required of an actor in this kind of work?

MA. My view of an actor is of an absolutely superb human being. Ideally, he needs versatility, truthfulness, openness, vulnerability, common sense, intelligence, imagination, generosity, daring, courage, taste, wisdom, a good body and a good voice . . . shall I go on?

One of the prerequisites for actors in the company – and you can only learn it by doing it – is to be able to stand in front of an audience without any clutter; to be simply and directly yourself without those mannerisms and tricks and winning ways that actors develop to protect themselves from any real exposure . . .

PH. Do you train the actors towards this end?

MA. It is very difficult to do so. One cannot really create performance conditions during rehearsal. All you can do in this period is to prepare them to expect these sorts of reactions from an audience. You can try to wean the actors away from the tricks they have developed to see them through difficult moments . . .

PH. The actor, therefore, has to call upon his physical and vocal skill to define the image.

MA. The actor has, first of all, to have a sense of space, because there is nothing (not even lighting) to define it but him. His imagination and energy has to radiate and fill the space as he requires it. Otherwise, the performance can seem very empty.

He has physically to be both strong and adept, because we use all sorts of movement and our own forms of mime. He also needs a wide vocal range of abilities to cope with multiple characterisations and create sound-effects. In fact, he needs every skill and talent he can lay his hands on. He is required to be a story-teller, narrator, commentator, performer, actor – in the sense of someone who transforms himself – a host to his audience, an MC, a stand-up comic. All those personae have to be available to him, to be used according to the levels at which the stories are functioning . . .

Apart from his text, the actor is on his own. If he doesn't create the image, nothing is there. The narrative will set the scene, but if the actor doesn't fulfil the expectations created by the text or enrich them by creating a counterpoint to what is said (an approach we prefer to that of doubling textual information with visual information), if he doesn't enhance or heighten the image he has already stimulated in the audience's mind, all is lost. If he convinces the audience, they will contribute their own imagination to his . . .

Let me say one final thing about story-telling. Because the nature of the work demands that each actor take full responsibility not only for his own roles and text, but for the conception and maintenance of the whole performance, it tends – in most cases – to take the actor's concentration off himself and his own difficulties, and even seems to release problems which otherwise might have seemed insoluble. If an actor has only one role to worry about, its failure or success can become obsessional. But in our work he has so many things to deal with that, if one of his performances isn't going so well, he has other more successful sections to carry him through. And I think that this sense of group endeavour helps to make the performance so satisfying for the audience.

Albert Hunt and Michael Kustow

US 'Narrative one', Albert Hunt, and 'Narrative two', Michael Kustow

Narrative one

Albert Hunt

US WAS, ABOVE ALL, A SEARCH. It was a collective search by a group of people who wanted to say something true and honest and useful about a subject we all felt was very important – the Vietnam War. The statement that was eventually made in the Aldwych Theatre on October 13, 1966, may not have satisfied all of us. But it was a statement that had grown out of a process of work, and not one that had been conceived in Brook's mind before the process began. And the possibilities opened up by the process are more important than the limitations of the show that was finally produced.

For me, the process began at a meeting between Brook, Reeves and myself at Brook's house the previous December. At that meeting Brook talked of two subjects which were very much on his mind. The first was the Vietnam War – not so much the war itself as what we, in London, could do about it, and how an awareness of the war could affect our lives . . .

The other question that was in Brook's mind that night was a very simple one from the *Bhagavad Gita*: 'Shall I fight?' Apparently simple, that is . . . Brook wanted to create a show in which this question would be raised in terms of the war in Vietnam. He felt, too, that the show would have to be made in a new way . . .

We studied Happenings and talked about ways of involving the audience physically. At Bradford, with the students of the art college, we invented a ritualistic game. From the ceiling, there hung a structure, built on two cross-pieces that would spin round if it were touched. Hanging from this structure were dummy bodies, tin cans that made noises, brightly coloured balloons, sheets of pink cellophane, rubber tyres. If anybody collided with these objects, the whole structure whirled round and up and down in colour and movement.

Through this constantly moving structure, five players felt their way, with paper bags over their heads. The bags made them look weird and helpless. Two carried blue flags, two carried red, and one, wearing a bag decorated with stars and stripes, carried a stick. The player with the stick hunted for the others. When he caught anybody, he raised his stick. A referee, wearing a frock coat and a black bowler, blew his whistle; everybody froze; the referee led the victim to the front of the stage; the lights went off, feed-back screamed through an amplifier, a girl shrieked – and when the lights came on, the victim, holding a flag, was lying dead at the front of the stage, and another player, pushed through a door at the back, had taken his place. The hunter never knew whether he had caught a red or a blue.

The game was a complete dramatic event in itself. But the paper bags found their way into rehearsal, and even into the first night: and the alternating sequences, of noise and silence, pointed towards an overall pattern . . .

July 4

We all met the actors for the first time in the ballroom of Bourne and Hollingsworth in Gower Street. Most of the actors had worked with Brook before, either in the Theatre of Cruelty or on the *Marat/Sade*. Several had recently been with the *Marat/Sade* in New York . . .

Brook began by re-stating his belief in a theatre that could speak directly about contemporary issues. The theatre ought to have a voice that could be listened to seriously. The trouble was that people found it only too easy to dismiss what they had seen as just another theatrical success. He talked about the *Marat/Sade*. The audience, particularly in London, had been able to avoid the play's political implications. If a man like Harold Wilson had seen it, he would have been able to take refuge in describing the play as theatrically exciting. We needed to make a statement that a Wilson or a Johnson would not be able to shrug off in this way . . .

At the end of the day, Brook said he had an idea for a final image in the show. After all the noise and violence there would be a silence. And in the silence there would be released – a butterfly.

July 5

In our pre-rehearsal discussions, we had talked a lot about Happenings. The aim of many of the Happenings we had examined was clearly to shock people into a new kind of awareness – something that the show itself was intended to do . . . We tried to analyse the connection between the society that had produced Happenings, and what was going on in Vietnam.

But at this point we were stuck. Apart from the obvious statement that both Happenings and the war were the products of American society, there seemed to be very little to say. And then Mike Williams suddenly demonstrated the kind of theatre language we were looking for. He found an image which made the connection in concrete terms. He put a chair on a table, crumpled some paper and took a match. Then, speaking very simply the words of the letter about the butterfly piece, he climbed on to a chair, and pretended to drench himself in petrol. As he reached the words 'Isn't it wonderful to listen to something you normally look at?', he struck the match.

The image suddenly pulled together the two worlds, so that they commented on each other. It did not say simply that Happenings were trivial, and that the real Happening was to burn yourself to death. The words revealed the immolation as a dramatic event – and the action placed the words in a wider context. It was this kind of revelation that we were looking for when we placed the material about Happenings in the middle of a discussion about burning in Act Two of the finshed production. But I don't think we ever in the end achieved anything as clear and penetrating as this very early, suddenly discovered act.

July 6, 7, 8

In the first two days, our search for a language had developed in three main directions: exploring American life through naturalistic improvisations; investigating American popular myths; and looking at the intellectual world of the Happenings . . .

The need to discover a new language of acting was dictated by the form we were reaching towards. We had felt all along that the material was too complex to be developed in conventional terms of story and character. There were too many elements; we had to be able to take in the world where political decisions were made, the cultural pressures behind those decisions and the effects of those decisions on anonymous people far away – and to make thematic links between these different worlds. It could only be done through a flow of imagery, with actors who could move rapidly backwards and forwards between several different styles. But since the training of actors in British theatre is limited, and largely centred on 'character' acting, the actors had to begin slowly and painfully at the beginning. What we were to do was phenomenally difficult. We were trying to discover images from the work of actors, and yet the actors had to learn new and basic techniques before the images could emerge. Two actors spent several hours on one Brecht exercise. They went through 'Good King Wenceslas', singing alternate lines – each moving quickly from Sinatra to Caruso and then to Mick Jagger. While they were struggling with this song, other actors were trying to discover ways of reacting to physical violence, without being struck . . .

July 11

The problems that had been apparent in the early work on pop culture were thrown into even sharper focus when Brook suddenly turned to the war and invited the actors to improvise their response to an air-raid . . . Brook threw a chair – it was the signal for the air-raid to begin. The actors dropped their work, and cowered on the ground, whimpering. When the raid was over, they began to crawl across the floor again.

One small incident suddenly called attention to the thinness of the work. At the start of one of the raids, the chair thrown as a signal nearly hit one of the actors. He reacted spontaneously, flinching instinctively from the *real* threatened pain. Then, when the chair missed, he became a Vietnamese villager again, simulating a wound . . .

Yet how could these actors begin to compete with those shots of the children whose faces had been turned to crust? All we had to offer in this show was ourselves – ourselves in London, not being burnt with jellied petrol. We – or rather the actors – could not convincingly simulate bombed villagers. They could only confront a particular audience on a particular night with their own, unblistered bodies. Whatever was communicated finally would come, not through a skilful imitation of pain, but through that confrontation. To this extent, each performance would be a Happening. The flinching from the thrown chair said more to me about Vietnam that morning than any of the tortured gestures of the actors. It was this quality of immediacy that we should have to look for . . .

July 20

In an attempt to approach the problem of depicting the Vietnamese, the actors had already done a little work on a Vietnamese legend – the Story of the Mosquito, about a hard-working farmer whose lazy wife is seduced by a rich man and then turned into a mosquito. The actors had tried to present the story in simple mime, but the result was both clumsy and coy.

A Chinaman, Chaing Lui, who had had some experience of Chinese theatre, was invited to come and watch the actors tell the story.

He began by correcting some basic errors. This, he said, is how the wife would cook rice, this is how she would sweep the hut, this is how the husband would say good-bye. He showed the actor playing the husband how to climb a mountain, how to depict the sunset. He showed the wife how to walk and bow.

For the actors, this was a most alarming experience. In the first place, Chaing Lui was fat and round and big, yet he danced lightly and gracefully every time he moved. He seemed to be able to leap gently into the air, and almost float from one step to the next. The much less heavily built actors moved gawkily beside him . . . I felt that a group of students tackling the same problem would have started from a rhythmic dance and worked in the opposite direction. For actors used to working inside a naturalist framework, even a Chinese exercise was seen, instinctively, as a 'realistic' problem . . .

July 25

Brook talked again to the actors, summing up the work of the previous three weeks . . . What had been achieved in these first four weeks? The rudiments of an acting style had been created – the actors were now able to move much more flexibly from one mood to another. A language of theatre, based on a bringing together of many different elements, was being tentatively formed. And most of the material that was to go into the first act had been thrown up in rehearsal at one time or another.

What was still lacking was a sense of disciplined control by the actors, either physical or emotional. What was needed, after all the exploration of different styles, was a tight concentration on one particular area.

This was what we were hoping for from Grotowski when this first period of rehearsal came to an end. The work he was going to do with the actors would inevitably determine the way the material we already had would be shaped and organised.

The actors were ready for the next step in the process of searching.

Narrative two

Michael Kustow

August 1

At this point in rehearsal, having conducted a first foray into the company's knowledge and images of America, Vietnam and Asia, Brook decided to shift the focus inwards for ten days. Jerzy Grotowski, director of the Polish Teatr Laboratorium at Wrocław, had been invited to work with our actors, putting them through an intensive course of the exercises and training with which his own actors have reached great physical and spiritual skill . . .

Brook wrote an article for the Royal Shakespeare Club newspaper, *Flourish*, which summed up Grotowski's impact on all of us at this stage:

Grotowski is unique.

Why?

Because no-one else in the world, to my knowledge, no-one since Stanislavski, has investigated the nature of acting, its phenomenon, its meaning, the nature and science of its mental-physical-emotional processes as deeply and completely as Grotowski.

He calls his theatre a laboratory. It is. It is a centre of research. It is perhaps the only avant-garde theatre whose poverty is not a drawback, where shortage of money is not an excuse for inadequate means which automatically undermine the experiments. In Grotowski's theatre as in all true laboratories the experiments are scientifically valid because the essential conditions are observed. In his theatre, there is absolute concentration by a small group, and unlimited time. So if you are interested in his findings you must go to a small town in Poland. Or else do what he did. Bring Grotowski here.

He worked for two weeks with our group. I won't describe the work. Why not? First of all, such work is only free if it is in confidence, and confidence depends on its confidences not being disclosed. Secondly, the work is essentially non-verbal. To verbalise is to complicate and even to destroy exercises that are clear and simple when indicated by a gesture and when executed by the mind and body as one.

What did the work **do**?

It gave each actor a series of shocks.

The shock of confronting himself in the face of simple irrefutable challenges.

The shock of catching sight of his own evasions, tricks and clichés.

The shock of sensing something of his own vast and untapped resources.

The shock of being forced to question why he is an actor at all.

The shock of being forced to recognise that such questions do exist and that – despite a long English tradition of avoiding seriousness in theatrical art – the time comes when they must be faced. And of finding that he wants to face them.

The shock of seeing that somewhere in the world acting is an art of absolute dedication, monastic and total. That Artaud's now hackneyed phrase 'cruel to myself' is genuinely a complete way of life – somewhere – for less than a dozen people.

With a proviso. This dedication to acting does not make acting an end in itself. On the contrary. For Grotowski acting is a vehicle. How can I put it? The theatre is not an escape, a refuge. A way of life is a way of life. Does that sound like a religious slogan?

It should do. And that's about all there was to it. No more, no less. Results? Unlikely. Are our actors better? Are they better men? Not in that way, as far as I can see, not as far as anyone has claimed. (And of course they were not all ecstatic about their experience. Some were bored.)

But as Arden says:

> For the apple holds a seed will grow,
> In live and lengthy joy
> To raise a flourishing tree of fruit,
> For ever and a day.*

Grotowski's work and ours have parallels and points of contact. Through these, through sympathy, through respect, we came together.

But the life of our theatre is in every way different from his. He runs a laboratory. He needs an audience occasionally. In small numbers. His tradition is Catholic – or anti-Catholic; in this case the two extremes meet. He is creating a form of service. We work in another country, another language, another tradition. Our aim is not a new Mass, but a new Elizabethan relationship – linking the private and the public, the intimate and the crowded, the secret and the open, the vulgar and the magical. For this we need both a crowd on stage and a crowd watching – and within that crowded stage individuals offering their intimate truths to individuals within that crowded audience, sharing a collective experience with them.

We have come quite a way in developing an overall pattern – the idea of a group, of an ensemble.

But our work is always too hurried, always too rough for the development of the collection of individuals out of whom it is composed.

We know in theory that every actor must put his art into question daily – like pianists, dancers, painters – and that if he doesn't he will almost certainly get stuck, develop clichés, and eventually decline. We recognise this and yet can do so little about it that we endlessly chase after new blood, youthful vitality – except for certain of the most gifted exceptions, who of course get all the best chances, absorb most of the available time.

The Stratford Studio was a recognition of this problem, but it continually ran up against the strain of a repertory, of an overworked company, of simple fatigue. Grotowski's work was a reminder that what he achieves almost miraculously with a handful of actors is needed to the same extent by each individual in our two giant companies in two theatres 90 miles apart.

The intensity, the honesty and the precision of his work can only leave one thing behind. A challenge. But not for a fortnight, not for once in a lifetime. Daily.

August 15

Over the weekend, Brook, Hunt and Reeves have gone through all the material we have explored, and decided (certainly influenced by the fiery commitment which Grotowski had succeeded in drawing from our actors) that BURNING, the act of burning oneself, could become the central image of the play's action. They discussed ways of working outwards from this naked act, bringing in history, politics, communications, all the other facets of the war . . .

August 30

In the tiny back room at the Donmar Rehearsal Theatre were: Brook, Hunt, Reeves, Mitchell, Kustow, Cannan and Mark Jones. A very delicate exercise was about to take place, based on the situation of Cannan's proposed final scene. 'You are in Grosvenor Square,' said Brook to Mark Jones, 'with your petrol-can and your matches. You have come to burn yourself.' Mark started to make preparations. Along came Cannan, working off a clipboard of questions. He stopped Mark in midstream, and probed the reasons for his action, the effect he hoped it would have, what he thought of other people and their capacity for change . . .

Brook sat down on the floor with Mark. Very close to him. 'Look me in the eyes. What is cruelty? Unlimited exercise of power over others. Do you have power over other people? Do you have power over yourself? Aren't you being cruel to your own flesh by setting it on fire? Aren't you alive? What is you? There is something called life and it's there in you. Have you the right to destroy it? What you want to do to yourself is what the world is doing to itself. You want life for the world, why don't you allow yourself to live? If you stop now, one less act of cruelty has taken place. It takes more courage to face the situation than to burn yourself. It takes the same kind of courage for the super-powers involved in this war to back down from their prepared positions.'

Mark put his head in his hands. There was silence for five minutes. The exercise had lasted nearly two hours. We all sat still. I was very aware of the different kind of contact Brook had made with the actor compared with the others. Brook's questioning had been much more physical, much closer to a confessional . . .

August 31

Into Donmar back room with five actors: Mark Jones, Michael Williams, Robert Lloyd, Glenda Jackson, Clifford Rose. Another very difficult and taxing exercise, relating to the problem of how to act self-burning.

Brook: 'I want you to start by searching deeply for the idea of being dead. It's nothing to do with imagination or the idea of having been; just try and get as close as you can to the problem of being nothing, now.

'Next; you're no longer dead, you're alive. Listen deeply to what, in the quietest sense, is the feeling of being alive. What is the smallest difference between that nothingness, that emptiness, and being alive. Listen to it.

'Now you have just one possibility: you may place beside you one person, one person who is breathing with you, the person who is closest to you. So you are now in a coma, but alive and aware that you are alive, with one person very close to you. That's all. There are no other elements available to you.

'Now you have a possibility of choice: you may have one of your faculties – speech, sight, touch, movement, sex, taste. But you can only have one. Listen deeply to the life in you. Move towards the person you need most. Let that one chosen faculty flower. Test your choice – is it satisfying? Can you find complete life in that one choice? Is this better than death? Is this a possible existence? Explore with the person beside you.

'Now you have another possibility: you may only bring to life one point of your body – your head or hands, or fingertips, or arms or legs or genitals. Bring life to this one point. Make it quite precise; which fingertip? Reach for the other person with this chosen point. Centre yourself on this point, move around it, caress it.

'Now a new possibility: you can live with your whole body – but only in a small closed room. Seek the things and people you need to live. What is the *least* you need to live? How many things? How many people? Throw out anything or anyone not strictly necessary. Check every object minutely. You may have to live with them for a long time. Now come out of the room into the outside world. As you put your hand on the door handle, decide on the one thing in the outside world that makes you want to go out – an experience, a light, a sound, a colour, people.'

The actors moved around the room, one leaping, one playing with levers on the wall, one swinging hips, one quietly wandering. The exercise lasted ninety minutes.

After a break, Brook set up five benches, and did the entire exercise in reverse. We called it privately 'walking the plank'. Each actor had to take six steps which would lead him to the end of the bench and off. But each step could only be taken after the actor had:

discarded the world and why it mattered
discarded the closed room with precious possessions
discarded the one living point of the body
discarded the one living faculty
discarded the one needed person
discarded the feel of being just alive, accepted death.

Each time the actor made one of these choices, he was to perform the action of stripping off a layer of skin. Most of the actors got to step four, Bob Lloyd got to step five, and stuck. Mark Jones had the greatest difficulty in making any of the steps, got to four, stuck, and then moved off the bench.

For the members of the team in the room it was also a pretty shaking experience. After a break, Brook talked to actors about the particular kinds of burning they were being asked to portray through their allotted character – an aged Buddhist monk, a young Buddhist nun, Norman Morrison, a desperate American avant-gardist, a young Englishman. He then asked them to do homework – to try and find a line through the many facets of the war we were presenting, a line that would concern their final decision to burn. In other words, to look back through all the material we had been assembling, and work out their attitude to each segment of the kaleidoscope.

Editors' Note

* These lines are from the closing scene of John Arden's *Sergeant Musgrave's Dance*, 1959/1960.

CHAPTER 38

Trevor Griffiths

Comedians

SECRETARY (*mic.*): Last, this evening, a young man from Clayton making his first appearance before an audience, I'm told . . . a warm hand for . . . Gethin Price.

(PRICE *emerges from the Audience, carrying the tiny violin and bow. He wears bagging half-mast trousers, large sullen boots, a red hard wool jersey, studded and battered denim jacket, sleeves rolled to elbows, a red and white scarf folded at the neck. His face has been subtly whitened, to deaden and mask the face. He is half clown, half this year's version of bovver boy. The effect is calculatedly eerie, funny and chill.*

He takes out a deeply filthy handkerchief, spreads it carefully, expertly across his right shoulder, slowly tucks the tiny violin on his left, stands perfectly still, looks for the first time at the Audience. Cocks the bow, stares at it intensely, apparently sinking into process. Notices a very fine thread of gut hanging down. Shakes the bow. Shakes it again. The thread hangs on. He brings the bow finally to his mouth, tries to bite the thread off, his teeth are set on edge, he winces mutely, tries again, can't. He thinks. Tries, bending oddly on one leg, to trap the thread under his huge boot. Fails. Thinks. Puts down the violin at last. Takes out a lighter. Sets fire to the thread. Satisfaction. Puts down the bow. Mimes, in slow motion, Lou Macari running back from his second goal against Burnley in the League Cup, ends up with back to Audience, picks up the violin (in right hand) and bow (in left), meticulously replaces handkerchief on other shoulder. Turns, slow and puzzled, prepares to play. The cocked bow slowly begins to smoulder at the far end. He rams it swiftly into his mouth, removes it fast, mimes a huge silent scream, the quenched bow held upright. Very slowly it begins to crumple. He watches it until it hangs loose in his hand, like a thickish piece of rope. On tape, a piece of intricate Bach for solo violin. Tape ends. He places the spent bow on the stage, puts the violin under his boot, dimps it like a cigarette until it's thoroughly crushed.)

PRICE (*to himself, not admitting the Audience's existence*): I wish I had a train. I feel like smashing a train up. On me own. I feel really strong. Wish I had a train. I could do with some exercise.

(He does a complicated kata, with praying mantis footsweeps, tan-tui, pa-kua dao, and other kung fu exercises. A spot suddenly illuminates dressed dummies of a youngish man and woman: well dressed, beautiful people, a faint, unselfconscious arrogance in their carriage. The man wears evening dress, gloves, etc., the girl a simple, stunning, white full-length dress and fur wrap. Her arm is looped in his. They stand, perhaps waiting for a cab to show after the theatre.

PRICE has continued his exercises throughout this 'arrival'. Becomes aware of them gradually: rises slowly: stares. Turns to the Audience, slowly smiles, evil and childlike. Sniffs. Ambles over. Stands by the man, measuring, walks round to stand by the girl. We sense him being ignored. He begins to inspect the girl minutely. Finally drops his rattle to the level of her buttocks, lets it rip, harsh, short, opens his eyes wide at the noise, looks covertly down at her arse, steps away from, carefully, scenting the air. Takes a tin from his pocket. Picks from it a badly rolled fag.)

Cigarette? (*Nothing. He offers it to the man.*) No? (*He withdraws the fag, tins it. Looking at them both again, up and down, turns, calls.*) Taxi! (*Sharply, out front, shakes his head as it disappears. Moves round to the man's side again.*) Are you the interpreter then? Been to the match, have we? Were you at t'top end wi' lads? Good, wannit? D'you see Macari? Eh? Eh? (*Silence.*) P'raps I'm not here. Don't you like me? You hardly know me. Let's go and have a pint, get to know each other. Here, don't you live in Salford? I swear I've seen you at the dog track. (*Nothing. He takes cigarette out of the man's top pocket.*) Very kind of you. Ta. (*He lights the cigarette, blows the smoke in slow separate puffs across the man's face.*) Do you fancy a quick game of crib (*Very fast.*) Taxi! (*Gone.*) Int this nice? I like a good chat. (*Intimate, man-to-man.*) Eh. I bet she's a goer, int she, sunshine? She's got a fair pair of knockers on her too. Has she been around? Does she ever go dancing at Belle Vue Saturdays? I think Eric Yates took her home one night. If her, she's a right goer, according to Eric. (*Pause.*) I don't know whether to thump you or what? I suppose I could give you a clout, just to let you know I exist. (*He blows smoke into the man's face.*) Is that hair dyed? Looks dyed. Are you a puff? Are you a pufter? (*Sniffs; front, fast.*) Taxi! (*Pause.*) That's not a taxi, lady, it's a hearse. (*Evilish grin.*) You're getting confused, lady. Unless you were thinking of getting a quick fun funeral in before retiring for the night. (*To man.*) Say something, Alice? She's calling hearses, he's talking to himself. (*He turns back to the man.*) You do *speak*, do you? I'm trying to *talk* to you. Say some'at. Tell us what kind of day you've had. Are you on the buses?. Eh. Shall I make you laugh? This feller pays twenty pounds for this whore, right? Only she dunt fancy him and runs out of the room. He chases her, stark nekkid, down t'street. Cop stops him, says: Where's the fire, lad? Feller says: I've no idea, but if you see a nude bird running down street, *fuck* her, it's paid for. (*Pause. Nothing.*) You can laugh, you know, I don't mind you laughing. I'm *talking* to you. There's people'd call this envy, you know, it's not, it's hate. (*Now very fast.*) Are you bisexual or is that your sister? You'll never get a taxi here, they're all up at Piccadilly waiting for t'last train from London. Ask me how I know. I work there that's why. Don't interrupt when I'm talking, dint your mother ever tell you, it's rude? (*He does a kung fu thrust, missing the man's head by inches.*) Bruce Lee, do you like him? God, he is, you're a stuck-up bastard aren't you? Give us a kiss then, go on, go on, Alice, give us a kiss, I love you. Give us a kiss. (PRICE *halts his burble. Blinks. Pads round to stand at woman's side.*) Say something? (*In her ear.*) Listen . . . I've got a British Rail delivery van round the corner, ditch Alice and we'll do the town. (*He notices a folded copy of* The Times *in the man's hand. Passes behind the figures, pops his head between them.*) Crosswords? (*Thinks a moment.*) Election. Nine across. Big poll in China question mark. (*Chinaman.*) E-lection. (PRICE *looks from one to the other, laughs suddenly. He takes hold of their handles, begins to lift them up and down, to indicate their mirth.*) Election! Election! Big poll in China. Laugh you buggers, laugh! (PRICE *laughs like a drain, throws himself around the stage, cartwheels and rolls mixed in with elaborate tai-chi gestures. Eventually he subsides, returns.*) Yeah. Here. (*He takes a flower out of his pocket, hands it out to the man.*) For the lady. Here's a pin. (*Pause.*) I'll do it, shall I? (*He pins the flower — a marigold — with the greatest delicacy between the girl's breasts. Steps back to look at his work.*) No need for thanks. My pleasure entirely. Believe me. (*Silence. Nothing. Then a dark red stain, rapidly widening, begins to form behind the flower.*) Aagh, aagh, aagh, aagh . . .

(*The spot fades slowly on the cut-outs, centring finally on the red stain.* PRICE's '*aaghs*' *become short barks of laughter.*) (*Innocence.*) I wonder what happened. P'raps it pierced a vein.

(*Their light goes altogether. We're left with his single, chill image.*)

I made him laugh though. (*Depressed.*) Who needs *them*? Hunh. Who needs *them*? We manage. Uni-ted. Uni-ted. Docherty, Docherty. You won't keep us down with the tiddlers, don't worry. We're coming up *there* where we can gerrat yer. (*Sings.*) Lou Macari, Lou Macari . . . I shoulda smashed him. They allus mek you feel sorry for 'em, out in the open. I suppose I shoulda just kicked him without looking at him. (*Pause. He looks after them. Calling.*) National Unity? Up yours, sunshine. (*Pause. He picks up the tiny violin, i.e. another, switched, uncrushed, and a bow. Addresses it. Plays* 'The Red Flag', *very simple and direct, four bars.*) Still. I made the buggers laugh . . .

(*He walks off.*

The concert SECRETARY, *probably shocked, embarrassed, not wishing to dwell. Lights fade.* WATERS *stands, face gaunt, grey.* CHALLENOR *tosses off a Scotch, sheafs his notes, pockets pen.*)

SECRETARY: That's the lot, ladies and gentlemen, you have your cards, I think, Charlie Shaw has 'em for them that hasn't and we're starting right away, settle yourselves down now. And it's eyes down for a full house . . . (*Lights fade gradually.*) Allus look after . . . Number One. (*Lights fade to black.*)

CHAPTER 39

Robert Kimball and Stephen Sondheim

'Introductory essay', by Robert Kimball and 'Beautiful', 'Sunday' (*Sunday in the Park with George*), by Stephen Sondheim

Introductory essay

Act 1 . . .

Another Sunday on La Grande Jatte. George sits drawing the Old Lady, who now seems loving and dreamlike in her attitude toward him. She urges him to capture all that is **Beautiful** in the changing world before it disappears.

People begin to fill the park, among them those we have seen George sketch. Dot, carrying her baby girl, whom she has named Marie after a character in her grammar book, goes over to where the painter sits. He does not look up from his pad. 'Can you not even look up to see your own child?' she asks. 'She is not my child. Louis is her father,' says George. 'Louis is not her father,' replies Dot. 'Louis is her father now,' says George as he continues to draw. Dot walks away, but George calls to her across the park to say 'I am sorry.'

All of the characters begin to congregate in the park, and squabbles and arguments break out, erupting into one big fight, which George observes. There is an arpeggiated chord, and, as George looks at them, everyone stops. When he calls for 'order', 'design', 'tension', and 'balance' the people take positions throughout the park. Music begins, and the group starts a peaceful promenade as George moves about rearranging trees, cutouts and figures. Finally he steps back and freezes everyone into their final poses in the painting. His picture is complete. He has created his 'harmony' – **Sunday**.

Act 2

When the curtain rises we see again the final tableau of the first act. The harmoni- ously achieved serenity is at an end, however, and we hear, separately and together, the complaints of the people in the painting – **It's Hot up Here**. The spell is broken; the figures depart; the landscape disappears . . .

BEAUTIFUL,
Another Sunday in the park. The Old Lady sits staring across the water. George is sketching her.

OLD LADY
Changing.
It keeps changing.
I see towers
Where there were trees.

Going,
All the stillness,
The solitude,
Georgie.

Sundays,
Disappearing
All the time,
When things were beautiful.

GEORGE
All things are beautiful,
Mother,
All trees, all towers,
Beautiful.
That tower –
Beautiful, Mother,
See?
A perfect tree.
Pretty isn't beautiful, Mother,
Pretty is what changes.
What the eye arranges
Is what is beautiful.

OLD LADY
Fading . . .

GEORGE
I'm changing.
You're changing.

OLD LADY
It keeps fading . . .

GEORGE
I'll draw us now before we fade, Mother.

OLD LADY
It keeps melting
Before our eyes.

GEORGE
You watch
While I revise the world.

OLD LADY
Changing,
As we sit here –
Quick, draw it all, Georgie . . .

BOTH
Sundays –

OLD LADY
Disappearing,
As we look –

GEORGE
Look! . . . Look! . . .

OLD LADY
(*not listening, fondly*) You make it beautiful.
Oh, Georgie, how I long for the old view.

SUNDAY,
(*The park is now crowded with people. Arguments break out among the strollers, erupting into total chaos.*)

OLD LADY
Remember, George.

GEORGE
Order.
(*Everyone turns to him. George looks at each of the people. He nods to them, one by one, and each takes a position in the park.*)
Design. Tension. Balance. Harmony.

(*They begin to promenade. George moves about, setting trees, cutouts and figures – making a perfect picture.*)

ALL
Sunday,
By the blue
Purple yellow red water
On the green
Purple yellow red grass,
Let us pass

Through our perfect park,
Pausing on a Sunday
By the cool
Blue triangular water
On the soft
Green elliptical grass
As we pass
Through arrangements of shadows
Towards the verticals of trees
Forever . . .
By the blue
Purple yellow red water
On the green
Orange violet mass
Of the grass
In our perfect park

GEORGE
Made of flecks of light
And dark,
And parasols:
Bumbum bum bumbumbum
Bumbum bum . . .

ALL
People strolling through the trees
Of a small surburban park
On an island in the river
On an ordinary Sunday . . .
(*They all reach their final positions.*)
Sunday . . .
(*They turn into their final poses.*)
Sunday . . .
(*George freezes them into the image of the painting.*)

Act II

IT'S HOT UP HERE
(*The strollers are still frozen in their poses.*)

SECTION 6

Bodies and Cultures

The memory of humankind

[Few collections have the scope of the British Museum] to challenge one of the great myths of our time – that civilisations are discrete entities that 'clash', according to . . . Samuel Huntington. Rather the BM can illustrate how civilisations are knitted together in a myriad of connections – economic, political, cultural – and are run through by common human preoccupations – birth, death, status, and the sacred . . .

Memory is the precondition of sanity, loss of memory is the loss of identity . . .
Madeleine Bunting, *The Guardian*, 15 March 2007

Essay 6

Assembling our differences

Bridging identities-in-motion in intercultural performance

■ David Williams

In memory of Ali Farka Toure, 1939–2006

If only a man can speak for a man, a woman for a woman, a Black person for all Black people, then we, once again, inhibit the *spirit* of theatre, which lives in the *bridge* that makes unlikely aspects seem connected. The bridge doesn't make them the same, it merely *displays* how two unlikely *aspects* are *related*. These relationships of the *unlikely*, these connections of things that don't fit together are crucial to [. . .] theatre and culture if theatre and culture plan to help us assemble our obvious differences.

(Anna Deavere Smith 1993: xxix)

MANY OF MY FORMATIVE experiences as a young teacher and performance maker in Australia and Europe in the 1980s and 1990s – those that provoked and extended my sense of what was possible, some of them indelibly leaving their fingerprints on my imagination – were events that fall under the broad and heterogeneous umbrella terms 'physical theatres' and 'interculturalism'. All of them implicated bodies and an amplification of their expressive and technical capacities; and all of them involved formal experiment drawing inspiration from training regimes, performance modes, representations and/or discourses from diverse cultural contexts. These included attending performances by, for example and most memorably, Robert Wilson, Pina Bausch, diverse Butoh practitioners, the Rustavelli from Georgia, Ninagawa, Suzuki, South African 'township' performers, Footsbarn, Théâtre de Complicité, Robert Lepage, Aboriginal artists in Australia, Bartabas's Théâtre Zingaro, and Alain Platel's Ballet C de la B. In addition I spent a lot of time looking closely at and writing about the work of two Paris-based directors and their companies, Peter Brook's CICT and Ariane Mnouchkine's Théâtre du Soleil. This writing was largely an excuse to try to think through something of what was at play in these rather different practices in terms of preparation, collaboration, scenography, narrative, bodies, musicality, the circulation and harnessing of energy, and the role of a director in devising ensembles. In addition, I participated in intensive workshops with members of Grotowski's Teatr Laboratorium, and with members of Brook's international group (most memorably the Japanese multi-instrumentalist and martial arts practitioner Toshi Tsuchitori), as well as becoming embroiled in a fractious ISTA session in Wales for young practitioners and scholars.

In retrospect these experiences look to me like a (predictable) hodge-podge of international festival circuit fare of the time interspersed with a very small number of genuinely immersive, electrifying and transformative encounter-events. Reflecting on them now, over twenty years after I first saw Peter Brook's production of *The Mahabharata* at the Bouffes du Nord, and a quarter of a century after Zygmunt Molik of Grotowski's Lab rather terrifyingly invited me to 'listen to the voices coming into your feet from underground, and let them sing you', I am struck by the degree to which my creative and intellectual energies remain connected to certain continuing concerns while at the same time having changed significantly. Although the forms and locations of my sites of enquiry might have shifted (towards, for example, interactions between humans and animals: more Beuys/coyote and Bartabas/horse than Brook/actor, rather different 'inter-cultures'), many of the underlying questions linger. What are the conditions for invention, and how to invent them with other beings? How might one meet, collaborate, co-exist with others affirming differences as productive, rather than resisting or rejecting them as a failure of plenitude? If cultures, like identities, are dynamic, heterogeneous, continually on the move, and if art making is a critical, inventive social practice of embodied, hopeful becoming, what forms and models of encounter-event and what ecologies of practice grant us the possibility of remaking ourselves and our cultures in an economy of relational exchange?

By the mid-1990s, I had grown frustrated at the degree to which many practitioners seemed to want to short-circuit or avoid critical debate, retreating into the mystificatory or the automatic-pilot rhetorical flourish. At the same time I was disappointed at the degree to which a great deal of academic thinking simply polarised ideas into fixed ideological positions. In addition, some theatre scholars seemed intent on overlooking the embodied *detail* of live events and their dynamics, or on rehearsing discourses of embodiment that seemed to suggest they had left their bodies behind in some evolutionary leap to an idealist domain of thought detached from phenomenal events and lived experience. Too often the detail of the messy and serendipitous histories of exchanges of cultural practices, and the complexities of circuits and flows, were overlooked or re-written in terms of a narrative of appropriative 'one-way-traffic'. At the point of embodied encounter between performers or forms from different contexts, inevitably the detail is very hard to track and map – it can be disorderly, anomalous, contradictory, multi-directional, barely or not at all acknowledged – and yet as in all encounters it is central to what can and does animate cultures and identities as 'works-in-progress'.

I think of the debates around so-called 'world music' in the 1980s, and the roles ascribed by some critical commentators to, for example, Paul Simon, Peter Gabriel, David Byrne *et al.* as complicit in dominant power relations. It is more complex than this, I believe. For the very mechanisms, circuits and flows of communication and distribution within international capitalism often establish the conditions for creative agency in diverse directions, *despite* capitalism's recuperative project, through acts of inventive listening, appropriation and re-invention far from the centres of capital. I remember with great joy encounters with the music of young Aboriginal bands in the North-West of Western Australia, who were using highly sophisticated tactics of assemblage and bricolage to make new hybrid forms of music (and new meanings) from a promiscuous coupling of traditional Aboriginal forms and instruments with aspects of those 'other' sounds available to them in remote communities via public radio: reggae (in particular Bob Marley), country and western, thrash metal.[1]

As a teacher in theatre and performance studies, I felt the most pertinent and exciting critical conversations about cultures and identities drew on writings in post-colonialism, cultural studies, feminisms, phenomenology, reflexive ethnographies and geographies, philosophy and critical theory. Theatre and performance studies raided these discourses freely and at times productively. Ultimately, however, the generative potential and urgent necessity of the debates around theatre interculturalism seemed to be repeatedly jeopardised by being hijacked by highly personalised denigrations of individuals as assumed stand-ins for their own 'culture', usually singularised as a nation from whom murky imperialist histories and practices have been inherited – and yet many of these artists have a questioning, critical or dissident relationship to their own culture and its histories, and understandably resist being constituted as its 'representatives'. Nonetheless the ensuing name-calling and finger-wagging across an unbridgeable discursive divide in part served to perpetuate certain problematic dualisms: East/West, First World/Third World, centre/margin, authentic/appropriated, intellectual/practitioner, and so on. As Joseph Roach suggests, such oppositions 'come less often in tidy pairs of either/or than in tangled bundles of perhaps/but' (Roach 1992: 14–15). Furthermore, critical positions often hardened into the ideological and creative dead-ends of a volatile opposition between, on the one hand, an absolutist identity politics of policed cultural ownership – rather than the more subtle 'strategic essentialisms' so thoughtfully articulated by Gayatri Chakravorti Spivak (1993: 3–4) – and, on the other, a free-floating, citational aesthetics of postmodern relativism at a purported 'end of history', freed from the constraints of context and its ethical implications.

* * *

AN UNTIMELY INTERRUPTION

In the face of contemporary frictions and violent collisions between cultures, within which countless bodies are implicated – many of them disabused, coerced, displaced, wounded, sick, starving, tortured, killed – the core tenets of liberal democracies and of international law in terms of individual and collective rights are under constant threat.

In Gaza, Iraq, Darfur, Afghanistan and many other areas of conflict and humanitarian crisis around the world, bridges are being systematically, and often literally, smashed in the name of 'freedom' and 'justice'. 'Culture' and 'identity' are being forcibly collapsed into two-dimensional silhouette versions of the assumed dominant ideology of the antagonists ('terrorist', 'Jew', 'Muslim', 'Shi'ite', 'Sunni', etc.), and these mutually exclusive performances of difference are all too often pursued into violence. Meanwhile those civilian others caught up in the conflict are consigned to the obscene discursive euphemism of 'collateral damage', or they are added to the growing numbers on the misery plains of the world's refugee camps. In such contexts, the bridging exchanges afforded by cultural practices, including theatre, seem fragile to say the least, if not wholly inadequate to the task. Elsewhere the exchange-based ideals of a liberal interculturalism might now appear hopelessly anachronistic, in large part dislodged by a particularly aggressive form of egological promiscuity – the 'free markets' of global capitalism, the contemporary avatar of imperialism – within which bodies are often commodities to be trafficked and fought over: in the territorial theatres of war, trade, pornography, prostitution, organ transplants, animal experimentation – even sport.

* * *

Some of the practitioners I admired further muddied the picture. Peter Brook, for example, made a number of slightly clumsy public utterances in relation to *The Mahabharata* which I read as the fruit of his utopian, universalising humanism and its blind spots rather than of any neo-colonialist malevolence, but inevitably these were picked up and used against him. (For example: 'To tell this story, we had to avoid allowing the suggestion of India to be so strong as to inhibit human identification to too great an extent . . .' Brook quoted in Banu 1991: 46). At the same time it became apparent to me that there was a critical gap between what Brook said and what he did as a director. In live performance *The Mahabharata*, for example, was culturally polyphonous, heteroglossic, underscored with physical and vocal discontinuities and uneasily coexisting cultural *differences*; it was a long way away from the staging of a syncretic myth or the seamless, trans-historical, Shakespearean drama that in Brook's idealist discourse purported to be 'all things to all people'. As a result, as embodied event the performance was much more complex, multiple and contradictory than is apparent either in the accounts of Brook or in those of some of his most vociferous critics. One might engage with this project as a collaborative cultural translation and displacement affirming difference, connection and the possibility of change, I believed, rather than simply as an orientalist claim to ownership and an assimilating reduction to the Same on Brook's part. I was thankful for the handful of scholars who looked and listened closely and generously enough to attend to this work's complexity and the embodied cultural work it undertook, whether Brook saw it in quite that way or not (see for example Chaudhuri 1998, Mishra 1991, Peters 1995, and Shevtsova 1991). As Una Chaudhuri notes in her fine essay about the cultural ambiguities of this *Mahabharata*:

> the goal of universality is confounded by the performance of difference. In working out of place, the cast works out a new place. [. . .] Whatever the magnificent philosophical vision behind [Brook's] play, for me its performance gave way to an altogether different vision, not universal and eternal but very much of our diasporic times and our multicultural places. For me, the place worked out by *The Mahabharata* points to the possibility of a place where no one is out of place, where interacting does not mean assimilating, where being 'unlike' does not automatically imply being 'unlikeable' .
>
> (Chaudhuri 1998: 95)

To my mind, certain kinds of music continue to offer models of practice in the performance of difference and similarity; they exist as an implicit provocation to refine qualities of listening in the making of theatre. Some musicians play dexterously with the possibilities of their instruments and the formal musical structures they inhabit, re-writing them continually in relation to other forms and instruments. As Jacques Attali suggests in his book *Noise* (1985), music can create audible mutations that prefigure new political models, 'possible worlds'; he claims that it can recuperate difference and herald change. The influential African musician Manu Dibango affirms the productive potential of an interest in difference in the following way:

> People who are curious search for sounds; they seek out harmony and melody because they are curious. Your curiosity can be limited by your environment, or you can expand it to take in things from outside: a bigger curiosity for a bigger world. The extent of your curiosity should not be determined by the village, or the town, or a city in another continent. The musician moves in these circles, but he moves to break out of his limits.
>
> (Dibango in Ewens 1992: 7)

The curiosities seem to move in diverse directions in, for example, Jan Garbarek's work (1994) with Anouar Brahem and Shaukat Hussein, Ry Cooder's with Vishwa Mohan Bhatt (1993) and Ali Farka Toure (1994), or Toure's final sublime recordings (2006) before his death in Mali. These are instances of a genuinely hybrid and radical interculturalism that makes so much theatre look extremely clumsy. The quality of listening is attentive and generous, and the embodied event of meeting audacious and inventive.

I have seen certain theatre performers explore representations of cultural identities and their inter-relations with similarly attentive qualities of listening. To take just one example – and it remains an important one for me – in the mid-1990s in Melbourne I saw Anna Deavere Smith's *Fires in the Mirror: Crown Heights, Brooklyn and Other Identities*, a solo performance about violent conflict between African Americans and Lubavitch Jews in Crown Heights, Brooklyn, in August 1991. (The Melbourne International Festival season of Smith's performance in October 1994 had a particular immediacy, for Yankel Rosenbaum, the young Hasidic scholar whose fatal stabbing was at the epicentre of the Crown Heights riots of August 1991, was on a study trip to New York from his home in Melbourne.) Smith performed almost thirty different personae, all of them people implicated in the Crown Heights events in some way, using verbatim transcriptions of their words as recorded by her in interviews. As each new voice in this multi-perspectival oral history of fractious cultural relations was introduced, the name of the individual being performed was projected onto a screen behind Smith, like a caption or credit. Through voice and body she represented African Americans, Jews, men and women, young and old, including the writer Ntozake Shange, the Reverend Al Sharpton, and the distraught father of seven-year-old Gavin Cato, the black child accidentally killed by a vehicle in a Lubavitcher motorcade. Smith allowed them to speak *through* her, her body hosted and re-pronounced their words, although in these re-presentations she was never quite transformed to the point of her own 'disappearance', and her own critical consciousness was apparent in the selection of material and the performance's dramaturgical structure. Richard Schechner described Smith's performance in terms of a quasi-shamanic 'incorporation' emerging from her 'uncanny empathy' (1993: 64) in looking, listening and opening herself up in face-to-face encounters with others. The quality of 'doubling' engendered was the result of 'the simultaneous presence of performer and performed' (ibid.): the layered complexity of possession without disappearance of the self.[2]

Smith the articulate shape-shifter played with mimesis, sliding from persona to persona, sometimes temporarily retaining some residual attribute from the previous persona and thus producing a slippage or blur. Physically she didn't impersonate as such; she signalled attributes in a mode related to the metonymic shorthands of Brechtian *gestus*. At the same time, she reproduced the precise vocal rhythms, cadences, inflections, tonalities, silences and other particularities of each individual's vocal *habitus* and speech gestures; in interviews, Smith has talked about the attempt to 'feel the song' within a voice, and employing that song as a mnemonic register of a body and a way of performing self (see e.g. Martin 1993: 57). The continuing presence throughout of her African American woman's body, her own voice and empathetic persona dipped in and out of focus to link and inform each of these polyphonic 'others' who flared into ephemeral appearance then passed through. Smith animated and inhabited the gap between them, and thereby opened up a critical space beyond mimicry, a relational field of multiple subject positions co-existing with both existential connection and cultural difference. Smith acted as a cross-roads, agora or *bridge* (her own term) for these contradictory identities and testimonies, as if they were in dialogue with each other through her interlocutory body; in this way, the apparently irreconcilable came into relation through her as materially unifying presence. They ghosted her and she ghosted them in this layered staging of a bridging of the dynamic axis between difference and identification, and the performance itself became a site for the negotiating and *working* of difference: in Smith's terms, 'a kind of cooperative dance' of 'identity in motion' (Smith 1993: xxv, xxxiii). Individuals had their say without their multiple perspectives being resolved into any singular point of view, and in the process identities became mutable, oppositional positions loosened to become slightly less fixed and absolute, the border lands more fluid, the relations associational and on the move.

In this way, Smith documented and explored issues and histories of identity, culture, race, difference and, above all in this context, community and inter-subjectivity, in extraordinarily immediate, compassionate and moving ways. As Carol Martin suggests, in *Fires in the Mirror* Smith rehearsed a cultural complexity of social relations that critiqued certain received ideas about pluralism in western liberal democracies, and at the same time affirmed the civic responsibilities and possibilities of performance making as public social action:

> neither a melting pot (we're all the same) nor multicultural (we're all different and must respect each other) perspectives were sufficient. Something more fluid and complex, more performative, was needed: a process of discovering who we might be as social, personal, political, and historical circumstances unfold within and around us; and as we accept our agency in relation to these circumstances, neither really being their author nor their subject.
>
> (Martin 1996: 89)

Of those other intercultural practices that strive to assemble differences and bridge identities-in-motion, there are two other instances I would like to mention here as of particular interest to me. First, in recent years the scholar and performance maker Mike Pearson has written with unsentimental compassion about his collaborations with Dave (now Lyn) Levett, a trans-sexual performer with cerebral palsy who 'lives in a sophisticated physical culture few of us can imagine'

(Pearson 2001: 19; see also Pearson 1998 [Chapter 26 within this volume]). Pearson addresses the questions their close work together seems to pose – about ability and disability, about training, timing, physical action, expression, representation, and the very nature of performing and its documentation:

> We meet. She hurls herself at me and I catch her: perhaps on some instinct, perhaps because that is what we always do, perhaps because we planned to do it, perhaps because we were instructed to do it. We have a history; we have a contract to suspend our social differences; we have an agreement to engage in extra-daily behaviours together, in a particular style, code or sub-code. So we touch and are touched; we operate and are operated upon. We commit without the need for recompense. *We build an empathy, a mutuality which only exists as 'the two', as 'we-performing', as an 'interculture'* [. . .] It is constituted as a series of sensual experiences, suspensions of personal decorum, patterns of body orientations and chains of altered demeanour. And it is impossible to notate; it resists the document.
>
> (ibid., 19–20, italics added)

Second, the remarkable collaboration of Daniel Barenboim and Edward Said produced contexts for cross-cultural dialogue and exchange that continue today in 2006, three years after Said's untimely death. At first sight they might appear unlikely allies: Barenboim, the internationally renowned Israeli pianist and conductor of Argentinian Jewish ancestry, former child prodigy, musical director of the Chicago Symphony Orchestra and the Berlin State Opera; and Said, influential cultural activist, literary critic and academic, author of numerous books including *Orientalism* (1978) and *Culture and Imperialism* (1993), a Palestinian Christian born in Jerusalem, educated in Cairo and long-term resident of New York. A chance meeting in 1991 marked the beginning of an enduring friendship between these two men of fluid identity, and a series of collaborations based on their mutual love of music and a recognition of its educational and cultural possibilities in the context of the Middle East. In a tribute to Said shortly after his death, Barenboim elaborated on the centrality of music to an understanding of his friend's work, in particular in terms of his acute sensitivities to the differences between power and force, the importance of detail, the interconnection of disparate elements, the combination of logic and emotional intuition, and the core principles of inclusion and integration: Said 'understood the fact that every musical masterpiece is, as it were, a conception of the world' (Barenboim in West-Eastern Divan 2006). Ultimately, Barenboim claimed, Said 'set fires in my brain' (Barenboim 2004).

In 1999, Barenboim and Said established the West-Eastern Divan Workshop, an annual three-week summer camp for Arab and Israeli musicians. The school took its name from a cycle of Persian-influenced poems by Goethe, which, according to Said, was 'an extraordinary act of homage to Islam' (West-Eastern Divan 2006). In this poetry and in his art, Said suggested, Goethe created 'an imaginative re-ordering of polarities, differences and oppositions, on the basis not of politics but of affinities, spiritual generosity and aesthetic self-renewal' (ibid.). With a group of young musicians from Lebanon, Syria, Egypt, Jordan, Tunisia, and Israel, the first workshop convened in Weimar, the home of Goethe, on the two hundred and fiftieth anniversary of the poet's birth. The summer school included masterclasses with Barenboim and the cellist Yo Yo Ma around a programme of Beethoven's work, and evening discussions with Said about music, literature, history and politics. Weimar is also the location of Buchenwald, the notorious Nazi concentration camp, and students were taken there by Said and Barenboim; in much of his work, Said endeavoured to invite people to open themselves compassionately to the suffering of others. The second workshop in the summer of 2000, also in Weimar, culminated in the formation of the West-Eastern Divan Orchestra, and a concert tour. Since then, from the workshop's base in Seville, the orchestra has toured widely in Europe and the Americas, in 2005 also performing in Morocco, Egypt, Turkey, and the Palestinian West Bank city of Ramallah.

Said and Barenboim conceived of the workshop and orchestra as part of a civic education in productive co-existence, listening, cultural dialogue, mutual respect and understanding, interconnection and collaboration – just as it was for Said and Barenboim themselves. This musical forum for exchange was proposed as a site for a modest integrative reparation of separation, and for the possibility of an 'alternative type of social model' (Said in ibid.). Reflecting on the early workshops in January 2003, shortly before his death, Said wrote:

> There has been an amazing crossing of borders and a disruption of the rigid lines that have circumscribed and organized our public as well as private lives. [. . .] [Music] is neither a sentimental panacea nor a facile solution for every problem, but rather *a practical utopia* whose presence and practice in our riven world is sorely needed and, in all sorts of ways, intensely instructive.
>
> (ibid.: italics added)

The final word on this educational and humanitarian project, as a contextual practice for bridging cultural and political differences and exchanging other stories through a shared, embodied, musical 'interculture', goes to Barenboim. Perhaps in part he offers a tentative response to my questions earlier in this essay about the kinds of relational art practices that might promote hopeful becomings in our plural and protean cultural identities:

> We don't see ourselves as a political project, but rather as a forum where young people from Israel and all the Arab countries can express themselves freely and openly whilst at the same time hearing the narrative of the other. It is not necessarily a question of accepting the narrative of the other, let alone agreeing with it, but rather the indispensable need to accept its legitimacy. [. . .] Music teaches us that there is nothing that does not include its parallel or opposite as the case may be; therefore no element is entirely independent because it is by definition in a relationship of inter-dependence. It is my belief that although music cannot solve any problems, since it is as Busoni said 'sonorous air', it can teach us to think in a way that is a school for life. In music we know and accept the hierarchy of a main subject, we accept the permanent presence of an opposite, and sometimes even of subversive accompanying rhythms.
>
> (Barenboim in West-Eastern Divan 2006)

Notes

1   For a remarkable discussion of such agencies within popular music, and the complex, connective, cultural affiliations and poly-lateral relations they can create, see Lipsitz 1994.
2   For Smith's own accounts of her work, see e.g. Smith 1993 and 2000.

References

Attali, Jacques (1985) *Noise: The Political Economy of Music*, Minneapolis: University of Minnesota Press.

Banu, Georges (1991) 'The Language of Stories: An Interview with Peter Brook', in David Williams (ed.), *Peter Brook and The Mahabharata: Critical Perspectives*, London: Routledge, pp. 45–51.

Barenboim, Daniel (2004) 'The Maestro' (re Edward Said), unpaginated: http://www.danielbarenboim.com/journal_maestro.htm

Barenboim, Daniel and Said, Edward (2002) *Parallels and Paradoxes: Explorations in Music and Society*, New York: Pantheon.

Chaudhuri, Una (1998) 'Working Out (of) Place: Peter Brook's *Mahabharata* and the Problematics of Intercultural Performance', in Jeanne Colleran and Jenny Spencer (eds), *Staging Resistance: Essays on Political Theater*, Ann Arbor: University of Michigan Press, pp. 77–97.

Cooder, Ry (1993) 'A meeting by the river' (with Vishwa Mohan Bhatt), Water Lily Acoustics CD (WLA-CS-29-CD).

Cooder, Ry (1994) 'Talking Timbuktu' (with Ali Farka Toure), World Circuit/Hannibal CD (HNCD 1381).

Ewens, Graeme (1992) *Africa O-Ye! A Celebration of African Music*, New York: Da Capo.

Garbarek, Jan (1994) 'Madar', with Anouar Brahem and Shaukat Hussain, ECM/Munich CD (ECM 1515).

Lipsitz, George (1994) *Dangerous Crossroads: Popular Music, Postmodernism and the Poetics of Place*, London: Verso.

Martin, Carol (1993) 'Anna Deavere Smith: The Word Becomes You', *The Drama Review* 37:4, 45–62.

Martin, Carol (1996) 'Bearing Witness: Anna Deavere Smith from Community to Theatre to Mass Media', in Martin (ed.), *A Sourcebook of Feminist Theatre: On and Beyond the Stage*, London: Routledge, pp. 81–93.

Mishra, Vijay (1991) 'The Great Indian Epic and Peter Brook', in David Williams (ed.), *Peter Brook and The Mahabharata: Critical Perspectives*, London: Routledge, pp. 195–205.

Pearson, Mike (1998) 'My Balls, Your Chin', *Performance Research* 3:2, Summer, 35–41.

Pearson, Mike (2001) with Michael Shanks, *Theatre/Archaeology*, Routledge: London.

Peters, Julie Stone (1995) 'Intercultural Performance, Theatre Anthropology, and the Imperialist Critique', in J. Ellen Gainor (ed.), *Imperialism and Theatre: Essays on World Theatre, Drama and Performance*, London: Routledge, pp. 199–213.

Roach, Joseph (1992) 'Cultural Studies; Introduction', in Roach and Janelle Reinelt (eds), *Critical Theory and Performance*, Ann Arbor: University of Michigan Press, pp. 9–15.

Said, Edward (1978) *Orientalism*, New York: Vintage.

Said, Edward (1993) *Culture and Imperialism*, London: Chatto & Windus.

Schechner, Richard (1993) 'Anna Deavere Smith: Acting as Incorporation', *The Drama Review* 37:4, 63–4.

Shevtsova, Maria (1991) 'Interaction-Interpretation: *The Mahabharata* from a Socio-Cultural Perspective', in David Williams (ed.), *Peter Brook and The Mahabharata: Critical Perspectives*, London: Routledge, pp. 206–27.

Smith, Anna Deavere (1993) *Fires in the Mirror*, New York: Anchor Books.

Smith, Anna Deavere (2000) *Talk to Me: Listening Between the Lines*, New York: Random House.

Spivak, Gayatri Chakravorty (1993) *Outside in the Teaching Machine*, London: Routledge.

Toure, Ali Farka (2006) 'Savane', World Circuit CD (WCD075).

West-Eastern Divan (2006) 'West-Eastern Divan Orchestra' (unpaginated), http://west-easterndivan. artists.warner.de

CHAPTER 40

Patrice Pavis

Introduction

Towards a theory of interculturalism in theatre

B UT HOW ARE WE TO GRASP THE *intercultural*, when *cultural* itself is already so difficult to imagine in all its senses? Let us consider as a point of departure that *human culture is a system of significations* which allows a society or a group to understand itself in its relationships with the world. It is

> a system of symbols thanks to which human beings confer a meaning on their own experience. Systems of symbols, created by people, shared, conventional, ordered and obviously learned, furnish them with an intelligible setting for orienting themselves in relation to others or in relation to a living work and to themselves.
>
> (Geertz 1973: 130)

We will make use of some more precise definitions of culture, in general inspired by the excellent formulation of Camille Camilleri (1982), and will try to establish what part of them is of equal value *mutatis mutandis* for the theatre experience.

Definition 1

'Culture', writes Camilleri,

> is a kind of shaping, of specific 'inflections' which mark our representations, feelings, activity – in short, and in a general manner, every aspect of our mental life and even of our biological organism under the influence of the group.
>
> (1982: 16)

On a theatre stage, every element of the production, animate and inanimate, is affected by such inflections. It is reworked, cited, inscribed in the signifying ensemble of the production and of the performances of the actors. As Valeria Tasca has shown here in relation to Dario Fo, the dramatic text accumulates innumerable sedimentations resulting from various languages and experiences, and re-forms them into a new text. The body of the actor is also penetrated and moulded by 'corporeal techniques' (Marcel Mauss) proper to his/her culture and by the codifications of his/her tradition of performing: Jerzy Grotowski and Eugenio Barba provide a demonstration of this; the 'femininity' of Asia seen by Cixous and Mnouchkine is inscribed on the bodies of actors and impregnates their roles. Theatrical performance and dance visualize this inscription of culture on and through the body. They show its movement, as if the skin were a palimpsest upon which, over and over again, cultural differences as well as similarities were inscribed. Actors simultaneously reveal the culture of the community where they have trained and where they live, and the bodily technique they have acquired, be this rigorously formalized by an established tradition (as in the Peking Opera, for example) or camouflaged by an ideology of the 'natural' (as with the Western naturalistic actor).

Definition 2

The cultural order is 'artificial' in the proper sense of the word; that is, it is created by human art. It is distinct from the natural order (Camilleri 1982: 16). Culture is opposed to nature, the acquired to the innate, artistic creation to natural expressivity. Such is the meaning of the famous Lévi-Straussian opposition between nature and culture:

> All that is universal in humankind arises from the order of nature and is characterized by spontaneity, all that is held to a norm belongs to culture and possesses the attributes of the relative and the particular.
>
> (Lévi-Strauss 1949: 10)

The body of the actor is the site where hesitant flesh instantly transforms itself into more or less readable hieroglyphics, where the person takes on the value of a sign or artefact in surrendering to a situation. The user of a culture indicates how it functions by revealing its codification and convention, just as the Chinese actors mentioned by Grotowski performed the realistic convention of an Ostrovski text as a 'received form', as a sign of everyday actions. It is the cultural 'strangeness' of the Chinese actors that allows them to transform apparent nature into culture, to expose what in the West would have appeared natural to spectators accustomed to the conventions of realism.

Definition 3

> Culture is transmitted by what has been called 'social heredity', that is, by a certain number of techniques through which each generation interiorizes for the next the communal inflexion of the psyche and the organism which culture comprises.
>
> (Camilleri 1982: 16–17)

In the theatre, this inflection is especially noticeable in certain traditions of performance for which actors and dancers have embodied a style and technique that is both corporeal and vocal. The parents physically transmit movements, of the *Topeng* for example, so that apprenticeship – by contact, the movement of muscles, impulses, the intensity of attitudes – becomes in fact a truly physical apprenticeship. The master organizes a resistance to 'natural' rhythm, substituting for it a new behaviour that is artificial and 'extra-daily' (cf. Barba, 1985: 144). Close observation will also reveal a comparable phenomenon in Western staging, an *implicit system* of techniques, experiences, citations, always employed in a coherent and functional manner. In the West, as in the East, actor-dancers have interiorized an ensemble of rules of behaviour, habits of acting according to unwritten laws which order all and are long-lasting.

> What lasts for only a short time is not theatre, but spectacle. Theatre is made up of traditions, conventions, institutions, and habits that have permanence in time.
>
> (Barba 1988: 26)

Definition 4

In the sense of collectivities possessing their own characteristics, certain cultures may be defined in terms of their power relationships and their economic or political strength. Here it is difficult to avoid the dichotomy between dominant and dominated, between majority and minority, between ethnocentric and decentred cultures. From there it is only a small step to seeing interculturalism as an ethnocentric strategy of Western culture to reconquer alien symbolic goods by submitting them to a dominant codification, an exploitation of the poorer by the richer. But this is a step we should avoid taking, since it is precisely the merit of a Barba or of a Mnouchkine never to reduce or destroy the Eastern form from which they gain inspiration, but to attempt a hybridization with it which is situated at the precise intersection of the two cultures and the two theatrical forms, and which is therefore a separate and complete creation. It is also true, as Schechner has stated (1982, 1985), that there is no 'pure' culture not influenced by others.

In these examples of intercultural exchange, the question of a colonialist or anti-colonialist utilization of forms borrowed from the contexts of Third World countries has not been addressed. Often intercultural theatre, even for Mnouchkine or Brook, is not placed directly at the service of a political struggle. Contemporary intercultural theatre, notably in the West, seems to have lost its militant virtue, tied to the search for a national identity, perhaps because it has already succumbed to the mirage of postmodern eclecticism and has relativized the historical and political inscription of cultural phenomena.

Both the enumeration of the various aspects of the idea of culture and the difficulty of applying them directly to theatre make it necessary to take into account all the constituent factors of the cultural act. But in order to grasp the relationship between cultures and to encompass the idea of the intercultural, we must first distinguish it from other concepts with which it is often implicitly associated . . .

All of the prefixes added to the *cultural* radically modify its significance, as well as limiting the meaning of the *intercultural*. Yet it is necessary to be even more precise and restrictive, and to envisage every sort of configuration where the theatre can be found at the 'crossroads of cultures' (Pavis 1990b), and in this way to set out several forms of theatrical interculturalism. Six varieties may be distinguished.

Intercultural theatre

In the strictest sense, this creates hybrid forms drawing upon a more or less conscious and voluntary mixing of performance traditions traceable to distinct cultural areas. The hybridization is very often such that the original forms can no longer be distinguished. The experiments of Taymor, Emig or Pinder, who adapted elements of the Balinese theatre for American audiences (Snow 1986), the creations of Brook, Mnouchkine or Barba, drawing upon Indian or Japanese traditions, belong to this category (Pavis 1989). One might also mention, in the North American context, Robert Lepage (*The Dragon Trilogy*), Lee Breuer (*The Warrior Ant*), Elisabeth LeCompte, John Jesurun, Winston Tong, Hou Hsiao-Hsien, and, in the area of music, David Byrne, Philip Glass, Bob Telson and the John Cage of *Europeras 1 & 2* (cf. Marranca and Dasgupta 1989).

Multicultural theatre

The cross-influences between various ethnic or linguistic groups in multicultural societies (e.g. Australia, Canada) have been the source of performances utilizing several languages and performing for a bi- or multicultural public (Shevtsova 1990; Rewa 1988). This sort of exchange is only possible when the political system in place recognizes, if only on paper, the existence of cultural or national communities and encourages their cooperation, without hiding behind the shibboleth of national identity. It is significant to note that few multicultural experiments are attempted in France or in Germany, although the composition of the population would lend itself well to this. The possibility of such a multicultural theatre does not seem to particularly interest these countries' public authorities. Have they even considered taking the risk? Cross-cultural influence is also and especially involved when a staging uses signs borrowed from a cultural universe without there being a direct relationship: for example, the neo-Shakespearean dramaturgy of Cixous on to which the Indian and Pakistani physical techniques and the proxemics of the actors was grafted. Meaning arises from the clash of contexts, not from the coexistence or multiplicity of cultural sources.

Cultural collage

If the intercultural theatre claims to be concerned with the cultural identities of the forms it utilizes, from which it seeks to draw a mutual enrichment, certain artists, like Robert Wilson, are 'resolutely indifferent to utopianist talk about transcultural communication' (Wirth 1990: 86). They cite, adapt, reduce, enlarge, combine and mix various elements without concern for a scale of importance or value. The intercultural becomes the unexpected and quasi-surrealist encounter of cultural debris or – more positively – of cultural material that has been repressed or discredited. There is nothing humanistic in these fortuitous encounters; affinities or similarities are far from being obvious, incongruities disturb or delight the public. This, James Brandon notes, is the way the productions of Suzuki Tadashi function; they

> rely upon a public consciously reacting to the discordant ambiguity of a Marlboro ad in a Greek temple – or of popular songs to pop music at Troy. Suzuki is participating in the postmodern process of a commentary with cultural fragments.
>
> (1990: 92)

Although these cultural collages have nothing blameworthy in themselves, and have resulted in productions of intense beauty and great power, they nevertheless do not pretend to understand a civilization, and they choose their forms and techniques without regard for their ethnological function in their home cultures. Yet it would be unjust to reserve the term *intercultural theatre* for experiments where the cultures are seen in their identity and specificity, particularly given that the declared intentions of the directors themselves are inadequate to judge this or to provide a seal of approval. Their appeal *expressis verbis* does not make their productions more justified and 'honest' than those of a Wilson, a Lavelli or a Suzuki, who attribute no humanist pretension whatsoever to their works.

Three more categories which demonstrate the same phenomena, but from quite specific points of view, should also be mentioned.

Syncretic theatre

A term used by Chris Balme (1995) for the creative reinterpretation of heterogeneous cultural material, resulting in the formation of new configurations (for example, the theatre of Derek Walcott or Wole Soyinka).

Post-colonial theatre

This takes up elements of the home culture (that of ex- or neo-colonization) and employs them from its indigenous perspective, thereby giving rise to a mixture of languages, dramaturgies and performance processes.

The 'Theatre of the Fourth World'

Created by authors or directors belonging to pre-colonization cultures, which have often become minority cultures in relation to that of the colonizers (e.g. the Maoris in New Zealand, Aborigines in Australia or Indians in Canada and America).

References

Balme, Chris (1995) *Theater im postkolonialen Zeitalter*, Tübingen: Niemayer.

Barba, Eugenio (1985) *Jenseits der schwimmenden Inseln,* Reinbeck: Rowohlt.

Barba, Eugenio (1988) 'Quatre Spectateurs', *L'Art du théâtre*, 10.

Brandon, James (1990) 'Contemporary Japanese Theatre: Interculturalism and Intraculturalism', in Fischer-Lichte *et al.*

Camilleri, Camille (1982) 'Culture et sociétés: caractères et fonctions', *Les amis de Sèvres*, 4.

Fischer-Lichte, Erika, J. Riley and M. Gissenwehrer (eds) (1990) *The Dramatic Touch of Difference: Theatre, Own and Foreign*, Tübingen: Günter Narr Verlag.

Geertz, Clifford (1973) *The Interpretation of Cultures*, New York: Basic Books.

Lévi-Strauss, Claude (1949) *Les structures élémentaires de la parenté*, Paris: Presses Universitaires de France.

Marranca, Bonnie and Gautam Dasgupta (eds) (1989) *Performing Arts Journal*, 33–34 ('Interculturalism').

Pavis, Patrice (1989) 'Danser avec Faust', *Bouffonneries*, 22–3.

Pavis, Patrice (1990b) *Le Théâtre au croisement des cultures*, Corti.

Rewa, Nathalie (ed.) (1988) *Canadian Theatre Journal*, 55 ('Theatre and Ethnicity').

Schechner, Richard (ed.) (1982) 'Intercultural Performance', *The Drama Review*, 26:2 (T94).

Schechner, Richard (1985) *Between Theatre and Anthropology*, Philadelphia: University of Pennsylvania Press.

Shevtsova, Maria (1990) 'Histoire/Identité. Le contexte sociologique du théâtre australien', *Théâtre/Public*, 91.

Snow, Stephen (1986) 'Intercultural Performance: The Balinese-American Model', *Asian Theatre Journal*, 3:2.

Wirth, Andrzej (1990) 'Iconophilia in the New Theatre', in Fischer-Lichte *et al.*

CHAPTER 41

Eugenio Barba and Nicola Savarese

Pre-expressivity

MANY SPECTATORS BELIEVE THAT the performer's nature depends on his or her expressivity and often also believe that expressivity in turn derives from the performer's intentions. In reality, above all in the traditions of codified theatre, the opposite occurs: the performers mould their body according to specific tensions and forms and it is these very tensions and forms which create lightning in the spectator. Hence the paradox of the performer who, unmoved, is able to move the spectator.

What name can be given to this level of the performer's tensions and forms?

(On the same topic, Stanislavski said to his actors:

> Without using the text, without a raise-en-scène, knowing only the content of each scene, if you play everything according to the line of physical action, your part will be at least thirty-five percent ready. First of all, you must establish the logical sequence of your physical actions. No matter what kind of delicacy an artist brings to a painting, if the pose of the model breaks physical laws, if truth is not in the pose, if its representation of a sitting figure, say, is not really sitting, nothing will make it believable. Therefore, the painter, before he can think of embodying the most delicate and complicated psychological states in his painting, must make his model stand or lie down or sit in a way that makes us believe that the model really sits, stands or lies.
>
> The line of physical actions of a role has precisely the same significance in the art of the actor. The actor, like the painter, must make the character sit, stand or lie down. But this is more complicated for us in that we present ourselves as both the artist and the model. We must find, not a static pose, but the organic actions of a person in very diverse situations. Until these are

found, until the actor justifies the truth by the correctness of his physical behaviour, he cannot think of anything else.

O. Toporkov, *Stanislavski in Rehearsal*)

When we see an organism alive in its totality, we know from anatomy, biology and physiology that this organism is organised on various levels. Just as there is a cellular level of organisation and a level of organisation of the organs, and of the various systems in the human body (nervous, arterial, etc.), so we must consider that the totality of a performer's performance is also made up of distinct levels of organisation.

Theatre anthropology postulates that there exists a basic level of organisation common to all performers and defines this level as *pre-expressive*.

The concept of pre-expressivity may appear absurd and paradoxical given that it does not take into consideration the performers' intentions, feelings, identification or non-identification with character, emotions . . . that is, psycho-technique. Psycho-technique has in fact dominated professional training and corresponding research into theatre and dance for at least the last two centuries.

Psycho-technique directs the performer towards a desire to express: but the desire to express does not determine what one must do. The performers' expression is in fact due – almost in spite of them – to their actions, to their use of their physical presence. It is the *doing* and *how the doing is done* which determine what one expresses.

According to 'result logic', the spectator sees a performer who is expressing feelings, ideas, thoughts, actions . . . that is, the spectator sees a manifestation of an intention and a meaning. This expression is presented to the spectators in its totality: they are thus led to identify what the actors are expressing with how they express it.

It is of course possible to analyse the performer's work according to this logic. This does, however, lead to a generalised evaluation which often does not offer an understanding of how that work has been done on the technical level.

The understanding of the how belongs to a logic which is complementary to 'result logic': 'process logic'. According to 'process logic', it is possible to distinguish between and to work separately on the levels of organisation which constitute the performer's expression.

The level which deals with how to render the actor's energy scenically alive, that is, with how the actor can become a presence which immediately attracts the spectator's attention, is the pre-expressive level and is theatre anthropology's field of study.

This pre-expressive substratum is included in the expression level, in the totality perceived by the spectator. However, by keeping this level separate during the work process, the performer can work on the pre-expressive level, *as if*, in this phase, the principal objective was the energy, the presence, the *bios* of his actions and not their meaning.

The pre-expressive level thought of in this way is therefore an operative level: not a level which can be separated from expression, but a pragmatic category, a praxis, the aim of which, during the process, is to strengthen the performer's scenic *bios*.

Theatre anthropology postulates that the pre-expressive level is at the root of the various performing techniques and that there exists, independently of traditional culture, a transcultural 'physiology'. In fact, pre-expressivity utilises principles for the acquistion of presence and the performer's life. The results of these principles appear more evident in codified genres where the technique which *puts* the body *in form* is codified independently of the result/meaning.

Thus theatre anthropology confronts and compares the techniques of actors and dancers at the transcultural level, and, by means of the study of scenic behaviour, reveals that certain principles governing pre-expressivity are more common and universal than would first have been imagined.

Inculturation and acculturation technique

In order to be more effective in his context, in order to make his historico-biographical identity emerge, the performer uses forms, manners, behaviour, procedures, guile, distortions, appearances . . . what we call 'technique'. This is characteristic of every performer and exists in all traditions. Making an analysis which goes beyond cultures (western, eastern, northern, southern), beyond genres (classical ballet, modern dance, opera, operetta, musical, text theatre, body theatre, classical theatre, contemporary theatre, etc.), going beyond all this, we arrive back at the first day, when the student begins to learn how to become effective relative to the spectator. And we find two points of departure, two paths. On the first path, the performers use their 'spontaneity', elaborating the behaviour which comes to them naturally, which they have absorbed since their birth in the culture and social milieu in which they have grown up. Anthropologists define as inculturation this process of passive sensory-motor absorption of the daily behaviour of a given culture. A child's organic adaptation to the conduct and life norms of his culture, the conditioning to a 'naturalness', permits a gradual and organic transformation which is also growth.

Stanislavski made the most important methodological contribution to this path of elaborated spontaneity, or 'inculturation technique'. It consists of a mental process which enlivens and dilates the performer's inculturated naturalness. By means of the 'magic if', by means of a mental codification, the performers alter their daily behaviour, change their habitual way of being, and materialise the character they are to portray. This is also the objective of Brecht's alienation technique or social gesture. It always refers to a performer who, during the work process, models his or her natural and daily behaviour into extra-daily scenic behaviour with a built-in social fabric or subtexts . . .

At the same time, in all cultures, it is possible to observe another path for the performer: the utilisation of specific body techniques which are separate from those used in daily life. Modern and classical ballet dancers, mimes, and performers from traditional Oriental theatres have denied their 'naturalness' and have adopted another means of scenic behaviour. They have undergone a process of 'acculturation' imposed from the outside, with ways of standing, walking, stopping, looking, and sitting which are different from the daily.

The technique of acculturation artificialises (or stylises, as is often said), the performer's behaviour. But it also results in another quality of energy. We have all experienced this other quality of energy when watching a classical Indian or Japanese actor, a modern dancer or a mime. Such performers are fascinating to the degree that they have been successful in modifying their 'naturalness', transforming it into lightness, as in classical ballet, or into vigour, as in modern dance. Acculturation technique is the distortion of usual (natural) appearance in order to recreate it sensorially in a fresh and astonishing way.

The

> 'acculturated' performer manifests a quality and an energetic radiation which is presence ready to be transformed into dance or theatre according to convention or tradition. But the path of inculturation also leads to rich variations and shades of daily behaviour, to an essential quality of the vocal action of language, to a flux of tensions, to sudden changes of rhythms and intensities which give life to a 'theatre which dances'. Both the inculturation path and the acculturation path activate the pre-expressive level: presence ready to re-present.
>
> It is therefore useless to over-emphasise the expressive differences between classical Oriental theatres, with their accultured performers, and Occidental theatre, with its inculturated performers, given that they are analogous on the pre-expressive level.
>
> (Eugenio Barba, *The Third Bank of the River*)

CHAPTER 42

Peter Brook

The world as a can opener

For Micheline Rozan who is the vibrant point from which so much in this
book found its life

IN THE MIDDLE OF AFRICA, I scandalized an anthropologist by suggesting that
we all have an Africa inside us. I explained that this was based on my conviction that
we are each only parts of a complete man: that the fully developed human being would
contain what today is labelled African, Persian or English.

Everyone can respond to the music and dances of many races other than his own.
Equally one can discover in oneself the impulses behind these unfamiliar movements and
sounds and so make them one's own. Man is more than what his culture defines; cultural
habits go far deeper than the clothes he wears, but they are still only garments to which
an unknown life gives body. Each culture expresses a different portion of the inner atlas:
the complete human truth is global, and the theatre is the place in which the jigsaw can
be pieced together.

In the last few years, I have tried to use the world as a can opener. I have tried to
let the sounds, shapes and attitudes of different parts of the world play on the actor's
organism, in the way that a great role enables him to go beyond his apparent possibilities.

In the fragmented theatre that we know, theatre companies tend to be composed of
people who share the same class, the same views, the same aspirations. The International
Centre of Theatre Research was formed on the opposite principle: we brought together
actors with nothing in common – no shared language, no shared signs, no common jokes.

We worked from a series of stimuli, all coming from without, which provided
challenges. The first challenge came from the very nature of language. We found that
the sound fabric of a language is a code, an emotional code that bears witness to the

passions that forged it. For instance, it is because the ancient Greeks had the capacity to experience certain emotions intensely that their language grew into the vehicle it was. If they had had other feelings, they would have evolved other syllables. The arrangement of vowels in Greek produced sounds that vibrate more intensely than in modern English . . .

With Avesta, the two-thousand-year-old language of Zoroaster, we encountered sound patterns that are hieroglyphs of spiritual experience. Zoroaster's poems, which on the printed page in English seem vague and pious platitudes, turn into tremendous statements when certain movements of larynx and breath become an inseparable part of their sense . . .

The second challenge, which also came to the actors from the outside, was the power of myths. In playing out existing myths, from myths of fire to myths of birds, the group was stretched beyond its everyday perceptions and enabled to discover the reality behind the fairytale trappings of mythology. Then it could approach the simplest everyday action, the gesture, the relation with familiar objects in the knowledge that if a myth is true it cannot belong to the past . . .

The third challenge came from allowing the outside world – people, places, seasons, times of day or night – to act directly on the performers. From the start, we studied what an audience means, and deliberately opened ourselves to receive its influence. Reversing the principle on which theatre tours are based, where finished work remains constant although circumstances change, we tried, in our travels, to make our work fit the moment of playing. Sometimes this came from pure improvisation, such as arriving in an African village with no fixed plans at all and letting circumstances create a chain reaction out of which a theme would arise as naturally as in a conversation. Sometimes we let the audience dominate the actors completely – as in Lamont, California, where, one Sunday morning under a tree, a crowd of strikers who had been listening to Cesar Chavez stimulated our actors into creating the images and characters that they needed passionately to cheer or hiss . . .

Two years later, in California, however, together with the Teatro Campesino, we played *The Conference of the Birds* to an audience of farmworkers in a park and it all fell into place: a Sufi poem translated from Persian to French, from French to English, from English to Spanish, played by actors of seven nationalities, had made its way across the centuries and across the world. Here it was no alien classic; it found a new and urgent meaning in the context of the Chicano struggle.

This was possible because we had learned many lessons on the way. From a shanty town near Paris to the villages of Africa, in front of deaf children, asylum inmates, psychiatrists, business trainees, young delinquents; on cliffs, in pits, in camel markets, at street corners, in community centres, museums, even a zoo – and also in carefully prepared and organized spaces – the question: What is theatre? had become for us a proposition that had to be faced and answered immediately. The constant lesson taught and retaught was respecting audiences and learning from them. Whether throbbing with excitement (I think of three hundred black teenagers in Brooklyn); or menacing, stoned on glue in the Bronx; or grave, immobile and attentive (in a Saharan oasis), the audience is always 'the other person': as vital as the other person in speech or love.

And it is clear that just pleasing the other is not enough. The relationship implies an extraordinary responsibility: something has to take place. What? Here we touched the basic questions: What do we need from the event? What do we bring to the event? What in the theatre process needs to be prepared, what needs to be left free? What is narrative, what is character? Does the theatre event tell something, or does it work through a sort of intoxication? What belongs to physical energy, what belongs to emotion, what belongs to thought? What can be taken from an audience, what must be given? What responsibilities must we take for what we leave behind? What change can a performance bring about? What can be transformed?

The answers are difficult and ever-changing, but the conclusion is simple. To learn about theatre one needs more than schools or rehearsal rooms: it is in attempting to live up to the expectations of other human beings that everything can be found. Provided, of course, one trusts these expectations. This is why the search for audiences was so vital.

Another aspect of the process we were following was that of interchange between working groups . . . 'In different ways,' Luis said on the first day, 'we are all trying to become more universal. But universal does not mean broad and generalized. Universal means, quite simply, related to the universe.' It was on this point that the work of our two groups began – trying to relate the smallest specific detail to the widest framework. For instance, to the Teatro, as to Chavez, the word 'union' not only means organized labour but also unity, with all its overtones.

The work with the Campesino was a major experiment, and it established that it is possible for different groups to help each other to search for the same goal. Once again it was the differences between the groups that made the strongest experiences occur.

Acknowledgement

'The World as a Can Opener', *The New York Times*, November 5, 1973.

CHAPTER 43

C.L.R. James

What is art?

To Learie Constantine and W.G. Grace for both of whom this book hopes to right grave wrongs, and, in so doing, extend our too limited conceptions of history and of the fine arts. To these two names I add that of Frank Worrell, who has made ideas and aspirations into reality.

I HAVE MADE GREAT CLAIMS for cricket. As firmly as I am able and as is here possible, I have integrated it in the historic movement of the times. The question remains: What is it? Is it mere entertainment or is it an art? . . .

It is a game and we have to compare it with other games. It is an art and we have to compare it with other arts.

Cricket is first and foremost a dramatic spectacle. It belongs with the theatre, ballet, opera and the dance.

In a superficial sense all games are dramatic. Two men boxing or running a race can exhibit skill, courage, endurance and sharp changes of fortune; can evoke hope and fear. They can even harrow the soul with laughter and tears, pity and terror. The state of the city, the nation or the world can invest a sporting event with dramatic intensity such as is reached in few theatres . . .

These possibilities cricket shares with other games in greater or lesser degree. Its quality as drama is more specific. It is so organized that at all times it is compelled to reproduce the central action which characterizes all good drama from the days of the Greeks to our own: two individuals are pitted against each other in a conflict that is strictly personal but no less strictly representative of a social group. One individual batsman faces one individual bowler. But each represents his side. The personal achievement may be of the utmost competence or brilliance. Its ultimate value is whether it assists the side to victory or staves off defeat. This has nothing to do with morals. It is the organizational structure on which the whole spectacle is built. The dramatist, the novelist, the choreographer, must *strive* to make his individual character symbolic, of a larger whole. He may or may not succeed . . .

The batsman facing the ball does not merely represent his side. For that moment, to all intents and purposes, he is his side. This fundamental relation of the One and the Many, Individual and Social, Individual and Universal, leader and followers, representative and ranks, the part and the whole, is structurally imposed on the players of cricket. What other sports, games and arts have to aim at, the players are given to start with, they cannot depart from it. Thus the game is founded upon a dramatic, a human, relation which is universally recognized as the most objectively pervasive and psychologically stimulating in life and therefore in that artificial representation of it which is drama.

The second major consideration in all dramatic spectacles is the relation between event (or, if you prefer, contingency) and design, episode and continuity, diversity in unity, the battle and the campaign, the part and the whole. Here also cricket is structurally perfect. The total spectacle consists and must consist of a series of individual, isolated episodes, each in itself completely self-contained. Each has its beginning, the ball bowled; its middle, the stroke played; its end, runs, no runs, dismissal. Within the fluctuating interest of the rise and fall of the game as a whole, there is this unending series of events, each single one fraught with immense possibilities of expectation and realization. Here again the dramatist or movie director has to strive . . .

The structural enforcement of the fundamental appeals which all dramatic spectacle must have is of incalculable value to the spectator. The glorious uncertainty of the game is not anarchy. It would not be glorious if it were not so firmly anchored in the certainties which must attend all successful drama. That is why cricket is perhaps the only game in which the end result (except where national or local pride is at stake) is not of great importance. Appreciation of cricket has little to do with the end, and less still with what are called 'the finer points', of the game. What matters in cricket, as in all the arts, is not finer points but what everyone with some knowledge of the elements can see and feel. It is only within such a rigid structural frame that the individuality so characteristic of cricket can flourish. Two batsmen are in at the same time. Thus the position of representative of the side, though strictly independent, is interchangeable . . .

Cricket, of course, does not allow that representation or suggestion of specific relations as can be done by a play or even by ballet and dance. The players are always players trafficking in the elemental human activities, qualities and emotions – attack, defence, courage, gallantry, steadfastness, grandeur, ruse. This is no drawback. Punch and Judy, *Swan Lake*, pantomime, are even less particularized than cricket. They depend for their effect upon the technical skill and creative force with which their exponents make the ancient patterns live for their contemporaries. Some of the best beloved and finest music is created out of just such elemental sensations. We never grow out of them, of the need to renew them. Any art which by accident or design gets too far from them finds that it has to return or wither. They are the very stuff of human life. It is of this stuff that the drama of cricket is composed . . .

The dramatic content of cricket I have purposely pitched low – I am concerned not with degree but kind. In addition to being a dramatic, cricket is also a visual art. This I do not pitch low at all. The whole issue will be settled here . . .

Lucian's Solon tells what the Olympic Games meant to the Greeks. The human drama, the literature, was as important to them as to us. No less so was the line, the curve, the movement of the athletes which inspired one of the greatest artistic creations we have ever known – Greek sculpture. To this day certain statues baffle the experts: are they statues of Apollo or are they statues of athletes? The games and sculpture were 'good' arts and popular. The newly fledged democracy found them insufficient. The contrast between life under an ancient landed aristocracy and an ancient democratic regime was enormous. It can be guessed at by what the democracy actually achieved. The democracy did not neglect the games or sculpture. To the contrary. The birth of democracy saw the birth of individualism in sculpture. Immense new passions and immense new forces had been released. New relations between the individual and society, between individual and individual, launched life on new, exciting and dangerous ways. Out of this came the tragic drama. After a long look at how the creation of the Hambledon men became the cornerstone of Victorian education and entertainment, I can no longer accept that Peisistratus encouraged the dramatic festival as a means of satisfying or appeasing or distracting the urban masses on their way to democracy . . .

The elements which were transformed into Greek drama may have existed in primitive form, quite apart from religious ceremonial – there is even a tradition that peasants played primitive dramas. However that may be, the newly fledged Greek democrat found his need for a fuller existence fulfilled in the tragic drama. He had no spate of books to give him distilled, concentrated and ordered views of life. The old myths no longer sufficed. The drama recast them to satisfy the expanded personality. The end of democracy is a more complete existence . . .

We may some day be able to answer Tolstoy's exasperated and exasperating question: What is art? – but only when we learn to integrate our vision of Walcott on the back foot through the covers with the outstretched arm of the Olympic Apollo.

CHAPTER 44

Edward W. Said

Orientalism now

On les apercevait tenant leurs idoles entre leurs bras comme de grands enfants
paralytiques.

(Gustave Flaubert, *La Tentation de Saint Antoine*)

The conquest of the earth, which mostly means the taking it away from those
who have a different complexion or slightly flatter noses than ourselves, is
not a pretty thing when you look into it too much. What redeems it is the
idea only. An idea at the back of it; not a sentimental pretence but an idea;
and an unselfish belief in the idea – something you can set up, and bow down
before, and offer a sacrifice to . . .

(Joseph Conrad, *Heart of Darkness*)

Latent and manifest Orientalism

IN CHAPTER ONE, I TRIED TO indicate the scope of thought and action covered
by the word *Orientalism*, using as privileged types the British and French experiences
of and with the Near Orient, Islam, and the Arabs. In those experiences I discerned an
intimate, perhaps even the most intimate, and rich relationship between Occident and
Orient. Those experiences were part of a much wider European or Western relationship
with the Orient, but what seems to have influenced Orientalism most was a fairly constant
sense of confrontation felt by Westerners dealing with the East. The boundary notion of
East and West, the varying degrees of projected inferiority and strength, the range of
work done, the kinds of characteristic features ascribed to the Orient: all these testify to
a willed imaginative and geographic division made between East and West, and lived

through during many centuries. In Chapter Two my focus narrowed a good deal. I was interested in the earliest phases of what I call modern Orientalism, which began during the latter part of the eighteenth century and the early years of the nineteenth. Since I did not intend my study to become a narrative chronicle of the development of Oriental studies in the modern West, I proposed instead an account of the rise, development, and institutions of Orientalism as they were formed against a background of intellectual, cultural, and political history until about 1870 or 1880. Although my interest in Orientalism there included a decently ample variety of scholars and imaginative writers, I cannot claim by any means to have presented more than a portrait of the typical structures (and their ideological tendencies) constituting the field, its associations with other fields, and the work of some of its most influential scholars. My principal operating assumptions were – and continue to be – that fields of learning, as much as the works of even the most eccentric artist, are constrained and acted upon by society, by cultural traditions, by worldly circumstance, and by stabilizing influences like schools, libraries, and governments; moreover, that both learned and imaginative writing are never free, but are limited in their imagery, assumptions, and intentions; and finally, that the advances made by a 'science' like Orientalism in its academic form are less objectively true than we often like to think. In short, my study hitherto has tried to describe the *economy* that makes Orientalism a coherent subject matter, even while allowing that as an idea, concept, or image the word *Orient* has a considerable and interesting cultural resonance in the West.

I realize that such assumptions are not without their controversial side. Most of us assume in a general way that learning and scholarship move forward; they get better, we feel, as time passes and as more information is accumulated, methods are refined, and later generations of scholars improve upon earlier ones. In addition, we entertain a mythology of creation, in which it is believed that artistic genius, an original talent, or a powerful intellect can leap beyond the confines of its own time and place in order to put before the world a new work. It would be pointless to deny that such ideas as these carry some truth. Nevertheless the possibilities for work present in the culture to a great and original mind are never unlimited, just as it is also true that a great talent has a very healthy respect for what others have done before it and for what the field already contains. The work of predecessors, the institutional life of a scholarly field, the collective nature of any learned enterprise: these, to say nothing of economic and social circumstances, tend to diminish the effects of the individual scholar's production. A field like Orientalism has a cumulative and corporate identity, one that is particularly strong given its associations with traditional learning (the classics, the Bible, philology), public institutions (governments, trading companies, geographical societies, universities), and generically determined writing (travel books, books of exploration, fantasy, exotic description). The result for Orientalism has been a sort of consensus: certain things, certain types of statement, certain types of work have seemed for the Orientalist correct. He has built his work and research upon them, and they in turn have pressed hard upon new writers and scholars. Orientalism can thus be regarded as a manner of regularized (or Orientalized) writing, vision, and study, dominated by imperatives, perspectives, and ideological biases ostensibly suited to the Orient. The Orient is taught, researched, administered, and pronounced upon in certain discrete ways.

The Orient that appears in Orientalism, then, is a system of representations framed by a whole set of forces that brought the Orient into Western learning, Western consciousness, and, later, Western empire. If this definition of Orientalism seems more political than not, that is simply because I think Orientalism was itself a product of certain political forces and activities. Orientalism is a school of interpretation whose material happens to be the Orient, its civilizations, peoples, and localities. Its objective discoveries – the work of innumerable devoted scholars who edited texts and translated them, codified grammars, wrote dictionaries, reconstructed dead epochs, produced positivistically verifiable learning – are and always have been conditioned by the fact that its truths, like any truths delivered by language, are embodied in language, and what is the truth of language, Nietzsche once said, but

> a mobile army of metaphors, metonyms, and anthropomorphisms – in short, a sum of human relations, which have been enhanced, transposed, and embellished poetically and rhetorically, and which after long use seem firm, canonical, and obligatory to a people: truths are illusions about which one has forgotten that this is what they are.[1]

Perhaps such a view as Nietzsche's will strike us as too nihilistic, but at least it will draw attention to the fact that so far as it existed in the West's awareness, the Orient was a word which later accrued to it a wide field of meanings, associations, and connotations, and that these did not necessarily refer to the real Orient but to the field surrounding the word.

Thus Orientalism is not only a positive doctrine about the Orient that exists at any one time in the West; it is also an influential academic tradition (when one refers to an academic specialist who is called an Orientalist), as well as an area of concern defined by travelers, commercial enterprises, governments, military expeditions, readers of novels and accounts of exotic adventure, natural historians, and pilgrims to whom the Orient is a specific kind of knowledge about specific places, peoples, and civilizations. For the Orient idioms became frequent, and these idioms took firm hold in European discourse. Beneath the idioms there was a layer of doctrine about the Orient; this doctrine was fashioned out of the experiences of many Europeans, all of them converging upon such essential aspects of the Orient as the Oriental character, Oriental despotism, Oriental sensuality, and the like. For any European during the nineteenth century – and I think one can say this almost without qualification – Orientalism was such a system of truths, truths in Nietzsche's sense of the word. It is therefore correct that every European, in what he could say about the Orient, was consequently a racist, an imperialist, and almost totally ethnocentric. Some of the immediate sting will be taken out of these labels if we recall additionally that human societies, at least the more advanced cultures, have rarely offered the individual anything but imperialism, racism, and ethnocentrism for dealing with 'other' cultures. So Orientalism aided and was aided by general cultural pressures that tended to make more rigid the sense of difference between the European and Asiatic parts of the world. My contention is that Orientalism is fundamentally a political doctrine willed over the Orient because the Orient was weaker than the West, which elided the Orient's difference with its weakness.

This proposition was introduced early in Chapter One, and nearly everything in the pages that followed was intended in part as a corroboration of it. The very presence of a 'field' such as Orientalism, with no corresponding equivalent in the Orient itself, suggests the relative strength of Orient and Occident. A vast number of pages on the Orient exist, and they of course signify a degree and quantity of interaction with the Orient that are quite formidable; but the crucial index of Western strength is that there is no possibility of comparing the movement of Westerners eastwards (since the end of the eighteenth century) with the movement of Easterners westwards. Leaving aside the fact that Western armies, consular corps, merchants, and scientific and archaeological expeditions were always going East, the number of travelers from the Islamic East to Europe between 1800 and 1900 is minuscule when compared with the number in the other direction.[2] Moreover, the Eastern travelers in the West were there to learn from and to gape at an advanced culture; the purposes of the Western travelers in the Orient were, as we have seen, of quite a different order. In addition, it has been estimated that around 60,000 books dealing with the Near Orient were written between 1800 and 1950; there is no remotely comparable figure for Oriental books about the West. As a cultural apparatus Orientalism is all aggression, activity, judgment, will-to-truth, and knowledge. The Orient existed for the West, or so it seemed to countless Orientalists, whose attitude to what they worked on was either paternalistic or candidly condescending – unless, of course, they were antiquarians, in which case the 'classical' Orient was a credit to *them* and not to the lamentable modern Orient.

And then, beefing up the Western scholars' work, there were numerous agencies and institutions with no parallels in Oriental society.

Such an imbalance between East and West is obviously a function of changing historical patterns. During its political and military heyday from the eighth century to the sixteenth, Islam dominated both East and West. Then the center of power shifted westwards, and now in the late twentieth century it seems to be directing itself back towards the East again. My account of nineteenth-century Orientalism in Chapter Two stopped at a particularly charged period in the latter part of the century, when the often dilatory, abstract, and projective aspects of Orientalism were about to take on a new sense of worldly mission in the service of formal colonialism. It is this project and this moment that I want now to describe, especially since it will furnish us with some important background for the twentieth-century crises of Orientalism and the resurgence of political and cultural strength in the East.

On several occasions I have alluded to the connections between Orientalism as a body of ideas, beliefs, clichés, or learning about the East, and other schools of thought at large in the culture. Now one of the important developments in nineteenth-century Orientalism was the distillation of essential ideas about the Orient – its sensuality, its tendency to despotism, its aberrant mentality, its habits of inaccuracy, its backwardness – into a separate and unchallenged coherence; thus for a writer to use the word *Oriental* was a reference for the reader sufficient to identify a specific body of information about the Orient. This information seemed to be morally neutral and objectively valid; it seemed to have an epistemological status equal to that of historical chronology or geographical location. In its most basic form, then, Oriental material could not really be violated by anyone's discoveries, nor did it seem ever to be revaluated completely. Instead, the work of various nineteenth-century scholars and of imaginative writers made this essential body of knowledge more clear, more detailed, more substantial – and more distinct from 'Occidentalism'. Yet Orientalist ideas could enter into alliance with general philosophical theories (such as those about the history of mankind and civilization) and diffuse world-hypotheses, as philosophers sometimes call them; and in many ways the professional contributors to Oriental knowledge were anxious to couch their formulations and ideas, their scholarly work, their considered contemporary observations, in language and terminology whose cultural validity derived from other sciences and systems of thought.

The distinction I am making is really between an almost unconscious (and certainly an untouchable) positivity, which I shall call *latent* Orientalism, and the various stated views about Oriental society, languages, literatures, history, sociology, and so forth, which I shall call *manifest* Orientalism. Whatever change occurs in knowledge of the Orient is found almost exclusively in manifest Orientalism; the unanimity, stability, and durability of latent Orientalism are more or less constant. In the nineteenth-century writers I analyzed in Chapter Two, the differences in their ideas about the Orient can be characterized as exclusively manifest differences, differences in form and personal style, rarely in basic content. Every one of them kept intact the separateness of the Orient, its eccentricity, its backwardness, its silent indifference, its feminine penetrability, its supine malleability; this is why every writer on the Orient, from Renan to Marx (ideologically speaking), or from the most rigorous scholars (Lane and Sacy) to the most powerful imaginations (Flaubert and Nerval), saw the Orient as a locale requiring Western attention, reconstruction, even redemption. The Orient existed as a place isolated from the mainstream of European progress in the sciences, arts, and commerce. Thus whatever good or bad values were imputed to the Orient appeared to be functions of some highly specialized Western interest in the Orient. This was the situation from about the 1870s on through the early part of the twentieth century – but let me give some examples that illustrate what I mean.

Theses of Oriental backwardness, degeneracy, and inequality with the West most easily associated themselves early in the nineteenth century with ideas about the biological bases of racial inequality. Thus the racial classifications found in Cuvier's *Le Règne animal*, Gobineau's *Essai sur l'inégalité des races humaines*, and Robert Knox's *The Dark Races of Man* found a willing partner in latent Orientalism. To these ideas was added second-order Darwinism, which seemed to accentuate the 'scientific' validity of the division of races into advanced and backward, or European-Aryan and Oriental-African. Thus the whole question of imperialism, as it was debated in the late nineteenth century by pro-imperialists and anti-imperialists alike, carried forward the binary typology of advanced and backward (or subject) races, cultures, and societies. John Westlake's *Chapters on the Principles of International Law* (1894) argues, for example, that regions of the earth designated as 'uncivilized' (a word carrying the freight of Orientalist assumptions, among others) ought to be annexed or occupied by advanced powers. Similarly, the ideas of such writers as Carl Peters, Léopold de Saussure, and Charles Temple draw on the advanced/backward binarism[3] so centrally advocated in late nineteenth-century Orientalism.

Along with all other peoples variously designated as backward, degenerate, uncivilized, and retarded, the Orientals were viewed in a framework constructed out of biological determinism and moral-political admonishment. The Oriental was linked thus to elements in Western society (delinquents, the insane, women, the poor) having in common an identity best described as lamentably alien. Orientals were rarely seen or looked at; they were seen through, analyzed not as citizens, or even people, but as problems to be solved or confined or – as the colonial powers openly coveted their territory – taken over. The point is that the very designation of something as Oriental involved an already pronounced evaluative judgment, and in the case of the peoples inhabiting the decayed Ottoman Empire, an implicit program of action. Since the Oriental was a member of a subject race, he had to be subjected: it was that simple. The *locus classicus* for such judgment and action is to be found in Gustave Le Bon's *Les Lois psychologiques de l'évolution des peuples* (1894).

But there were other uses for latent Orientalism. If that group of ideas allowed one to separate Orientals from advanced, civilizing powers, and if the 'classical' Orient served to justify both the Orientalist and his disregard of modern Orientals, latent Orientalism also encouraged a peculiarly (not to say invidiously) male conception of the world. I have already referred to this in passing during my discussion of Renan. The Oriental male was considered in isolation from the total community in which he lived and which many Orientalists, following Lane, have viewed with something resembling contempt and fear. Orientalism itself, furthermore, was an exclusively male province; like so many professional guilds during the modern period, it viewed itself and its subject matter with sexist blinders. This is especially evident in the writing of travelers and novelists: women are usually the creatures of a male power-fantasy. They express unlimited sensuality, they are more or less stupid, and above all they are willing. Flaubert's Kuchuk Hanem is the prototype of such caricatures, which were common enough in pornographic novels (e.g. Pierre Louÿs's *Aphrodite*) whose novelty draws on the Orient for their interest. Moreover the male conception of the world, in its effect upon the practicing Orientalist, tends to be static, frozen, fixed eternally. The very possibility of development, transformation, human movement – in the deepest sense of the word – is denied the Orient and the Oriental. As a known and ultimately an immobilized or unproductive quality, they come to be identified with a bad sort of eternality: hence, when the Orient is being approved, such phrases as 'the wisdom of the East'.

Transferred from an implicit social evaluation to a grandly cultural one, this static male Orientalism took on a variety of forms in the late nineteenth century, especially when Islam was being discussed. General cultural historians as respected as Leopold von Ranke and Jacob Burckhardt assailed Islam as if they were dealing not so much with an anthropomorphic abstraction as with a religio-political culture about which deep generalizations were possible and warranted: in his *Weltgeschichte* (1881–1888) Ranke spoke of Islam as defeated by the Germanic-Romanic peoples, and in his 'Historische Fragmente' (unpublished notes, 1893) Burckhardt spoke of Islam as wretched, bare, and trivial.[4] Such intellectual operations were carried out with considerably more flair and enthusiasm by Oswald Spengler, whose ideas about a Magian personality (typified by the Muslim Oriental) infuse *Der Untergang des Abendlandes* (1918–1922) and the 'morphology' of cultures it advocates.

What these widely diffused notions of the Orient depended on was the almost total absence in contemporary Western culture of the Orient as a genuinely felt and experienced force. For a number of evident reasons the Orient was always in the position both of outsider and of incorporated weak partner for the West. To the extent that Western scholars were aware of contemporary Orientals or Oriental movements of thought and culture, these were perceived either as silent shadows to be animated by the Orientalist, brought into reality by him, or as a kind of cultural and intellectual proletariat useful for the Orientalist's grander, interpretative activity, necessary for his performance as superior judge, learned man, powerful cultural will. I mean to say that in discussions of the Orient, the Orient is all absence, whereas one feels the Orientalist and what he says as presence; yet we must not forget that the Orientalist's presence is enabled by the Orient's effective absence . . .

Notes

1   Friedrich Nietzsche (1954) 'On Truth and Lie in an Extra-Moral Sense,' in *The Portable Nietzsche*, ed. and trans. Walter Kaufmann, New York: Viking Press, pp. 46–7.
2   The number of Arab travelers to the West is estimated and considered by Ibrahim Abu-Lughod (1963) *Arab Rediscovery of Europe: A Study in Cultural Encounters*, Princeton, NJ: Princeton University Press, pp. 75–6 and *passim*.
3   See Philip D. Curtin, ed. (1972) *Imperialism: The Documentary History of Western Civilization*, New York: Walker & Co., pp. 73–105.
4   See Johann W. Fück, 'Islam as an Historical Problem in European Historiography since 1800,' in *Historians of the Middle East*, ed. Bernard Lewis and P. M. Holt (1962), London: Oxford University Press, p. 307.

Afterwords

Utopias in performance

The force of the utopian text . . . is not to bring into focus the future that is coming to be, but rather to make us conscious precisely of the horizons or outer limits of what can be thought and imagined in our present.

Frederic Jameson in Jill Dolan (2005) Utopia in Performance: 13

Index

Abramovic, Marina 120
Abramson, R.M. 72
acculturation 257–8
action art *see* Happenings
actor 17–19, 152, 217–20
Adams, J.A. 70
Adams, Richard 73–4
Adèle Myers Company 120
Adler, Stella 52
Aeschylus 45, 49, 50, 60
Aldwych Theatre 221
Alembert, Jean le Rond D' 31
Alexander, Gerda 10
Alfreds, Mike 217–20
Allain, Paul 153
Animate Theatre 117, 118
Anthonisson De Morgan, Peter 115
Antoine, Andre 49, 50
The Arabian Nights 218
Arden, John 226
Aristophanes 50
Aristotle 29, 39, 52, 57–9, 60
Armbruster, G. 72
Arnold, Malcolm 71
Arnold, Peter J. 92–4
Artaud, Antonin 23, 119, 142, 225;
    The Theater and the Plague 103–5

Arthur, Robin 137
Arts Council 118, 119, 120
Arturius Rex 145
Asmus, Walter 215
Attali, Jacques 243
Ausdruckstanz 24
avant-garde theatre 21–5
Avery, John 137
Avner the Eccentric 117

Bach, J.C. 71
Baddeley, A. 68
Bahm, A. 73
Baker, Bobby 120
Balinese theatre 252
Ballet C de la B 239
Ballet Rambert 153
Balme, Chris 253
Banu, Georges 242
Barba, Eugenio 13, 47–8, 118, 119,
    151, 250, 251, 255–8
Barenboim, Daniel 245–6
Barker, Clive 9, 118; *Theatre Games* 12
Bartabas 239
Barthes, Roland, *The Rhetoric of
    the Image* 11–12
Bartok, Bela 134–5

Basserman, Albert 101–2
Bastick, T. 74
Bausch, Pina 24, 135, 239
Beckett, John 127
Beckett, Samuel 3, 23, 127–30, 214–16;
    'Come and Go' 199; *Krapp's Last Tape* 135;
    Waiting for Godot 214, 215–16
Beijing opera 151, 153
Bel, Jerome 115
The Bells (Leopold Lewis) 63–4
Benny, Jack 79
Bentley, D. 67
Berghaus, Günter, 120
Bergson, Henri 73
Berkoff, Steven 5, 117, 123–6
Bernstein, N. 68
Bhagvad Gita 221
Bhatt, Vishwa Mohan 243
Billington, Michael 203
Bing, Suzanne 50, 151
Birringer, J. 24
Biswas, Ansuman 120
Black Mime 117
Black and White 144
Bluebeard (Bela Bartok) 134–5
Boal, Augusto 32–7, 120, 151
the body 21, 22–3, 25, 42–3, 114, 142, 151,
    152, 204, 308; breath 185; dualistic
    thinking 161; dynamic 6, 14, 74, 93,
    165, 189; elements of movement 185–6;
    engineering principles 162; function of 163,
    164; immobility 184–5; and movement
    162; neutral 184; no pain, no gain ideology
    162; primacy of 159; in space 186;
    still/stillness 11, 64, 107, 132, 184–5,
    227, 229; and training 159–64
Body Art 120
body techniques, concept 38–9; general
    considerations 39–40
Boleslavsky, Richard 52
Bouge-de-là 152, 154
Brahem, Anouar 243
Brandon, James 253
Braun, Edward 14, 49
Brecht, Bertolt 3, 22, 23, 134, 151, 223,
    257; *On everyday theatre* 209–12
Breuer, Lee 252
Brith Gof 145–50

British Museum 237
Brook, Peter 221–8, 240, 242, 251,
    259–61
Brooks, D.N. 68
Brooks, V.B. 69
Brouhaha 152
Brown, I.C. 69
Bubb, Les 117
Bunge, M. 73
Bunting, Madeleine 237
Burgess, Hovey 193–5
Byrne, David 252

Cable Street 5
Cage, John 252
Callery, Dymphna 120, 121
Camilleri, Camille 249, 250
Campbell, Patrick 109–11
Cannan, Denis 227
capitalism 42
Cardiff Laboratory Theatre 142
Carnicke, Sharon 51
Castrillo, Edouardo 151
Cato, Gavin 243
Centre for Performance Research
    (CPR) 145
Chaikin, Joseph 52
Chaing Lui 224
Chamberlain, Franc 117–21, 120, 151–5
Chaplin, Charlie 20, 79
Chapter Arts Centre 145
Charnock, Nigel 119
Chaudhuri, Una 242
Chekhov, Anton 3
Chekhov, Michael 52, 151, 169–83, 206
Chinese theatre 224
Chinoy, Helen 51
choral dancers 60–1
choreography 61
Christopher, Karen 7
Chronegk, Ludwig 51
CICT 240
circus performance 193–5
Cixous, Hélène 250
Claid, Emilyn 131–2
Club of No Regrets 136–7; structure
    of performance 137–41
Cluman, Harold 51

cognition/cognitive 5, 10, 12, 14, 27, 29–30, 30, 37, 66–70, 74, 75–6
Coker, J. 71
Cole, Toby 51
Coleman, S.N. 72
Comdians 229–32
Comédie-Française 49
comedy 49, 50, 57, 58, 79, 159, 163
Commedia dell'Arte 49, 50, 51, 151, *see also lazzi*
Commotion 152
Comte, Auguste 39
The Conference of the Birds 260
Conrad, Joseph, *Heart of Darkness* 265
Constantine, Learie 262
Cooder, Ry 243
Copeau, Jacques 48–50, 52, 53, 79, 119, 151, 152
CORR-I-ADOR 120
counter-mask 189, 191
Craig, Edward Gordon 63, 79; 'The Actor and the Ubermarionette' 152; *On the Art of the Theatre* 151
creativity 73–5, 152
cricket 262–3
Croce, Benedetto 73
Crown Heights (Brooklyn) 243
Czerny, Karl 72

dance-sport relationship *see* sport-dance
dance-theatre 24–5, 112–13; angelology 114; Artemisian 113; choreographic 113–14; conversion/contradiction 113–14; musical integration 134–5; performance 131–2
dancing 101, 153
Dartington 154
Dastée, Jean 50
Davis, R. 70
de Keesmaeker 120
Decroux, Étienne 9, 13, 14, 17–20, 50, 119, 151, 165
Delgado, Maria 7, 157
Dennis, Anne 184–6
Descartes, René 161
Dibango, Manu 243
Diebold, Bernhard, *Anarchy in the Drama* 102
Doblin, Alfred 100

Dodin, Lev 52
Doerschuk, B. 71
Dolan, Jill 273
Downer, Alan S. 63–5
dramatic gymnastics 187–90, 191
dramatic spectacle 262–4
Duchartre, Pierre L. 79
Dullin, Charles 50
Dumas fils, Alexandre 49
Dumas, Georges 39
Duncan, Isadora 24, 101
DV8 Physical Theatre 119, 120, 153

Eagleton, Terry 42–3
East Scene 4 124–6
eclosion 189, 191
Edschmid, Kasimir 99, 101
Edwards, Nigel 137
The Elephant Vanishes (2003) 121
Emmel, Felix, *The Ecstatic Theatre* 101
Erickson, J. 23
Etchells, Tim 136–41
eukinetics 101
eurhythmics 101
Euripides 61
European Mime Federation 119, 152
European Mime and Physical Theatre Workshop Symposium 119
Evans, Mark 50, 154
Evreinov, Nikolai 79
Ewens, Graeme 243
Ewing, A. 73
exercise *see* protocol
Expressionism 99
Expressionist acting, modes of 102; theory/roots of 100–2
expressive mask 189, 191
expressivity 255
Extemporary Dance Theatre 118
Eyre, Richard 45

Fabre, Jan 120
Farr, Ju Row 137
Fedotov, Alexander 51
Feldenkrais, Moshe 10
Felner, Myra 193–5
Fields, W.C. 79
First Studio 151

Flaubert, Gustave, *La Tentation de Saint Antoine* 265
Flesh 142
Fo, Dario 117, 119, 250
Foe 153
Foltin, B. Jr 72
Footsbarn 117
Forced Entertainment 137
Franko B. 109–11
Fratellini Brothers 151
Freehold 118
French theatre 48–50, 52
Furse, Anna 157

Gaburo, K. 71
Gaines, David 118
Galas, D. 71
Garbarek, Jan 243
Gardner, Lyn 199
Gardzienice 119, 120
Garner, S.B. 22
Gaulier, Philippe 202
Gautam, Dasgupta 252
Geertz, Clifford 249
George, David E.R. 26–30
German Expressionism *see* Expressionism
Giannachi, Gabriella 121
Gibbs, C.B. 69
Gilman, Richard 215
Glass, David 117, 152
Glass, Philip 252
Goethe, J.W. von 245, 246
Gorder, W.D. 74
Gordon, Mel 79–87, 99–102
Gore-Booth, Celia 120
Goulish, Matthew 7
Grace, W.G. 262
Griffiths, Trevor 229–32
Grotowski, Jerzy 10, 14, 118, 119, 149, 151, 194, 195, 224, 225–6, 240, 250
Group Theatre 51
Guilford, J.P. 74–5

habitus 38–9
Hamel, P.M. 71
Hansa Gallery 106
Happenings 106–8, 221, 223, 224
Hartung, Gustav 100

Haunted, Daunted and Flaunted (1997) 131–2
Hayman, R. 22
Hébert, Georges 50
Heggen, Claire 9–15
Hermann, Bernard 201
Herodotus 60
Hidden Risk Performance 119
Hillman, James 114
Hixson, Lin 7
Hoepfner, R. 74–5
Houstoun, Wendy 131–2
Hsiao-Hsien, Hou 252
Hughes, Ted, *Gaudete* 201
Hulton, Peter 217–20
Hunt, Albert 221–4, 224, 225–6, 227
Huntington, Samuel 237
Hussein, Shaukat 243
Husserl, Edmund 27
Hybrid 120

Imperial Maly Theatre 51
improvisation 57, 60, 66; anticipation, preselection, feedforward 70; development of skills 75; feedback/error correction 69–70; interest of 204–5; intuition/creativity 73–5; motor control 68; motor memory 71; musical 71–2; physiology/neuropsychology 66–8; process of 75–6; and scripted plays 205; skill classification 69; skilled performance 68; time scales for control of movement 70; timing/movement invariants 70–1
inadvertent interpretation 213–16
inculturation 257–8
Innes, C. 23
intercultural theatre 252
interculturalism 249; and cultural collage 252–3; definitions 249–52
International Centre of Theatre Research 259
International Schools Theatre Association (ISTA) 119
intuition 73–5
Ionesco, Eugene 22, 23
Irving, Henry 63–5

Jackson, Glenda 227
Jacques-Dalcroze, Émile 71–2, 101
James, C.L.R. 262–4

Jameson, Frederic 273
jazz 71, 72
Jeffery, Mark 7
Jesurun, John 252
Johnstone, Keith 204
Jones, Mark 227
Jones, Richard 202
Jovet, Louis 50

kabuki 151, 153
Kalb, Jonathan 213–16
Kaprow, Allan 106–8
kathakali 151, 152, 153
Kayssler, Friedrich 101, 102
Kean, Edmund 65
Keaton, Ben 117–18; *Intimate Memoirs of an Irish Taxidermist* 117
Keefe, John 1–6, 45, 142, 145, 147, 149
Kelso, J.A.S. 68
Kemble, Charles 65
Kimball, Robert 233–4
Knebel, Maria 52
Kokoschka, Oska 100
Kompany Malakhi 120
Konishi, M. 67
Koonen, Alice 52
Kornfeld, Paul, *The Seduction* 100
Kortner, Fritz 100–1
Krauss, Werner 101
Krell, Max, *German Theatre of the Present* 101
Kuhn, Thomas 4
Kustow, Michael 221, 225–8, 227

Laabs, G.J. 71
Laban, Rudolf von 24, 101
Ladzekpo, K. 72
Lahr, Bert 79
Lancaster University 145
Laneri, Roberto 71
Lashley, Karl 68
Laurel (Stan) and Hardy (Bert) 79
lazzi 79; definition 80; function of 80–1; scenario 85–7; sexual/scatological 83–4; sources 81; stage properties 81, 83; stupidity/inappropriate behaviour 84–5, *see also* Commedia dell'Arte
Le Page, Robert 203, 252
Leabhart, Tom 152

LeCompte, Elisabeth 252
Lecoq, Jacques 61, 119, 151, 187–92, 202
Lee, John 117
The Lesson of Anatomy 142
Levett, Dave (now Lyn) 143–4, 244–5
Lévi-Strauss, Claude 250
Lily, Peter 117
Littlewood, Joan 3, 95–6
Live Art 120
Living Theatre 23
Lloyd, Robert 227, 228
London International Mime Festival 9
London Theatre Group 123
Lowdon, Richard 137
Lucian 263
Lyubimov, Yuri 52

McCaw, Dick 9–15
McClucas, Cliff 142–50
McDermott, Phelim 12, 201–8
Machado, Antonio 15
The Machine Wreckers 153
McLucas, Cliff 142, 148–9
Macready, William 63, 65
The Mahabharata 240, 242
Malaev-Babel, Andrei 169–83
Man Act 120
The Man Who Ate His Shoes 154
Marat/Sade 221
Marceau, Marcel 14, 119
Market Theatre Johannesburg 12
Marranca, Bonnie 252
Marshall, Claire 137
Marshall, Lorna 159–64, 196–8
Martin, Carol 244
Marx Brothers 79
Mason, Bim 117
Mauss, Marcel 38–40, 250
Meiningen Troupe 51
Melbourne International Festival 243
memory 34, 37, 39, 68, 71, 72, 74, 75, 110, 143, 210, 237
Mersenne, Marin 71
method acting 151
Meyerhold, Vsevolod 48, 49, 52, 79, 119, 151, 194
Milner, B. 68
mime 9, 117, 118–19, 127–30, 152

Mime Action Group (MAG) 119, 120, 152, 154–5
Mime and Physcal Theatre 119
Mime Theatre Project 117
Mind the Gaps conference 145–6
mind-body dichotomy 12–13, 15, 23, 161, 163
A Minute Too Late (1984) 121
Mirecka, Rena 118
Mishra, Vijay 242
Mitchell, C.J. 7
Mnouchkine, Ariane 240, 250, 251
Molière 49, 95
Molik, Zygmunt 240
monologues 34
morality 42–3
Morrison, Norman 228
Moscow Arts Theatre (MAT) 51, 52
Motionhouse 120
movement, analysis 189; balance 194; breathing 188; communicator of feeling 185; design 185–6; directions of 196–8; dramatic gymnastics 187–9; eclosion 190; giving meaning to 187–9; glossary 191; intensity 186; living immobility 184–5; natural everyday movement 189–90; play 188; rhythm 186; technique 187–90; theatrical space 186; undulation 189–90
Moving into Performance (*MIP*) 120, *see also* European Mime and Physical Theatre Workshop Symposium
Moving Picture Mime Show 117, 152
Mowat, John 117
multicultural theatre 252
Mummer&dada 152
Murray, Simon 1–6, 142, 146
music 134–5, 240

Nada Theatre 154
Naden, Cathy 137
National Student Drama Festival 204
National Theatre 153, 203
Nelson, O. 71
Nemirovich-Danchenko, M.V. 51
Nettl, B. 72
neurological 5, 68
neutral mask 165, 189, 191
neutrality, neutral state 191

New Man 100
New York Performance Art 120
Newson, Lloyd 119
Nin, Anaïs 103–5
Noh 151, 153
Noh theatre 49, 50
Nuttall, Jeff 88–91

O'Connor, Terry 137
Odin Teatret 47, 48, 52
Oedipus Rex (1912) 100
Oida, Yoshi 196–8
Old Vic 202
Oliveros, P. 71
Oppression of the Innocent (1995) 153
Orientalism 265–71
Orpheus and Eurydice (Gluck) 134
Ostrovski, 250
Ouspenskaya, Maria 52

Paines Plough 157
pantomime 20, 187, 191, 263
Pardo, Enrique 112–14, 119, 151
Parons, W. 72
Partchey, K.C. 69
Pavis, Patrice 249–54, 252
Pearson, Mike 120, 142, 146, 147, 149, 244–5
Peisistratus 264
Peking Opera 250
The People Show 120
performance 154; cognitive aspects 27, 30; comparison with theatre 29; definitions 26–7; epistemiology 27–30; expressionist 102; as flux 28; methodology 27; phenomenological 27; post-physical 117–21; as 'present' 29; primacy of 28; pushing the limits 109–11; realist/naturalistic 123–4; and spectators 28–9; surviving 109–11; and text 28
performance art 120
Peters, Julie Stone 242
physical theatre 153; benefits of 203–4; as body-focused 21, 22–3, 25; classification difficulties 118–21; complexity of tradition 52–3; concept 21; as contested term 119; contextualizing 21–2; courses on 120; and dead collaborators 205–6; definitions 154;

development of 21, 202; discursive practices 23, 24; dislike of 202–3; establishment of 24–5; experience of 201; heuristic 120; key features 117; as mainstream 202; mainstream perception of 203; in the mid-eighties 202; new terminology 120–1; provocative statements for adventures in 207–8; and ritual of the curtain call 206–7; roots of practice 48–52; terminology 48; and Whelan's recording technique 206; and wrestling with text 204

physical-based performance 151–5

Pinero, Arthur Wing 65

Pitches, Jonathan 47–53

Platel, Alain 239

Plato 161

play/playfulness 4, 5, 12, 14–15, 49, 50, 90, 150, 162, 188, 189, 191, 204, *see also lazzi*

Plexus 117

poetry 57–9

Polish theatre 52, 225

Pollock, Jackson 106

post-colonial theatre 253

Poulton, E.C. 69

pre-expressivity 255–7

Pressing, Jeff 66–76

Price, Joe 194

protocol, activity/passivity mixture 11–12; body/mind interaction 12–13, 15; and habitual/fictitious body 13; Heggen's system 10–15; heuristic approach 11, 15; journey 10–11; and play 14–15; restriction/movement contradiction 14; and (un)predictability 13–14; use of senses 12

psychological gesture (PG) technique 169–70; imaginary space/time 181–3; role as a whole 170–1; score of atmospheres 174–7; separate scenes 171–4; for speech 17881

Quantz, Johann 71

Ra-Ra-Zoo 117, 118

Rae, Nola 117

Randle, Frank 88–91

RAT Theatre 118, 142, 147

Rees, Roger 204

Reeves, 221, 226, 227

Reinhardt, Max 79, 100

replay 191

Rewa, Nathalie 252

Richardson, C.P. 74

Riley, Terry 71

Rite of Spring (Igor Stravinsky) 134

ritual 61, 113, 149, 206–7, 221–2

Roach, Joseph 241

Roads, C. 72

Robertson, Thomas 65

Rockaby 213–16Lyons, Charles R. 214

Rose, Clifford 227

Rosenbaum, Yankel 243

Rousseau, Jean-Jacques 31

routes/roots 5, 47, 53

Royal Ballet 153

The Royal Hunt of the Sun (Peter Shaffer) 203

Royal Shakespeare Company (RSC) 119

Rudin, John 49

Rueda, Lope de 49

Russian theatre 49, 51–2

Sage, G.S. 67, 70

Said, Edward W. 245–6, 265–71

St Denis, Michel 50, 151

Salvini, Tommaso 51

Sánchez-Colberg, Ana 21–5, 119

Saner, Bryan 7

Sannio 61

Saporta, Karine 113

Savares, Nicola 255–8

Schauspielhaus theatre 100

Schechner, Richard 118, 151, 243, 251

Schepkin, Mikhail 51

Schmidt, R.A. 70

Servos, Norbert 134–5

Shaffer, L.H. 69

Shakespeare, William, *The Tempest* 26, 30

Shange, Ntozake 243

Shared Experience 217

Sharpton, Al 243

Shepherd, G.M. 67

Sher, C. 72

Shevstsova, Maria 242, 252

Simmons, R.W. 71

Simon, Barney 12

Slonimsky, N. 71

Smart, Roger 117

Smith, Anna Deavere 239; *Fires in the Mirror: Crown Heights, Brooklyn and Other Identities* 243–4

Smith, Phil 120

Snow, Stephen 252

Society of Art and Literature 51

Sondheim, Stephen, *Sunday in the Park with George* 233–6

Sonny Roy the Funny Boy 88–91

Soyinka, Wole 253

Spackman, Helen 109–11

Sparrow, W.A. 69

spectators 28–9, 36

Spinoza, Baruch 73

Spivak, Gayatri Chakravorti 241

Spolin, Viola 12

sport-dance relationship 92; artistic activities 94; non-aesthetic 92; partially aesthetic 92–4

Staniewski, Wlodzmierz 119

Stanislavsky, Konstantin 48, 51–2, 151, 255, 257

states 191

Station House Opera 120

Stelarc 121

Sternheim, Carl 100

Stockhausen, Karlheinz 71

Stocks, J. 73

storytelling 6, 118, 132, 204, 217–20, 218–20

Strasberg, Lee 52

The Street of Crocodiles (1992) 121

Strindberg, August 100

Summers, J.J. 68

Suspension (1980) 121

Suzki, 151

Svitch, Caridad 7, 157

SymbioticA 121

syncretic theatre 253

Tai Chi 160

Talking Pictures 152

Tanztheater 24

Taoism 40

Tasca, Valeria 250

Teatr Laboratorium 225, 240

Teatr Piesn Kozla 120

Teatro Campesino 260, 261

Telson, Bob 252

Terry, Keith 117

theatre, aesthetic space 36–7; centricity of 6; collaboration in 95–6; as communal event 218; contemporary practices in 5; and cultural exchange 6; definitions 18–19, 34; and human beings 34; hybrid nature of 3, 5; landscape of 5; official/unofficial work 2–3; personal meditations on 4; physicality of 3–4, 5–6; plurality of perspectives on 2–4; preparation/training for 5; primacy of 32–3; roots/routes of 5; stage/audience separation 36–7; traditions of 5

Theatre of Cruelty 221

Théâtre de Complicité 117, 120, 121, 152, 153, 203, 239

Théâtre du Mouvement 9

Théâtre du Soleil 240

Theatre of the Fourth World 253

Theatre Workshop 95

Théâtre Zingaro 239

Three Lives (Tri Bywyd) 149

time-space 181–3, 196–8

Tolstoy, Leo 264

Tong, Winston 252

Too Clever by Half 202

Toporkov, O. 256

Total Theatre Group (TTG) 120, 153, 154, 155

Total Theatre Magazine 120

Toure, Ali Farka 243

Tourischeva, Ludmilla 93

Tovstonogov, Giorgi 52

tragedy 58–9, 60–1, 63

training 151–2, 153, 153–4; applications 160, 161, 163–4; and the body 159–60; outcome 160–1; process 160, 161–2; warm-ups 163–4

Trestle Theatre 118, 120, 152

Triple Action Theatre 118

Tsuchitori, Toshi 240

Turvey, G. 68

Ubu 154

UEA Phoenix 118

UK Mime and Physical Theatre Training Directory (1984) 119

undulation/inverse undulation 189, 191–2

University of Western Australia 121
US 221–8
utopias 273

Vakhtangov, Eugene 52
Vasiliev, Vladimir 52
Vaughan, M.M. 74
Vega, Lope de 34, 36
Verma, Jatlinder, *Journey to the West* 47
Vietnam War 221–8
Vieux Colombier 49, 50, 51
Vijayakumar, Kalamandalam 153
Vincent Dance Theatre 120
The Visit 153

Walcott, Derek 253, 264
Webster, R.P. 74
Wedekind, Frank 100, 101
Weill, Étienne Bertrand 165–8
Weill, Kurt 134
Weimar 246
Welford, A.T. 68, 69

West-Eastern Divan Workshop 245–6
Westcott, M.R. 73
Whelan, Jeremy 206
Whitelaw, Billie 214
Wilding, Faith 121
Wiles, David 60–1
Williams, David 1, 239–47
Williams, Michael 221–2, 227
Wilson, Robert 239, 252
Wirth, Andrzej 252
Wissel Theatre 117
world as can opener 259–61
world music 240
Worrell, Frank 262
Wrights & Sites 120

Yeats, W.B., *The Circus Animals'
    Desertion* 65
Yefremov, Oleg 52
Yellow Earth 120

Zidane, Zinedine 1

Physical Theatres:
A Critical Introduction

Simon Murray and John Keefe

This essential new textbook on physical theatre is the first to synthesise history, theory and practice of this field in a useful way for students new to the subject and considers the issues surrounding the body in theatre.

Simon Murray and John Keefe – both experienced lecturers in the field – unpack the term 'physical theatre', explaining the range and variety of concepts that it incorporates. *Physical Theatres: A Critical Introduction* surveys:

- traditional forms – such as popular theatre and French mime
- contemporary practice – including examinations of successful theatre companies such as Theatre du Complicité
- training techniques
- physicality in text-based-theatres
- the relationship between western and non-western traditions.

Complemented by *Physical Theatres: A Critical Reader*, also available from Routledge, this book provides a necessary and fascinating introduction to this broad field of theatre.

ISBN13: 978–0–415–36249–8 (hbk)
ISBN13: 978–0–415–36250–4 (pbk)

The Twentieth-Century Performance Reader

Edited by Michael Huxley and Noel Witts

The Twentieth-Century Performance Reader provides a pioneering introduction to all types of performance (dance, drama, music, theatre and live art) through the writings of forty-two practitioners, critics and theorists which together reaffirm performance as a discipline in its own terms.

Organised alphabetically, rather than chronologically or according to art form, this reader invites cross-disciplinary comparisons. Each piece is fully supplemented by a contextual summary, detailed cross-references and suggestions for further reading. The editors' introductory essay provides an invaluable analysis of the field, and the definitive bibliography offers an essential reference source.

The reader, which makes it possible to compare major writings on all types of performance in one volume, is an essential sourcebook for researchers, practitioners and students. It will also be of interest to anyone who enjoys innovative live performance.

ISBN13: 978–0–415–25286–7 (hbk)
ISBN13: 978–0–415–25287–4 (pbk)

The Performance Studies Reader, 2nd edition

Edited by Henry Bial

'A collection of this type has been needed for a long time.'

Sally Harrison-Pepper, *Miami University*

'Clearly an important collection of essays that will provide an excellent resource for levels II and III specialist courses.'

Nick Kaye, *Exeter University*

The Performance Studies Reader is a lively and much-needed anthology of critical writings on the burgeoning discipline of performance studies. It provides an overview of the full range of performance theory for undergraduates at all levels, and beginning graduate students in performance studies, theatre, performing arts and cultural studies.

The collection is designed as a companion to Richard Schechner's popular *Performance Studies: an Introduction* but is also ideal as a stand-alone text. Henry Bial collects together key critical pieces from the field, referred to as 'suggested readings' in *Performance Studies: an Introduction*. He also broadens the discussion with additional selections. Featuring contributions from major scholars and artists such as Richard Schechner, Eugenio Barba, Marvin Carlson, Judith Butler, Jon McKenzie, Homi K. Bhabha, Eve Kosofsky Sedgwick and Jerzy Grotowski, this important collection offers a wide-ranging introduction to the main areas of study.

ISBN13: 978–0–415–77274–7 (hbk)
ISBN13: 978–0–415–77275–4 (pbk)

Related titles from Routledge

Theatre of Movement and Gesture

Jacques Lecoq

Jacques Lecoq was probably the most influential theorist and teacher of what is now known as physical theatre. *Theatre of Movement and Gesture*, published in France in 1987, is the book in which Lecoq first set out his philosophy of human movement, and the way it takes expressive form in a wide range of different performance traditions. Lecoq traces the history of pantomime, sets out his definition of the components of the art of mime, and discusses the explosion of physical theatre in the second half of the twentieth century.

This unique volume also contains:

- interviews with major theatre practitioners Ariane Mnouchkine and Jean-Louis Barrault
- chapters by Jean Perret on Etienne Decroux and Marcel Marceau
- a final section by Alain Gautre celebrating the many physical theatre practitioners working in the 1980s
- a wealth of illustrations, included previously unpublished photographs from the Lecoq collection.

Lecoq's poetic, incisive writings form the backbone of this extraordinary text. The pieces gathered here represent a precious testimony to his special vision of the art of acting and of its close relationship with the history of mime and of masked performance.

ISBN13: 978–0–415–35943–6 (hbk)
ISBN13: 978–0–415–35944–3 (pbk)

Available at all good bookshops
For ordering and further information please visit:
www.routledge.com